WRITING EROTICA

Edo van Belkom

Self-Counsel Press
(a division of)
International Self-Counsel Press
USA   Canada

*Self-Counsel Press acknowledges the financial support of the Government of Canada
through the Book Publishing Industry Development Program for our publishing
activities.*

Printed in Canada.

First edition: 2001

Canadian Cataloguing in Publication Data
Van Belkom, Edo
   Writing Erotica

   (Self-counsel series)
   Includes bibliographical references.
   ISBN 1-55180-307-0

   1. Erotic literature — Authorship.   2. Erotic literature — Authorship —
Marketing I. Title. II. Series.

PN3377.5.E76V36 2001   808.3   C2001-910086-8

Self-Counsel Press
(a division of)
International Self-Counsel Press Ltd.

1704 N. State Street	1481 Charlotte Road
Bellingham, WA 98225	North Vancouver, BC V7J 1H1
USA	Canada

CONTENTS

A Few Words with...

Samples

Tables

ACKNOWLEDGMENTS

I'd like to thank the people at Self-Counsel Press: Richard Day for getting this project started; Catherine Bennett for seeing it through to the end; Roger Kettyls for spreading the word; and Brenda Cline for getting things done.

I am grateful to all of the interviewees who gave up some of their precious time to enrich this book with their invaluable advice and experience: Nancy Kilpatrick, Cecilia Tan, Michael Bracken, Lawrence Block, Michael Thomas Ford, Caro Soles (Kyle Stone), Michael Crawley, James Marriott, Lynda Simmons, Loren L. Barrett, Susie Bright, and Kathryn Ptacek.

And of course, thank you to my wife Roberta, without whose help this and all my other books would never have been written.

INTRODUCTION

So Who Wants to Be a Pornographer?

So, who wants to be a pornographer?

Oh, excuse me — I meant, purveyor of erotic literature?

I sure didn't.

At least not at first.

I began my writing career as a newspaper reporter, but my ultimate goal was to write short stories like those of science fiction and fantasy author Ray Bradbury. Reading his stellar collection *The October Country* had me in awe, not only of the man's talent but also of the effect great writing can have on an individual.

I was turned on to writing fiction (short stories in particular) and knew it was what I wanted to do with my life — writing erotica, however, was still the furthest thing from my mind.

And so I began writing stories during my spare time. At first I tried to write stories like Bradbury, full of a naive sort of wonder and purple prose that lacked Bradbury's vision and poetry. But it was a start. Once I had a few stories written, it was time to find a place to publish them.

Pornography: Written or other material designed to stimulate sexual excitement. In general, "hard-core" pornography explicitly describes or depicts sexual acts such as intercourse, whereas "soft-core" pornography usually describes or depicts men or women in sexually provocative poses or situations.

— *Miriam Stoppard, MD*
The Magic of Sex

Like all writers, I wanted to share my work with anyone and everyone, even if that work wasn't exactly ready to be shared. Rejection followed rejection, but I didn't let that get me down.

In high school, I had been one of those people who managed to get by on doing just the minimum amount of work. My grades were okay, I never fell behind (and I never surged ahead, either), and everyone seemed happy with my progress. In university, it was much the same, except that I worked diligently for the university newspaper as a sports editor. It was more interesting than my classes, and when I wrote something, it appeared in print almost immediately. When I left university and got a job as a sports reporter at a small daily newspaper, I was once again back to doing an okay job. I was never considered for advancement or promotion, nor was I ever in danger of being canned.

But I was writing fiction on the side. And despite many rejections (here comes the point to this tangent), I stuck with it because I realized that writing fiction was a lot more difficult than anything I'd tried up to then. Fiction writing was the first thing in my life at which I'd had to work really hard. I was determined to stick with it because I wanted more than anything else to succeed at it and I would do whatever I needed to do to make that happen.

While I was writing stories in imitation of Ray Bradbury, I was also looking to expand my horizons. Could I try other kinds of stories and see how they worked out? I bought a copy of the Writer's Digest Books annual *Novel and Short Story Writer's Market* and studied the listings. (For me, the *Market* was like one of those picture books or reference books about something really interesting that you can look through a hundred times and never get tired of.) I remember a listing for a magazine called *Corvette,* which published fiction as long as a Corvette was featured in the story. I tried for months to come up with a Corvette story, but never did. There were also listings for a juggling magazine and a gambling magazine, and I tried very hard to come up with a story that might fit their requirements, but I always came up empty.

In addition to all the mainstream magazines, the *Novel and Short Story Writer's Market* also included listings for men's magazines such as *Hustler, Cheri, Oui,* and *Cavalier.* Each one had its own specific guidelines, but none sparked an idea in my mind. Then I read the listing for *Gent* magazine, which required that any fiction submitted prominently feature a woman with large breasts. That seemed simple enough, so I began thinking about possible story ideas.

I came up with one.

I originally called the story "Woman As Art." It was about an artist who is given a lump of magical clay by a fellow artist whose wife seems to be a whole lot curvier than she'd been just a few weeks before. It turns out that the clay could be used to alter a person's body shape. The artist sculpts a figure from the clay (with large breasts, of course) and places a few of his wife's hairs in the figure's head — sort of like a voodoo doll. Voila — his wife is a busty babe, and he's having the sex of his wildest dreams. The story ends with the artist realizing he has a bit of the clay left over, which he can use to make a figure of himself that is significantly better endowed than the original.

It seems like a silly premise now, and embarrassingly like some primal male fantasy, but it was the best I could do at the time. (Remember, I was trying to write fantasy like Bradbury, so maybe this story was the inevitable mixing of fantasy and erotica.) And I did work hard on the story, making sure characterization, plot, and everything else I had learned by writing the other stories was written into this effort.

Since I had written it for *Gent,* that's where I sent it.

And damned if they didn't accept it.

I was stunned.

"Woman As Art" was the 14th story I had written, the second I'd sold, and the first I had published, seeing print in *Gent*'s July 1990 issue under the title "Artistic License." I was paid $175 US for the story, which absolutely amazed me because I had started writing not to make money, but to tell stories. Getting paid for the story came as a pleasant surprise. Perhaps more important was that I had written the story for a specific market, sent it to that market, and sold it on the first try. Success like that had to be followed up, so the 15th story I wrote was "The Zero Gee Spot," and I sold that to *Gent* as well.

Meanwhile, I had placed a few other stories ("placed" as opposed to "sold," because most of my fantasy stories at the time were being accepted at small, pay-in-copies magazines) and was slowly getting better at my craft. But although my "straight" stories were getting a better reception, I was still being rejected a lot. To compensate, I continued to write and sell erotic stories for men's magazines.

One unexpected benefit of this was that my third sale to *Gent,* "Night Vision," qualified me for active status in the Science Fiction and Fantasy Writers of America (SFWA). Active status is the "pro" level of

I use that term [erotica] when I don't know people because the "P" word puts people off. I've also discovered, to my horror, that if you do say it's "erotica," people have no idea of the kind of strength it has, and how powerful and disturbing it is for some people.

— *Caro Soles*
(writing as Kyle Stone)

membership and is earned through the sale of a science fiction or fantasy novel, or the sale of three short stories to a professional market. The markets are usually such magazines as *Asimov's, Analog,* or *The Magazine of Fantasy and Science Fiction,* but *Gent* was just as professional, paid better, and had a larger circulation, so I was in — much to the chagrin of the other members of my writers' group at the time, all of whom looked upon active status within SFWA as some faraway and virtually unattainable milestone.

The more erotic stories I wrote, the more I sold, and in no time my sales count was up past 30. In addition to having an impressive number of sales, something else was going on with the erotic stories I was writing.

They were teaching me how to craft a story.

One misconception about erotic fiction is that it is somehow easier or takes less ability to write than other types of fiction. I say that it takes just as much craft, and perhaps even more. Along with all the usual things you must do in creating fiction, in erotica you have to establish character quickly, explain the plot economically, and move your story along at a good clip. You also have to write to a certain length to ensure that your story is usable by the magazine for which you intend it. (Science fiction writer James Alan Gardner once looked at my chapbook collection *Virtual Girls* and marveled at how each story was exactly ten pages long. "It requires a talent," he said of writing a specific kind of story to a specific length each and every time. I was also once asked by horror writer Brian Hopkins if I had a computer program that turned out perfectly plotted 3,000-word horror stories with twist endings. I took it as a compliment, of course, because the program does exist: it's loaded into the wetware inside my head, and it got there by the trial and error experience of writing dozens and dozens of erotic short stories for men's magazines.)

I've now been writing erotic stories for more than ten years. During that time there were periods when erotica was all I was writing, because that was all that was selling. Inevitably, though, I've been writing fewer erotic stories in recent years, as my other writing enjoys more success. I've now won the Bram Stoker Award from the Horror Writers Association and the Aurora Award (Canadian science fiction and fantasy award) for my short fiction, and I've had a collection published, *Death Drives a Semi,* which has brought me a little closer to my goal of emulating my idol, Ray Bradbury. But that doesn't mean I've forgotten about erotic stories. I still enjoy writing them from time to time, and

I've also used what I've learned about erotica to spice up my horror writing. In 2001, my collection of erotic horror stories, *Six-Inch Spikes*, will be published, extending the learning curve that began with writing erotic stories more than ten years ago.

And Now to This Book

As is the case with most books on the subject of writing, the advice and instruction in *Writing Erotica* is based on the experiences of the author — namely me — in the field of erotica. As most of my experience comes from writing short stories for heterosexual men's magazines, you'll find that the examples and instruction in this book lean toward that market. However, I have also written many erotic stories that could be considered literary in nature, one of which, "The Terminatrix,"was published in *Best American Erotica 1999* and reprinted in an Italian erotica anthology called *Latex*. I've done my best to fill in the gaps in regard to other forms of erotica, but the basics of good writing are universal. Whether you write erotic short stories or sex novels, the same principles apply.

However, since erotica is a field in which there can be dozens of special niches, I have interviewed twelve purveyors of erotica (as opposed to pornographers, but more on that in the next chapter) and covered such subjects as fetish fiction, gay and lesbian erotica, sex novels, and erotic fiction markets. In addition, I've peppered the manuscript with examples of my work in the hope of showing you how erotic fiction works.

I hope that *Writing Erotica* will serve as an introduction to the genre and turn you on to the possibility of writing your own erotica.

And remember: You can write for pleasure. You can write for profit.

If this book does its job, you'll be doing it for both.

Technically, this book itself is part of that industry — the exchange of money for sexual stimulation or gratification, in this case in the form of smut/ erotica/porn. . . . Whatever you wish to call it, this is, without a doubt, a book intended to stimulate. The content of the stories is intended to get the juices flowing.

— *Cecilia Tan*
Introduction to
Selling Venus

Part One
THE EROTIC GENRE

Erotic literature — straight, lesbian, gay — has become mainstream.
During the past decade, it has blossomed into a literary genre of its
own. Publishers big and small are including it in anthologies, novels
and short stories.

— The Toronto Star
"Erotomania"

I
WHAT IS EROTICA?

Erotica versus Pornography

Erotica. Pornography.

Pornography. Erotica.

What's the difference?

Opinions on this are numerous and varied. Some might consider anything to do with sex and sexuality to be pornography, while others might say that erotica is material that has literary merit and pornography is simply debasing and degrading.

Here are the dictionary definitions of the two terms:

Erotica: literature or art dealing with sexual love.

Pornography: obscene writings, drawings, or photographs, or the like, esp. those having little or no artistic merit.

> — *The Random House Dictionary*
> *of the English Language,* 2nd edition

The roots from which each of these words was derived do nothing to dispell the idea that erotica is artistic and pornography is not. *Erotica* comes from "Eros," the Greek god of erotic love, while *pornography* comes from words that were used to describe the writings of prostitutes.

But in the 21st century, the line between pornography and erotica has become somewhat blurred, and one can conclude that both erotica and pornography are now produced with pretty much the same goal in mind — that of sexually stimulating the reader. The deciding factor in whether material is deemed pornography or erotica is usually the manner in which this goal is achieved, and there's something to be said for that. I have had stories published first in men's magazines, where they would certainly be considered porn, and later reprinted in small-press anthologies, where they would be considered erotica. Indeed, one of the best lines I've ever heard on this subject is this: *The difference between pornography and erotica is the annual income of the reader.*

However, I sincerely doubt that anyone has picked up this book with the intention of creating literature that is without artistic value or merit or which is degrading to either men or women; therefore, I will consider all that follows to be talk about erotica and leave the word pornography behind.

Who Writes This Stuff, Anyway?

Sometimes people have difficulty separating the writer from his or her work. Horror writer James Herbert summed it up best in an interview with Stan Wiater when he said, "People expect us to look like Christopher Lee and wear a black cape, don't they?"

People expect that horror writers look like vampires or ghouls who live in foul castles and write their tomes by candlelight in the small hours of the morning. People imagine that military-thriller writers live in bomb-shelters, play with weapon systems in their spare time, and take the kids to school in a fully armed Hummer. And they'd like to think that erotica writers are dirty old men who drool over the keyboard, or are sexually liberated women who spend their days in bed, trying out new positions before they write about them in their next novel or short story.

Nothing could be farther from the truth.

While there are some erotica writers who indulge in the activities they write about (things such as S/M or dominance and submission), most erotica is simply an extension of a writer's own fantasies and imagination.

The function of erotic literature is to express the secret part of our lives which periodically rules us no less than money or death.

—*Michael Perkins*

Furthermore, it's a popular misconception that writers mostly just put a thin veil over events in their lives — or the lives of people they know — and proceed to pass it off as fiction. Readers who believe this see the disclaimer beginning most works of fiction — "This is a work of fiction. The characters, incidents, and dialogues are products of the author's imagination and are not to be construed as real. Any resemblance to actual events or persons, living or dead, is entirely coincidental" — as nothing more than a legal loophole to prevent the author from being sued by those about whose lives he or she has written.

Some novels are indeed based on real occurrences and the characters in them based upon the people involved in the actual events, but most often, works of fiction are just that: fiction. Novels and short stories are born into this world because a writer sat down and wrote about what he or she had first imagined.

This is especially true for works of erotica.

Instead of being dirty old men and sex-craving young vixens, writers of erotica are apt to be middle-aged housewives or professional freelance writers who write a variety of things to earn a living. And, though some authors such as Erica Jong or Susie Bright have been able to establish very successful careers writing nothing but erotic fiction or nonfiction about sex and erotica (as well as doing things associated with the writing, such as lectures and seminars), the majority of erotica writers are also busy working in other genres.

I myself write erotica, but I also writer horror, science fiction, fantasy, and mystery. I edit and review books, teach writing classes, give talks on writing, and write magazine and book-length nonfiction. If you saw me on the street, you'd think I was an insurance salesman before you'd guess that I write erotica.

In his article "Lust in My Art," which appeared in the October 1992 issue of *Hot Talk,* Daltrey St. James put it this way: "Portrait of a DC-area porn author: a happily married agnostic libertarian nondrinking nonsmoker who's never even tried illegal drugs. . . . If you saw me on the street, you'd think I was just another boringly conventional WASP breadwinner."

There's no prerequisite to being a writer of erotica other than having a fantasy or two about a sexual encounter. That pretty much encompasses the entire human race, so if you've been putting off writing erotica because you felt unqualified to do it, push those thoughts aside and get on with it.

Literature — creative literature — unconcerned with sex, is inconceivable.

— *Gertrude Stein*

2
TYPES OF EROTICA

There are countless different ways to enjoy sex, and there are just as many different ways to write about sexual relations. It would be impossible to list them all here, but what follows is an attempt to at least touch on some of the major subgenres of erotica. Keep in mind that within each subgenre is a multitude of smaller areas of specialization.

Straight Erotica/Vanilla Sex

Erotica featuring sex between heterosexual men and woman is often called "vanilla sex." Although there can be no end to the various ways men and women can make love and please each other, this term covers all of them.

"Vanilla sex" is sometimes used as a derogatory term by publishers of more spicy or risqué erotica to mean boring old missionary-position sex between members of the opposite sex. However, there are still plenty of readers out there who enjoy reading about loving sexual relations between men and women. It's the kind of sex that makes a best-selling romance or thriller sexy. Look at it this way: Even though Baskin and Robbins has 31 kinds of ice cream from which to choose, tried and true vanilla remains one of the company's most popular flavors.

Selected magazines featuring vanilla sex

Penthouse

Penthouse Letters

Club

Genesis

Forum

Hustler

Velvet

Gay Erotica

Gay erotica has experienced tremendous growth over the last few years, with many magazines and publishing houses starting up and thriving in the marketplace. Furthermore, gay erotica has even begun to enter the mainstream, thanks to writers such as John Preston and his *Flesh and the Word* anthology series.

Newsstand gay magazines have included the likes of *Honcho, Mandate,* and *Dude,* which publish gay erotica as well as nonfiction relating to gays and better sex. This is a burgeoning market, and publications are always looking for new writers. You don't have to be gay to write for these publication, but it wouldn't hurt. Many women also write for gay magazines, since straight women appreciate a sexy, good-looking man every bit as much as gay men do. You can write stories for these magazines from a straight perspective — gay men love straight men, since they are forbidden fruit, so to speak — but make sure that what you write isn't derogatory or a put-down, and always remember that the story should be erotic from the gay-male point of view.

(My only gay stories were written at the request of editor Michael Rowe, who first asked me to contribute a gay vampire story to an anthology he was editing with Thomas S. Roche called *Sons of Darkness.* I included a single sex scene, which Michael promptly removed. Seems I couldn't get the gay sex right, and Michael enjoys relating the story of my straight-boy faux pas to anyone who'll listen. However, the story worked well enough without the sex scene for Michael to ask me to contribute to another of his gay horror anthologies, *Queer Fear.* The story I wrote for that one also contained a sex scene that didn't work. This

A Few Words with...

Michael Thomas Ford

On Writing Gay Erotica

EDO VAN BELKOM: Did you start out writing gay fiction, or was it something you came to after publishing your work elsewhere?

MICHAEL THOMAS FORD: Well, gay erotica and gay fiction are entirely different things. I write gay fiction and gay nonfiction because I'm a gay man and I like to write about my life and the lives of the community I am a part of. Gay erotica is a genre within that.

I started writing gay erotica simply because what I was reading wasn't very good. I thought I could do better, so I tried. I sent out my first story and two days later it was accepted. I wrote gay erotica for about three or four years, off and on, publishing it in various magazines and ultimately putting out two collections of my stories, *Hitting Home & Other Stories* and *Tales from the Men's Room,* written under the name Tom Caffrey. But I was also writing other kinds of material during this time, both gay and non-gay, and I continue to do so. The erotica was more for fun than anything else, as you certainly can't make a living doing it, or at least not a very good one.

EDO VAN BELKOM: How much has the market for gay erotica and gay-male fiction in general expanded over the past few years?

MICHAEL THOMAS FORD: Again, gay erotica and gay fiction are two entirely different things. The erotica market is still fairly strong. The gay porn magazines, which are the primary outlet for gay erotic fiction, always need good writing, and there are always new anthologies being put together. Also, several gay presses have begun publishing collections of gay erotica, where for many years there was primarily only one publisher for gay erotic books (BadBoy Books, which is no longer publishing).

Gay fiction is a different thing. For a couple of years, mainstream publishers were very interested in gay books. That has slowed down a lot, not because the books don't sell well, but because they don't sell well when mainstream, largely heterosexual publishers compare their sales figures to the sales figures for non-gay books. The fact is, gay books generally have a limited readership, which is gay people. Even a gay bestseller won't sell enough copies to make most mainstream publishers, who are completely focused on the bottom line, take a chance on more gay titles. That's why we've seen a lot of the gay books published in hardcover from mainstream houses come out in paperback from smaller, gay presses, and often the authors of those books go on to do subsequent books with gay presses.

EDO VAN BELKOM: You've written dozens of books ranging from young adult titles to gay erotica. What sort of challenges does writing for the gay market present that other genres don't?

MICHAEL THOMAS FORD: In general, I think writing is writing. It's all about learning how to get your message across in the most effective way. When you're writing erotica — be it gay or straight — your primary objective is to help the reader experience some aspect of sexual arousal. One of the things I enjoyed about writing erotica for gay men was challenging readers to explore avenues of desire they might not have been down before. That can certainly be a challenge, but I don't think it's peculiar to writing for a gay audience. I've written gay, lesbian, and straight erotica, and it's all fun and challenging in that same way. I know a lot of people make a fuss about how men can't really write erotica about women and vice versa, or how gay men can't write straight erotica, and there have even been anthologies centered around writing across gender or orientation. But I think that's largely an empty argument.

I think the challenge of writing — all writing — is being able to honestly and effectively describe how characters react to whatever situations you put them in. Writing erotica is about understanding desire, and while writing about being a woman getting fucked is certainly different from writing about being a man getting fucked, in the end it's all about being able to capture the moment.

EDO VAN BELKOM: Gay-male erotica can range from literary soft-core porn to hard-core sex, with the envelope expanding all the time. Is there anything that is still taboo, or are there markets for anything and everything?

MICHAEL THOMAS FORD: The market is limited primarily by Canadian censorship laws. If a magazine or a book is going to be distributed in Canada, where the laws are much more draconian than they are in the States, then there are a lot of taboos. For example, one magazine I used to write for started out having only a few taboos, such as rape and incest. As the Canadian laws tightened, we kept getting lists of more and more things we couldn't do. The word "boy," for example, became taboo, both in descriptions and dialogue, even if the people involved were clearly stated to be over the age of 21. Similarly, we couldn't use any language or imagery that suggested force, even if it was clearly consensual. Eventually, writing for this magazine became no fun, and I stopped when they asked me to write a story for their special leather fetish issue but said the story could have nothing in it even suggesting S/M or rough sex.

Aside from the censorship laws, though, most magazines are self-censored, depending upon what their readership wants. You don't write S/M scenes in stories for a vanilla magazine, for example, or stories about big, hairy men for a magazine whose readers like pictures of smooth, thin guys. Luckily, there are magazines for almost every fetish you can imagine, so if you want to write about a particular thing, you probably can.

EDO VAN BELKOM: Someone like John Preston was a celebrated writer inside the gay community and fairly well-known outside it. Are other gay writers making strides toward the mainstream or is it a closed genre?

MICHAEL THOMAS FORD: John Preston was widely acknowledged outside of the gay community. In fact, his *Flesh and the Word* series of gay erotica was the first erotica series to really get the attention of mainstream publishers and reviewers, and it launched a revolution in erotica publishing that is only now starting to slow down. And Preston's acclaimed series of essay anthologies earned him critical attention in many mainstream venues. Many gay writers are, in fact, acknowledged by the mainstream, and have successful careers selling to non-gay audiences. The mystery novelists Michael Nava and Steven Saylor, for example, have enormous audiences among non-gay readers. Armistead Maupin's *Tales of the City* books are hugely popular with gay and non-gay audiences.

Now, this isn't to say that everyone is embracing gay writing and gay writers. But there's no reason they should. Critical attention and praise are different from wide readership. Many gay writers get excellent reviews in important places, and their skill is acknowledged. But readers, in general, read books that are of interest to them, so writers who write about gay characters and gay life are, by and large, going to be read by other gay people. There's nothing wrong with that, although certainly it can disappoint writers who like to think that what they write is universal enough to have wider appeal.

I think that, too often, people equate being popular primarily with a specific readership with not being successful, especially if that readership is in the minority. But the point of writing, for me, is to reach the audience you have in mind. If you do that, and they enjoy and understand what you write, then that's all that should matter. The rest is just a bonus.

Michael Thomas Ford is the Lambda Literary Award–winning author of numerous books, including the essay collections Alec Baldwin Doesn't Love Me, That's Mr. Faggot to You, *and* It's Not Mean If It's True. *His fiction, essays, and criticism have appeared in numerous anthologies and periodicals.*

time, I had to rewrite the story, always keeping in mind the gay point of view. The result was a much better story, and one of the most violent tales I've ever written.)

It also wouldn't be a bad idea to read a few gay magazines — and this is true for any new genre in which you write — and rent a few videos if you're not sure of what sex between two men might be like. Subject matter for gay erotic stories runs the gamut from soft-core love stories to gang bangs and bondage.

In addition to slick magazines, there are many small presses publishing gay-male erotica, such as Alyson Publications and Circlet Press. In fact, gay fiction has become one of the larger erotic subgenres and features everything from soft- and hard-core sex novels to gothics and detective novels. Some of the latter have broken out of the gay marketplace and been published by large mainstream houses.

Selected magazines and publishers of gay erotica

Magazines

Advocate Men

Beau

Dude

Honcho

Manscape

Torso

Book Publishers

Alyson Publications

Circlet Press

Cleis Press

Idol (Virgin Publishing)

Lesbian Erotica

Like gay-male erotica, lesbian erotica has been enjoying increased popularity over the past few years, and now there are many anthologies of lesbian erotica published by both small presses and large mainstream publishers. While many books of gay and lesbian erotica can be found in the large chain bookstores, the best selection of material can always be had at gay and lesbian specialty stores such as Glad Day Bookshop in Toronto and Boston, Little Sisters Book and Art Emporium in Vancouver, and Good Vibrations in San Francisco.

One of the first lesbian magazines was *On Our Backs,* and it has grown in popularity over the years. It is published out of San Francisco — probably the gay and lesbian capital of the world — and has thrived in the last decade. One of the most prominent lesbian publishers also happens to be located in San Francisco — Cleis Press, which specializes

The sensitive novel of female homosexuality constituted a small but quite popular category in the '50s. I probably read the books more for information and titillation than anything else . . . and one day I finished [reading] one and realized that I could have written it myself.

— *Lawrence Block*

in books such as the annual *Best Lesbian Erotica* anthology series (they also publish select gay titles, including *Best Gay Erotica*), nonfiction books about lesbian sex and lifestyles by such noted writers as Pat Califia and Susie Bright, and even cooking and travel books like *Betty and Pansy's Severe Queer Review of San Francisco.*

(As with my two gay stories, my lone lesbian story was written at the request of an editor. Nancy Kilpatrick had edited a series of erotic horror anthologies for Masquerade Books under the name Amarantha Knight. In 1996, she was putting together *Seductive Spectres,* an anthology of vengeful-ghost stories, and she asked me to contribute to it. Shortly after that, she called me up and asked that I write a lesbian story because it looked as if the anthology was going to be short on that particular type. I agreed to give it a try, and ended up writing "The Terminatrix," about a woman who is killed by her husband and returns as a ghost, only to discover her husband had killed her so he could be with another woman. Needless to say, she evens the score, starting with the new woman in his life. I knew very little about lesbians, and the sex between the women in the story probably reads like a straight-male fantasy about two women having sex, but it worked and was picked up by Susie Bright for her anthology, *Best American Erotica 1999.* My suggestion is that if you want to read erotica that contains lesbian sensibilities and point-of-view, seek out those publications that are written and published by lesbians, for lesbians.)

Selected magazines and publishers of lesbian erotica

Magazines

On Our Backs

Books

Best Lesbian Erotica (annual)

Hers

Hers 2

Dark Angels (lesbian vampire stories)

Book Publishers

Alyson Publications

Circlet Press

Well, that's it, isn't it? Erotica is the safest fantasy arena for sexual expression and experimentation.

— *John Preston*

Cleis Press

Sapphire (Virgin Publishing)

S/M and B&D

S/M stands for sado-masochism and has to do with pleasure and pain, or more specifically, the relationship between the two. Sadists are those who derive pleasure from other people's pain, often by inflicting that pain on others themselves. Masochists are those who enjoy experiencing pain themselves, and that pain is often integral to the sex act and their sexual satisfaction. In many ways, erotica is an ideal outlet for fans of S/M because the fiction can be as wild and as violent as publishers will allow and no one gets hurt. Most often in fiction — and in magazine pictorials — it is women who take on the dominant role over slave-type men, since this type of depiction is most acceptable in today's politically correct society. Having said that, one must keep in mind that even for those who practice S/M as part of their adventurous sex lives, S/M is consensual as well as a form of fantasy role-playing.

B&D stands for bondage and discipline. B&D fiction is usually about some sexual encounter in which someone was tied up. Even in fiction, the sex has to be consensual — as in, "My wife wanted to know what it felt like to be tied to the bed and made love to for hours on end, and I had to admit the thought of it turned me on like nothing else before or since" — or else all in fun, as in, "I was determined to do a strip show for Jerry, and if I had to tie him in a chair to show off my tits and pussy, well then, that's the way it had to be."

Selected magazines and publishers of S/M and B&D erotica

Magazines

Drummer

Nugget

Book Publishers

Olympia Press

Silver Moon Books

But certainly a [horror] story can be erotic. And it can be frighteningly erotic. And there can be strong hints of sadomasochism in it; it's simply a question of the intelligence of the writers and how they handle what they're doing.

— *Graham Masterton*

Oh, I feel horror fiction is very erotic. People have written brilliant essays on that subject. It's absolutely inherent in vampire material: the drinking of the blood, the taking of the victim; all of that is highly erotic.

— *Anne Rice*

Erotic Horror

Erotic horror has been one of the most popular subgenres of horror over the past few years, with dozens of anthologies and novels filling up the shelves. Horror easily lends itself to tales of sex and lust; hence the success of erotic horror. Both genres involve providing the reader with an emotional charge: with horror, you're scared; with erotica, you're turned on. When erotic horror's really working, you're both afraid and just a little bit turned on. A lot of vampire fiction falls into the realm of erotic horror, since the vampire is usually a romantic figure.

A Few Words with...

Nancy Kilpatrick

On Writing Erotic Horror

EDO VAN BELKOM: Why do you think erotica has had such a successful union with the horror genre?

NANCY KILPATRICK: It's a natural marriage. The history of human sexuality is impregnated with guilt that often leads to death, or worse; we have always taken a grim approach to a natural function. The best horror tends to be both visceral and psychological; sensuality blends nicely with both realms. And we humans seem to prefer our sex a tad scary, and for our fears to have impact, we need them to tap both the psychological and the physical so that they are tied up with our drive towards pleasure. Shrewd writers capitalize on this. For one thing, it's fun and challenging to blend genres. Also, in today's market, it makes good marketing sense.

EDO VAN BELKOM: Have you found anything to be off limits or taboo in terms of subject matter?

NANCY KILPATRICK: Not really. As a writer, I've had only one story pulled — by the publishing house, not by the editor. As an editor, none of my publishers have rejected any material I've selected. There are tricky subjects, of course, but good writing can deal with even the most taboo material, like incest, snuff, and bestiality. At the turn of the millennium, we have collectively experienced it all, at least vicariously, and people are jaded. One of the challenges for a writer is to come up with a view of material that actually "melts the frozen sea within," as Kafka put it. A story evocative and vivid, one that cuts deep enough that the reader will again feel something. In the case of erotic horror, the writer aims for feelings of arousal and revulsion combined. No easy task. But pulled off successfully, it becomes a remarkable and rewarding story for both the writer and the reader.

EDO VAN BELKOM: As the editor of several anthologies, is there any aspect of erotic horror in which you think writers often miss the mark?

NANCY KILPATRICK: The biggest problem with blending any genres is to make the story work in both worlds. This is simply good writing. The story itself becomes a double entendre. It can be read as horror or erotica, and it works for either or both. Writers usually slight one genre in favor of the other, so the story reads as either erotic or horrific but not erotic horror, which is a hybrid unto itself.

Nancy Kilpatrick has published 13 novels, including the Power of the Blood *series, more than 100 short stories (winning the Arthur Ellis Award for best mystery story), two collections, four comic books, and has edited seven anthologies, most recently* Grotesques: A Bestiary, *an Ace Books release. Nancy also teaches writing courses on the Internet and can be contacted through her Web site: <www.sff.net/people/nancyk>.*

There are two kinds of erotic horror. The first kind is horror with some sexual content or subject matter, such as the stories you might find in the *Hot Blood* anthology series. The stories don't necessarily have to be sexy, or even provide a turn-on to the reader, but they must deal in some way with sex and adult situations. For this reason, this kind is often called "sexual horror" rather than "erotic horror." The second kind is erotica that is just a little bit dangerous, meaning more graphic and explicit, bordering on what some might call pornography.

Selected authors and works of erotic horror

Ramsey Campbell, *Scared Stiff*

Jeff Gelb, Michael Garrett, eds., *The Hot Blood Series Vols. 1–10*

Amarantha Knight, ed., *Flesh Fantastic, Seductive Spectres, Demon Sex, Love Bites*

Michele Slung, ed., *I Shudder at Your Touch*

Lucy Taylor, *Unnatural Acts and Other Stories*

Thomas Tessier, *Finishing Touches*

Erotic Romance

It used to be that romance novels depicted virgin women and morally steadfast men making eyes at each other against backdrops of sunny skies and lush forests. They would carry on in this manner, wending their way through 200 pages, until a single soulful kiss was consummated in the final chapter before the characters set off into the sunset to get married and have a life full of (sex and) children.

Romances have come a long way since gothics and nurse novels cluttered the shelves. The change started in the 1970s, when sex started to make an appearance in historical romances. It was referred to in the softest of terms or often shrouded under the pretense of rape or otherwise forced sexual activity, which the heroine resists, then accepts, and finally enjoys, being overcome with passion. But while romance novels have gotten hotter over the years, they still haven't made the leap to outright erotica. The sex, although explicit at times, is seldom anything but heterosexual vanilla sex.

Some specific imprints published by the major romance publishers have more adventurous scenes. Non-series mainstream romance novels are freer in terms of sexuality, and the descriptions of the sex act are far more graphic than category romances.

Selected romance novels and imprints with erotic content

Imprints

Intimate Moments (Silhouette Books)

Silhouette Desire (Silhouette Books)

Temptation Blaze (Harlequin)

Horror and sexuality have always been linked. Good horror writing is almost always sensuous writing because the threat posed in horror fiction is usually a veiled erotic threat.

—*Anne Rice*

Novels

Susan Andersen, *Be My Baby, Baby I'm Yours*

Thea Devine, *All I Desire, By Desire Bound*

Linda Howard, *After the Night, All the Queen's Men*

Elizabeth Lowell, *Pearl Cove, Jade Island*

Beatrice Small, *Besieged, Bedazzled*

Adult Westerns

Although the western genre is quite small compared to others such as science fiction, mystery, and romance, one area in which the western thrives is series publication. Check the men's action-adventure section in your local bookstore, and along with the usual series published by Worldwide (an imprint from the Harlequin Romance people), you'll find a few shelves of western novels. A large percentage of that shelf space will be taken up by series novels, some of them quite long-running, with a current issue number well over 200.

These westerns are aimed at a male audience and usually follow a format that gives the reader what he wants, much in the same way that series romance novels do. These novels always feature a love interest and one or more sex scenes, which usually occur toward the middle or end of the book, and which are fairly soft-core by today's standards. The placing of the sex scenes allows a suitable amount of sexual tension to build up between the hero and his love interest, and can often provide a respite between shoot-em-up action scenes.

Series westerns are usually published under a house name to allow several authors to write for the series simultaneously and to keep the series fresh and published on schedule. Copyrights to the series are usually owned by the publisher, who will create the series and hire established professional authors to produce the books. The only way a new writer would be able to crack this market is by creating and writing a totally new series, or by writing several original western novels and then expressing interest in writing series westerns to the editor of a particular series.

Selected adult-western series

Tabor Evans, *Longarm* (more than 250 installments)

Jack Hanson, *Wildgun*

Jake Logan, *Slocum* (more than 250 installments)

J.R. Roberts, *The Gunsmith* (more than 220 installments)

Fetish Fiction

There's a wonderful aspect of human sexuality that ensures that there will always be someone who is interested in someone else, no matter how that person looks — beautiful, homely, fat, thin, tall, short, whatever. It's called "partialism," and it means that there will always be *someone* who is attracted to *some thing*, no matter how different or strange that thing might be. Women might be partial to a man's tight butt and hairy chest, while men might be partial to a woman's large breasts or long legs. Or someone might enjoy a particular type of clothing, from lingerie to latex rubber, from high-heels to gas masks.

These specialized sexual interests are called fetishes, and in the world of erotica, fetish fiction can be quite popular. Several erotica publishers have lines of books devoted to different types of dominant/submissive behavior and S/M, and mass-market magazines run the gamut from legs to breasts, young girls to mature women, tiny women to voluptuous matrons, ethnic groups, and a whole range of even more specialized niches.

One way to discover what's out there is by taking a trip to your local newsstand (the one that sells all the slick magazines, not just *Playboy* and *Penthouse*) or to a gay or lesbian specialty bookstore. Spend some time scanning the shelves. You'll be amazed at the diversity, and you never know for just which specialty magazine you'll have a talent.

Over the years I've sold dozens of stories to *Gent* (published by Dugent), which calls itself "Home of the D-Cups." I didn't have a particular interest in this specialty at the time but I lucked into selling to the magazine after my first submission. (See the Introduction for a more detailed report on how this came about.)

After I'd sold a number of stories to *Gent*, I was asked to provide stories for other magazines in the Dugent stable, so I wrote for their magazine about large-sized women, *Plumpers and Big Women*, and for their short-lived, all-black magazine, *Sugah*. One excellent piece of advice I can give you about writing for these types of markets is make sure you put a positive spin on the women in your story. For instance, if you're writing for a magazine that features older women, at some point put in a line like, "He'd been with plenty of women, but the best always seemed to be mature, full-figured women who really knew how please a man and have a good time while they were at it." These publications are appreciations and celebrations of the specialized fetish in their pages, and this sort of line reinforces that, especially to the reader.

The only other specialized markets I've been able to regularly sell to are those specializing in legs — you know, stockings, high heels, pantyhose, and the like. I've tried other markets, such as those concentrating on young girls (18 and older) with older men, but haven't been able to get it right. And there are other magazines for which I've considered writing but just could not understand what the erotic attraction was, so I didn't bother. (Some people find latex and leather sexy; I don't.) It's not surprising that many of these specialized magazines have contributors who themselves specialize in a certain subspecialty of the magazine's already small niche.

If you want to write erotica but aren't sure what type you'd like, don't be afraid to try different things. You might even surprise yourself along the way.

Selected fetish magazines

40-Plus (older women)

Babyface, Petite (young girls — 18 and over)

Gent, Score (large breasts)

Leg Show, Leg Sex (legs, high heels, stockings)

Outlaw Biker (bikers, leather)

The Rubberist (latex)

Erotic Nonfiction

Erotic nonfiction appears in both magazine and book format, with some of the latter becoming national bestsellers.

Just about every adult magazine, whether it's for heterosexual men and women or gays and lesbians, has an article or two in it, frequently about ways to improve your sex life. If the article appears in a specialty magazine, then the nonfiction will be about improving your sex life by exploring an aspect of that magazine's specialty. One of my nonfiction articles was called "The Well-Dressed Leg: A Gift-Giving Guide for Leg Lovers." It outlined the best gifts for leg-loving men to give to the women in their lives, and covered everything from short skirts and high heels to pantyhose and stockings. It even delved into ankle bracelets, tattoos, and tanning. The purpose of such an article is to both turn on and to inform the reader, so I spent plenty of time on descriptions of high heels, stockings, etc., and what they do to the female form.

Other articles I've done have been actual "how-to" articles about sex. This sort of nonfiction requires some research to ensure that you at least sound as if you know what you're talking about. If you're writing for a men's magazine, these stories are often best told from a woman's point of view and under a female pseudonym. After all, what better advice can there be than that from a woman who's speaking directly from experience? These articles are also frequently peppered with plenty of quotes from "Janine, a 24-year-old waitress, who admits she's had her share of men compliment her on her legs." The anecdotes and quotes are usually embellished — or outright fabricated — to suit the article you're writing. Of course, if you're writing basic articles for a men's magazine, which are practically fiction anyway — "The Ten Best Places to Meet Women" — then creating quotes and the people who say them is no big deal.

Having said that, writing erotic nonfiction doesn't mean you have to check your journalistic integrity and standards at the door. It all depends on the magazine for which you're writing and the expectations of its editors and readers. If you're writing an advice column for *Playboy* or *Cosmopolitan,* you'd better have interviewed the people you're quoting and have done plenty of firsthand research, talking to doctors, psychologists, and sex therapists. Even so, because of the explicit nature of erotic nonfiction, sometimes details must be changed to protect the privacy of those being quoted. For example, here is the disclaimer on the copyright page of Carol G. Wells's 1991 book, *Naked Ghosts: Intimate Stories from the Files of a Sex Therapist,* which is a clinical study, but one with plenty of erotic details from people's sex lives:

> *This book is the work product of Carol Wells' experience through the years as a therapist. Each of these case histories is a composite of people she has known and worked with throughout her career. Names of the patients described in the case histories have been changed.*

Selected authors and works of erotic nonfiction

Wendy Dennis, *Hot and Bothered: Men and Women, Sex and Love in the 90s*

Nancy Friday, *My Secret Garden: Women's Sexual Fantasies, Women on Top, Forbidden Flowers: More Women's Sexual Fantasies*

Graham Masterton, *Wild in Bed Together, Single, Wild, Sexy . . . and Safe, How to Drive Your Woman Wild in Bed, More Ways to Drive Your Man Wild in Bed*

Carol G. Wells, *Naked Ghosts: Intimate Stories from the Files of a Sex Therapist*

True Confessions

Magazine confessions are 2,000- to 6,000-word stories written in the first person that are designed to sound to the reader as if a friend is relating an event from his or her own life. These are basically "problem" stories — the people involved confront and try to deal with a problem. That problem can be something as small as low self-esteem or as big as spousal abuse. Like most stories, the main character must fix the problem and learn something about himself or herself along the way — which will usually be summed up at the story's end. Confessions are most often written in the first person from a middle- or working-class woman's point of view and are published without a byline.

Contrary to what you might think, most confessions stories are based, however loosely, on the lives of real people. In fact, confessions-magazine editors will expect you to sign a release attesting to the veracity of your story.

Author Michael Bracken, who has written dozens of confessions stories for magazines such as *Black Confessions, Intimate Romances, Jive,* and *True Secrets,* says, "While my imagination certainly plays a role in the development of a confession from concept through completion, nearly all are based on a real-life event which happened to me or to someone I know. I've found that reality-based confessions are both easier to write and easier to sell."

Sex is often the main subject of a confession — from not enough to too much, from boring to too kinky — and if it's not the main subject, sex almost always plays a part in the story. However, sex scenes in confessions don't get much more explicit than those in many romance novels in which loving couples "discover the rhythms of love," "lose control," and "shudder together in love."

Selected magazines publishing true confessions

Black Confessions

Black Secrets

Bronze Thrills

Intimacy

Jive

True Confessions

True Life

True Love

True Romance

True Secrets

True Story

(Note: All titles published by the Sterling/Macfadden Partnership, 233 Park Ave. S., NY, NY 10003.)

Letters

Every magazine dealing with sex has a section for readers' letters. In the upscale magazines such as *Playboy* and *Penthouse*, these letters relate readers' "true life" sexual encounters. They are written in the first person and usually run a few hundred to 1,000 words. These are the letters about guys coming home late from work one night, taking a dip in the condo pool to unwind, and ending up having sex in the showers with the woman upstairs. Some of these letters recount actual events that happened to readers; some don't. The most telling aspect of these letters is that they often follow trends in specific magazines. For a few months, young men with older women might be popular, then the focus might switch to multiple partners. If you're thinking of writing some erotic letters, read some, then try to write something completely different. Publishing lead times are such that by the time you spot a trend and write a similar piece, the letters section will be on to something new.

Erotic letters are such a popular part of most magazines that there are even magazines focusing solely on letters. *Penthouse Letters* and *Hot Talk* are two such publications. There are plenty of letters in their pages, all of them fairly well written and full of explicit sex. Because so many publications use letters, letters can be a great way to break into writing magazine erotica. You may or may not be paid for your letters, depending on where they are published. However, if you do enough letters for a specific magazine, the editor will likely take note and be receptive to a fiction or nonfiction piece from you.

Other magazines (*Gent*, for instance) feature reader fantasies, which are like one long letter describing a sexual encounter in detail, or a fantasy some reader has had about one of the magazine's more popular models. That gives the editor the opportunity to sprinkle the piece with nude photos of the model, and saves the letter section for actual letters.

A Few Words with...

Michael Bracken

On Writing Erotic Letters

EDO VAN BELKOM: How does writing erotic letters differ from writing other erotic fiction?

MICHAEL BRACKEN: Good erotic fiction often has theme and structure beyond simply the mechanics of sex. A good erotic letter introduces the characters and immediately places them in a sexual situation.

An erotic letter nearly always follows a three-step structure: 1) the set-up, where the characters are introduced; 2) the body, where the characters engage in a sexual activity; 3) the climax, where one or more characters achieves orgasm, followed by a short summation of the events or a teaser which leads the reader to believe there's even more the narrator hasn't told.

Unlike other forms of erotic fiction, erotic letters are always written in first person. An erotic letter is usually 3 to 5 pages, typed double-spaced, where erotic short stories often run 10 to 15 pages.

EDO VAN BELKOM: How much of an erotic letter is fiction, and how much is based on truth? Do editors care whether a letter is "real" or not?

MICHAEL BRACKEN: Some publications claim to publish only true, reader-written letters, but I doubt those claims. Most editors don't care if the erotic letter is true, only that it could be true. Sex with the neighbor's spouse could happen, but sex with a three-headed dwarf from Mars couldn't.

When writing erotic letters, it's essential to keep track of the participants' body parts, and not have vaginas suddenly sprout from armpits. Most editors also want the characters in letters to have body parts that are reasonably proportioned. Not every man is hung like a horse and not every woman has breasts the size of a blimp.

EDO VAN BELKOM: What are the markets like for erotic letters?

MICHAEL BRACKEN: The market is wide open and opportunities abound. Included among the many publications which use erotic letters are swingers' publications printed in tabloid-newspaper style, digest-sized publications that print nothing but letters, and many slick men's magazines that use a handful of erotic letters in each issue to supplement the pictorials, short stories, and articles.

Payment ranges from $10 to $100 per letter, but pay rates range from nothing on up. As in all areas of publishing, some publishers and editors are a joy to work with, responding to submissions promptly and paying on acceptance, and others fail to respond at all or delay payments forever. There are so many opportunities that a dedicated letter writer should be able to quickly ferret out the good editors and publishers.

EDO VAN BELKOM: Is there any stigma attached to writing erotic letters? Is it a kind of writing that other writers look down upon?

MICHAEL BRACKEN: Because erotic letters are published pseudonymously, no one need know you ever wrote them.

EDO VAN BELKOM: Do you think writing letters is a good way for a new writer to learn the craft of erotica? What about simply learning the craft of writing?

MICHAEL BRACKEN: Writing letters is an excellent first step for would-be erotica writers and can be a good step in learning the craft of writing. Because erotic letters are so short, and because they usually follow the pattern I outlined earlier, any writer who already has a basic command of the English language and is not afraid to use sexually explicit words can easily master erotic letter writing.

The danger a writer faces is the lure of "easy" money. After sufficient practice, any competent erotic letter writer can easily complete a letter in two hours or less. A short story, erotic or not, takes much more time to complete and requires more attention to plot, characterization, description, dialogue, etc. New writers must consider erotic letters as a good early step, not the final step in a writing career.

Another advantage to writing erotic letters is the opportunity to put work in editors' hands, to receive rejections and acceptances, and to cash a few checks.

Michael Bracken is the author of Deadly Campaign, Even Roses Bleed, Just in Time For Love, Psi Cops, *and nearly 700 shorter works. In addition to numerous science fiction, fantasy, horror, and mystery short stories, he has sold erotica — both letters and full-length erotic short stories — to such publications as* BabyFace, Bust Out!, Chic Letters, Fling, Gent, Gentleman's Companion, Hustler Fantasies, Mantalk, Max, Naughty Neighbors, Nugget, Oui, Outrageous Letters, Playgirl, Score, Screw, Swinging Times, Taboo Letters, Turn-on Letters, Uncensored Letters, Voluptuous, *and many, many more.*

These letter sections contain a variety of letters, ranging from readers' questions about models in the magazine ("She was fantastic! Let's see more!") to accounts of how the magazine played a part in some hot sex had by the reader, either on his own or with a girlfriend. This again allows the editor to use photos of models who appeared in past issues.

Some words of advice to anyone wanting to write erotic letters for publication: Get to the sex quickly. If you want to write about characters, setting, and plot, your time will be better spent on fiction. If you want to write about hot sex, give letters a try.

Selected magazines publishing erotic letters

Fox Magazine

Hot Talk

Lusty Letters

Penthouse Letters

Turn-On Letters

Uncensored Letters

3
STORY FORMAT

What's Best for an Erotic Tale?

Before you start writing erotica, you'll first have to make a few decisions about the kind of erotica you would like to create. But regardless of whether you decide you'd like to try to write literary erotica or fiction for one of the specialty markets, you'll still have to decide on the format or medium in which you'd like to work.

Just as an artist has to choose between oil and watercolor paints, or between canvas and modeling clay, a writer of erotica also has a similar choice to make. Fiction or poetry? Publication of either can be equally rewarding. Novel or screenplay? The story can be the same, but the end products are very different.

Perhaps the following will help you decide.

Novels versus Short Stories

It used to be easier to break into print by writing a sex novel than by writing any other type of prose. In the 1950s and 1960s, there were dozens of publishing companies producing countless sex novels each month. This was a time when men's magazines sold their product by

I served my own novelistic apprenticeship in the field of paperback sex novels. In the summer of '58, I had just finished my first novel and was wondering what to do next. My agent got in touch with me to say that a new publisher was entering the field of sex novels. Could I read a few and try one of my own? I bought and skimmed several representative examples in the field. I then sat down at the typewriter with the assurance of youth and batted out three chapters and an outline of what turned out to be the start of a career.

— *Lawrence Block*

showing only exposed breasts and erect nipples. It was also before adult films were available on video, and before the Internet brought live porn into the home. Back then, the only place people could get their sexual fix was at the newsstand or drugstore, where books with titles such as *Fun Girl* and *The Strangest Marriage* were available for just 50¢ a pop.

These sex novels were nothing more than stories (crime, adventure, romance) with sexual themes or in which the characters found themselves in sexual situations more often than not. A single novel might have 10 or 12 sex scenes in it (each one slightly different from the next in terms of partners and activity) before the story came to an end — or, dare I say, climax. The neat thing about these books was that, just like the best adult films, they contained real stories.

More recently, sex novels became the bottom of the barrel in terms of publication credentials for a young writer. Companies such as Beeline produced books through the 1980s and 1990s, but their distribution was erratic and it sometimes seemed that the companies didn't want anyone to know they were in business. The most recent Beeline title that I purchased at a local convenience store, *Desires of the Flesh*, has an ISBN number but no company address. There is a notice that says —

All Rights Reserved
Interlude Press
Toronto, Ontario

— but a check of the Toronto phone book reveals no Interlude Press, and in the end, locating the company seemed more trouble than it was worth. Perhaps the decline of the sex novel is best summed up by Lawrence Block, the bestselling mystery writer who toiled at writing sex novels early in his career. In his nonfiction book, *Writing the Novel: From Plot to Print*, he writes:

> *Is the sex-novel field a good starting place for a beginner today? I'm afraid not. Their equivalent in today's market is the mechanical, plotless, hard-core porn novel, written with neither imagination nor craft and composed of one overblown sex scene after another. The books I wrote were quite devoid of merit — let there be no mistake about that — but by some sort of Gresham's Law of Obscenity they've been driven off the market by a product that is indisputably worse. Any dolt with a typewriter and a properly dirty mind could write them; accordingly, the payment is too low to make the task worth performing. Finally, the books*

are published by the sort of men who own massage parlors and peep shows. You meet a better class of people on the subway.

Daltrey St. James, in his October 1992 *Hot Talk* article "Lust in my Art," talks about trying to sell a sex novel after having great success writing erotic short stories:

> *Payment would be four hundred dollars for a novel of at least thirty-five thousand words, which works out to a little more than a penny a word. That four hundred dollars would cover outright purchase; the author would receive no royalties or further payment of any kind and the publisher would own the copyright.*

Ouch!

Hardly worth it, when four hundred dollars is what an average men's magazine pays for a short story less than one-tenth the length of a novel.

But, like the weather, trends in publishing go through changes, and sex novels aren't exactly the literary ghetto they were just a few years ago. Recently, publishers have discovered that the people who most often buy erotic literature are women. As a result, erotic novels are now published by erotica imprints from major mainstream publishers, and are sold in the "Erotica" sections of major bookstore chains, as well as in specialty stores that sell gay and lesbian books.

A Few Words with...

Lawrence Block

On Writing Erotic Novels

EDO VAN BELKOM: Since you probably never planned on a career writing sex novels, how did it all come about?

LAWRENCE BLOCK: I had worked for a year as an editorial associate at the Scott Meredith agency, and had been writing and selling magazine fiction. A month or so after I left the job, I got a note from Henry Morrison with an assignment to write three chapters and an outline of a spicy novel for Harry Shorten of Midwood Books. So I did, and one thing led to another.

EDO VAN BELKOM: What did writing over 100 sex novels teach you about the craft that you might not have otherwise learned?

LAWRENCE BLOCK: Hard to say. The form was a very forgiving one, and as long as the story moved along and the sex scenes were right, you could pretty much do as you pleased. Writing's like most things in that you learn by doing.

EDO VAN BELKOM: Repetition can often be boring, even when you're writing about sex. At what point did writing erotica become a chore for you, or at least not much fun anymore?

LAWRENCE BLOCK: I don't know, but I guess it happened. I've noticed that the sex scenes in my subsequent crime fiction have been quite circumspect. Maybe I got all that out of my system. Or perhaps it's all part of aging.

EDO VAN BELKOM: After writing so many novels so quickly, did writing a single mystery or crime novel seem almost easy to complete, or did it present a whole new set of challenges?

LAWRENCE BLOCK: My apprenticeship helped make me confident that I could start and finish novels. But nothing ever writes the book for you. You have to do it yourself, and it's new each time.

Lawrence Block is the author of several books for writers, including the classic Telling Lies for Fun and Profit. *His most recent Bernie Rhodenbarr mystery is* The Burglar in the Rye. Hit List *is his second book about the wistful assassin Keller.*

If there is now a market for sex novels, is it a place to start a fiction writing career?

Well — yes and no. You can publish erotic novels, but unless your erotic novel has made a splash in the mainstream (much like Erica Jong's *Fear of Flying* did when it was published), you might have to satisfy yourself with a small number of avid readers. Even if you publish a number of erotic novels, the advances and royalties probably won't amount to enough for you to make a living. The reason sex novels used to be a great training ground was that you could write them in six to ten days and they would sell very well, earning you more than a so-called "straight" writing job would. Those days are gone.

If there is a market today that is as voracious and well-paying as the sex-novel industry of the 1950s and 1960s, it would have to be in men's magazines. Go to your local newsstand or convenience store and take a quick survey of the number of magazines on the shelves. Most of these magazines publish fiction, and all of them use some sort of letters in their pages. Then keep in mind that your local store likely doesn't stock half of the titles that are available. Finally, if you consider the Internet as an additional market for short-form erotica, there appears to be almost no limit to the number of markets out there for letters and short stories. If you can write erotica well and fast, there are markets that want and need what you write.

Of course, if you have your heart set on writing novels, there are novel markets out there as well, more than you'd imagine if you include mainstream publishers as publishers of erotica. Jacqueline Susann's *Valley of the Dolls* was little more than soft-core pornography, and the same has been said of the novels of Jackie Collins. It all depends on your viewpoint and what you consider to be a work of erotic fiction. Perhaps the best thing about erotica is that it doesn't matter what kind of package it's wrapped in; the maxim "Sex Sells" still holds true.

I tried some other things, but the real passion was for the erotic.

— *Larry Townsend*

Erotica Other Than Prose Fiction and Nonfiction

Short stories and novels aren't the only forms of erotic writing out there. In fact, they make up only a small part of the erotica field. Other forms, such as poetry, won't pay as much, but you will nonetheless likely receive the same amount of satisfaction from having created and published the work. At the other end of the spectrum, writing for erotic films might not be personally satisfying, but the financial rewards will probably make up for that.

Writing erotic poetry

If you're interested in writing erotica for money, you can skip this section altogether. Poetry, no matter in what genre, even if it's literary, isn't going to earn you anything more than a token payment. If you want to write erotic poetry, you'll be doing it simply for the love of expressing yourself in a provocative or sensual way. And if you use plenty of sexy-sounding words and make your subject matter sexy as well, you might

find yourself and your readers getting turned on by it. But no matter how good a job you've done or how hot your poetry is, you'll have an awfully hard time finding a market.

None of the men's magazines publish poetry — unless it's a limerick for their humor page, beginning with the line "There was an old lady from Mundt. . . ." Some women's sex magazines or mainstream magazines that deal heavily with sexual subject matter (such as *Cosmopolitan* or *Flare*) might use poetry, but only as filler or with a special section or article on sex. Which is not to say that it's impossible to place an erotic poem in such magazines (remember that there are always exceptions to every rule), but that it's almost impossible.

It's more likely that you'll publish erotic poetry in small literary magazines (some of which are barely more than pamphlets) that embrace exotic or even bizarre material. *Paramour* is one such magazine, but other zines — the type you might find in a university or college bookstore — might be better markets to explore. If you place a poem in one of these publications, be prepared to be satisfied with seeing your work in print and receiving nothing more than a copy of the zine as payment.

Perhaps a better use of your erotic poetry might be on your lover. What would taping an explicit poem to the refrigerator door do for your love life? Or how would an erotic poem e-mailed to your lover at work perk up his or her day?

Finally, if you're absolutely determined to write erotic poetry and see it in print, consider including it in your erotic fiction. Write a story called "The Pleasure Poet" and provide samples of the poet's hot verse. Or write an erotic novel called *The Poet's Pleasure* and start each chapter with a sample of your own ribald verse.

As with all else in the writing game, anything can be achieved through imagination and perseverance.

Writing erotic comics

Erotic comic books are quite popular just now. Comic-book artists and writers have begun to explore sexual themes in great detail and have the benefit of being able to use both words and pictures to convey not only the story, but also the mood of their work.

One advantage comic books have over text erotica is that both the men and women depicted can be drawn to suit the situation. Scantily clad, well-endowed women, well-hung men, and sexual positions unimaginable under the gravitational pull of planet Earth are all possible in erotic comic books. If erotic fiction is mostly fantasy, erotic comics take that fantasy to new heights. American erotic comic books feature the best artists, who can render beautiful women and handsome men with ease and grace. For storylines, it's the Europeans who have the edge in handling the fantasy and sexual tension that make erotica work.

If you're interested in writing for erotic comics, explore the market by visiting a local comic shop (or a comic shop in a big city) and study the racks. You're not going to find erotic comics published by Marvel and DC, but you will probably stumble on dozens of titles produced by small and independent comic-book publishers. Once you've found a publisher, write a letter explaining who you are and that you'd like to write for a comic-book line.

Don't expect anyone to jump at the chance to sign you on. The best you can hope for is to be asked to send in some samples of your work. If you don't have any published samples, you might be asked to show a few sample storylines, either for the company's erotic-comic line or for some other line for which you've written (even if the work wasn't accepted). Still, you've got an uphill battle and will be asked to write a sample story on spec (short for on speculation) — which means that you're just trying out and won't be paid. If they do like your work, then they might use it for an upcoming issue, or they might hire you on and instruct you in what they're looking for from a new writer and the direction they want the current story to take.

Sound like a lot to go through? Maybe, but you'll have to go through the same thing to publish in any field. If you don't have any publishing credits, there has to be some way for a publisher to find out if there is a reason you haven't published before.

It might be easier to establish yourself as a writer of prose erotica and then approach a comic-book publisher. This way, you've already proven that you can write well and tell stories. The only question is whether or not you can write in the comic-book format. The good thing is, format can be taught. Storytelling cannot.

I've written only one comic-book storyline, for an erotic-horror comic series called *Vampire Girls*. I'd thought I'd written a bang-up storyline, filled with naked women and a nice twist ending, but I never heard a word from the company after I submitted it. (Perhaps I had written it like prose fiction rather than as a comic-book story.) I suppose

I could have pursued the matter to find out why I'd failed and ask for a second chance, but my heart wasn't in writing for comics.

I'll be hanging on to the storyline, though. That I'll always be able to use.

Writing phone scripts

Look in just about any erotic magazine or entertainment weekly in North America and you'll notice ads for telephone-sex lines. For entertainment, a client will call one of the advertised lines and, after credit-card verification, will either get a recorded message or have a live, one-on-one chat with the man or woman at the other end.

While some services simply have their employees follow the customer's lead, most make use of scripts, because the phone calls are often limited to a few minutes and a script is useful in helping to get the customer off in the allotted time. As every company is eager for repeat business, scripts are always in demand, and for some of the busier phone services, the use of as many as 30 or 40 a month is not uncommon.

The scripts themselves are a few hundred words long, and must establish an immediate connection between the caller and the person on the other end. Scripts often begin like this: "Hey, remember me? I thought you might. I sure remember you. How could I forget that sweet voice, not to mention your body? Ohhh, I sure remember that!"

If you're interested in writing phone scripts, call up one of the advertised numbers and wait until the end of the message. There is often information or additional numbers to call, which will give you a contact to follow up.

Writing for adult videos

Getting a foot in the door in the adult film industry isn't all that much different from trying to establish yourself in any other business or artistic endeavor.

If you want to write scripts for adult films, or "pornos," you're going to have to do some research. And yes, that means you'll have to rent a few movies, see what makes them work — and what makes them not work — and try to write one yourself on spec. No one at this point will be paying you for your work, and when you're done you'll have to sell it on your own. Once you are established in the field, you might be lucky enough to be commissioned to write a script.

Adult films come in many different formats. A trip to your local adult store will reveal different sections devoted to the different kinds of films, which in turn are devoted to specific fetishes or sex acts. However, when you narrow it all down, there are really just two types of adult films: compilations featuring nothing but sex; and films listed under "couples appeal," which feature costumes, sets, and — most important of all — storylines. This is where you, the writer, come in.

Once you've seen enough films and you know the kind of film you want to write — keeping in mind budgets, number of actors, number of sex scenes, and other aspects of production — you have to find out which company produces those types of films. Pick a company or two and find out where their head offices are located, either by going through the distributor who supplies the store from which you rent, or from the address or contact information on the video box. When you've got the right address, you might want to call the company up and ask to whom you should send a spec script, or at least whom you should query about making a submission.

Next comes the query letter, which tells the person at the other end who you are and explains what your script is about. If they're interested, they'll ask to see the completed script, or might ask that you send them another script — which is why you should have the script completed and ready to go before you query anybody. If you've never sold a porn script, then there's no reason for anyone to be interested in one of your ideas. As with any other business, in the adult-film industry you have to prove yourself before people will trust in your ability.

So you send in your script and hope it's the sort of thing they'll want, and if you've done your homework, there's a good chance that it will be.

If you're interested in a career in the adult-film industry, either as a scriptwriter or producer, it helps if you live near an area where these films are made — Hollywood or New York, or even Montreal. If you're near where they make the films, it's more likely that you'll be able to get work in the industry and make contacts with the people who read and choose the scripts. For years, people have gotten breaks in this way in the music and publishing industries, and it's no different in the adult-film industry.

Perhaps the best thing about writing adult-film scripts is that there is a ready market for them. Thousands of videos are released each year, putting scripts in demand, just as erotic letters and other fiction are in demand in the magazine market.

Things to avoid in adult videos

There are certain things that you should avoid in all erotic writing, but if you're serious about a career writing adult-film scripts, here is a list of five things you would do well to learn before you submit that first spec script.

Avoid —

1. *Sex without a story.* Since the whole point of writing a script is to tell a story, make certain your script tells a compelling story that has room for plenty of sexual tension. The best sex, the sexiest sex, is the kind that arises naturally (or as naturally as possible in these sorts of films) from the storyline.

2. *Unnatural dialogue.* Actors in the adult-film industry aren't widely know for their ability to turn a phrase, so any phony or stiff dialogue will sound doubly so coming out of the mouths of these performers. Your dialogue should sound as much like two real people talking as possible. When you've completed your script, read it out loud or get some friends together to do a reading, just to be sure everything sounds as natural as it can be.

3. *No ending.* Stories have beginnings, middles, and ends, and although many adult films are made up mostly of middles (where all the sex happens), there must be a scene that brings the film to a close. Even better is a scene that brings the film to a close, but hints that the sex between the characters will be going on for a long, long time.

4. *Predictability.* Adult films must have a certain number of sex scenes, and the female lead usually gets two sex scenes instead of just the one in which the other women appear, but don't be afraid to mix things up a bit and provide the viewer with a twist or two. This could be something like a character observing two others having sex, or characters meeting under unusual circumstances — the more unique, the better.

5. *Too much time between sex scenes.* Sure, you want to tell a story, but the story is there to compliment the sex scenes, not the other way around. Be as economical as possible when telling the story, and allow the characters to get on with the task at hand — which is, of course, having sex.

Part Two
WRITING EROTICA

Some people get in the writing game with high-minded ideals about the seriousness of their calling. I have no such constraints. I'm not blind to the fact that porn fiction as a genre (cliterature?) isn't held in particularly high esteem . . . but so what? Classical music gets more respect than rock, but that doesn't make *Ziggy Stardust* a bad album.

— Daltrey St. James
"Lust in My Art," *HOT TALK,* October 1992

4
WHAT TURNS YOU ON?

Exploring Your Fantasies in Fiction

Erotica is a genre anyone can write. Perhaps not all can write it well, but since every one of us is a sexual being and every one of us has fantasies, we all have the essential ingredients to produce erotic fiction.

Because of this, erotica is one of the most fun genres in which to write. Unlike other genres, erotica allows you to explore the inner workings of your own sexual psyche, to make use of your fantasies as subject matter and discover what you find exciting about your fantasies.

If you think your fantasies are too wild to be committed to paper, or you wouldn't be caught dead divulging your innermost secrets by writing about them and having them published so that everyone in the world can read them, relax. Your erotic fiction doesn't have to be based on your fantasies; your fantasies need only to serve as a catalyst for your writing. If having multiple partners is one of your fantasies, you don't have to get into specifics, but it would help your fiction if you could convey in your writing why you consider multiple partners a turn-on. Conveying the feeling of sexual excitement and tension is what erotica is about.

On the other hand, if you are interested in turning your sexual fantasies into fiction, you're more than likely on your way to producing something that, if nothing else, turns *you* on. And if it turns you on, chances are it will turn someone else on as well. All this is a roundabout way of saying that you already have the ideas. What you need to do is to learn how to develop them into stories.

However, if you're not willing to admit that you have sexual fantasies, then think of writing erotica as a way of helping you discover what those fantasies might be. Remember, too, that erotic writing doesn't always have to be created with publication in mind. Perhaps you'd like to write down your fantasies and give them to your partner as a gift. Or, by writing erotica, you might come to terms with your fantasies and understand more about yourself in the process.

Finally, if you're still of the opinion that you shouldn't have sexual fantasies, or if you think only perverts or degenerates have wild fantasies, or you'd just like to know if your erotic fantasies are abnormal, I suggest that you pick up one of books on the subject of fantasies written by Nancy Friday. As the author of books such as *My Secret Garden, Forbidden Flowers,* and *Women on Top,* Friday has chronicled several hundred sexual fantasies of both men and women. If reading about these doesn't loosen up your mind and bring your own fantasies to the fore, at the very least the books can serve as a comprehensive guide to what turns on the human mind and body, and why.

More sexy women have romance fantasies, however, than sexual ones. And it has been learned that readers of romance novels tend to be sexier and enjoy sex more than non-readers.

— *Julia Grice,*
What Makes a Woman Sexy

Erotica for Men and Women

In her book *The Magic of Sex,* Dr. Miriam Stoppard says that men and women have similar responses to erotic material:

> *Reading or watching sexually explicit material can produce genital sensations in both women and men, and can have an effect on sexual behavior. Many men use pornography as an aid to masturbation, and many women find that racy material increases their interest in having sex, though few will admit it.*

While men and women might equally enjoy erotica, there is generally a distinct difference in the *kind* of erotic material each sex enjoys, so you should be aware of your readership.

In her book *Dr. Ruth's Encyclopedia of Sex,* Dr. Ruth Westheimer says that the things that turn on each sex in terms of erotica are very different. "Women are often interested in reading a story with greater emphasis

The difference between male- and female-generated erotica lies in the treatment of the subject matter. Men tend to put a lot of emphasis on anatomy. To the man, there is nothing erotic without the body of the woman. To the woman, the male body is a nice addition to an already sensual world. The female erotic imagination is more diffuse than obsessive.

— *Black Lace guidelines*

Sexually, I have a fetish about truth telling. It does help in my work.

— *Dorothy Allison*

on teasing anticipation and a gradual build-up than two people meeting, tearing their clothes off, and jumping into bed."

Men, on the other hand, are stimulated by visual images, primarily of women's bodies, and, in erotic literature, by descriptions of the sex act itself. For years, image- and action-oriented erotica was all that was available because it was produced by men, for men. These days, women produce as much erotic fiction as men do, or more, and they produce it for women, because — let's face it — no one knows better what will appeal to the female libido than another female. And while a good writer can use his or her imagination to gear a piece of fiction toward a specific market, in erotica it's often a case of "It takes one to know one." With very few exceptions, erotica for women is written by women, and most erotica for men is written by men.

If you don't believe it, consider the Black Lace imprint, which produces erotica for women, written by women. Here is the line from their guidelines that spells it out:

> *We accept submissions only from female authors, with no exceptions. We have found that, in this genre, authors tend to write better for their own gender. The fact that all our authors are guaranteed to be women is a valuable part of our marketing strategy.*

Fortunately, Virgin Publishing, the publishers of the Black Lace line, also publish other lines of erotica that are open to both male and female authors.

Making Use of Your Own Fantasies

Just about every writer who has published a work of fiction has been asked the question "Where do you get your ideas?"

That question isn't an easy one to answer.

In my short story collection, *Death Drives a Semi*, I included an essay with the story "And Injustice for Some" that explained how the story came to be written. In the end, I summed up the essay by answering the question "Where do you get your ideas?" with the word "Life."

It sounds like a very simple answer, but it happens to be true. Since everyone has sexual thoughts throughout the day, no one should ever find themselves short of ideas for erotic stories.

For example, if you're a woman who takes the bus to work every day, think about a liaison with a handsome man you see every day on the bus but to whom you never speak —

One day your eyes meet, and you know he's been thinking about you the same way you've been thinking about him. The next few days you sit next to him, saying nothing. Then one day his hand makes its way between your legs. Before you realize it, he's probing the area between your legs. You're shocked by what's happening, but your body is excited by it and you feel yourself spreading your legs wider. Then, just as he's about to touch you there, the bus arrives at his stop and he's gone . . .

I'll leave you to use your own imagination to take it from there.

Now, if you're a man who goes to the library every week or so to do a little reading, you might have thoughts about a good-looking librarian with a friendly smile —

One week she gives you a book and says that since she's been helping you find books that interest you the last few months, she thought that this was the kind of thing you'd enjoy reading. You thank her and take the book home with you. When you get home you realize there's a note inside the book that says — The library closes at 9 p.m. if you'd like to go for a drink somewhere. *You head back to the library and wait for the librarian. She gets into your car, dressed a bit more sexily than she was for work, and you ask her where she'd like to have a drink. She answers, "My place."*

Fantasies, plain and simple.

They are a staple of erotica and a gold mine for writers of erotic literature. And perhaps the best thing about using your own fantasies and everyday experiences for your writing is that you'll be expanding your mind in the meantime. Who knows — you might learn something about yourself you never would have imagined possible.

However, if you're convinced your own life is boring and your thoughts are devoid of any erotic spark, you might need to jump-start your writing with a few fantasies that other people think about all the time. Here is a list of the top ten sexual fantasies, as selected by my alter ego and erotic *nom de plume*, Evan Hollander. (There'll be more on him in chapter 9.) At least one of these will be sure to generate an erotic thought or two in you:

Evan Hollander's Top 10 Fantasies for Men and Women

1. Group sex. Threesomes.

2. Watching others have sex. Being watched having sex.

3. Having sex with someone other than your usual partner.

4. Being forced/forcing someone to have sex against his or her will.

5. Having sex somewhere unusual, exotic (outdoors, an elevator).

6. Using sex toys to enhance the sex act.

7. Having sex with someone who has a large penis/breasts/vagina.

8. Having/being a sexual slave.

9. Interracial sex.

10. Homosexual sex.

Where Else Do You Get Your Ideas?

If you still haven't got any ideas for an erotic story, ask friends what their fantasies are, pick up a newspaper or magazine, or even watch television. (Talk shows can be especially fruitful.) You'd be surprised at the variety of sexual situations, and the lengths to which humans will go to satisfy the sexual urge.

The best idea I ever got from watching television came while viewing the *Geraldo* show one day. On the screen was a very beautiful and sexy woman along with her very fat and overweight husband. The woman told Geraldo that she refused to have sex with her husband until he lost between 50 and 100 pounds.

How insensitive! I thought.

How cruel! I thought.

What a great idea for a story! I thought.

And so I began to write the erotic-horror story "Sex Starved," which is about a man who marries a woman from another country. He thinks she's in love, but she only wants to live in the United States. She refuses to have sex with him, but works as a stripper (and perhaps even as a porn actress). He starves himself and loses 150 pounds, but he ends up hallucinating, mistaking food for human body parts and human body parts for food. In the end she feels sorry for him and agrees to have sex with him, but by this time he can't tell the difference between his wife and a T-bone steak. So when he goes down on her, he eats her — literally.

The story was published in 1994 in volume four of the *Hot Blood* series of erotic-horror anthologies and is reprinted in my erotic-horror collection, *Six-Inch Spikes*.

I have none other than Geraldo Rivera to thank for providing the story's inspiration.

Ideas Are Easy; Writing Stories Is Hard

An idea for an erotic story can range from a single image to a complete storyline.

Say you're a man walking through your neighborhood mall, and you spot a woman who's sitting by herself with her legs crossed. She's got nice legs, which are made even more attractive by the pantyhose she's wearing, and by the way her black high heels shape her feet and the rest of her legs.

Is that an idea? Yes and no. If you think it's not an idea, then it's just an attractive image that can be either innocent or erotic, depending on your point of view. But if you think it is a story idea, then you can use it as such and form a story around it.

The impulse stems from this single image of an attractive woman sitting on a bench in the mall. To turn the idea into a story idea, you have to use it in a story. How about this:

> *A man is on his lunch break walking through the mall. He sees an attractive woman with terrific legs sitting on a bench. Her legs are crossed, and her right leg is exposed past the thigh. It looks sexy, and the man is a bit intrigued. He sits down, starts talking to her, and she's very friendly. He boldly decides to put a hand on her leg — it's just too tempting — and she doesn't seem to mind. They keep talking, keep flirting, and she eventually says that she has the afternoon off and would he like to spend it with her?*

He says yes. They go back to her place and they have great sex.

A week later he's walking through the mall again. He spots her from the upper level and decides to go down and talk to her. But by the time he reaches the bench where's she's sitting, there's another guy sitting next to her. He's talking away, and then he puts his hand on her leg. She smiles at him, and a few minutes later they leave together.

And our man realizes that the woman wasn't just sitting there, she was trolling for a man, waving her sexy leg as bait for any sex-starved man who flowed by in the stream. He understands he's been caught and released like a fish, but remembering the afternoon he had, he doesn't seem to mind all that much.

He walks the rest of the mall, curious to see if any other women are out angling today.

So, there you have it, SI, SI, SL:

Sexy Image

Story Idea

Story Line

But even though there's a storyline, it still isn't a complete story. Ideas are easy to come up with; it's the writing of the complete story, paying attention to all the details that make fiction interesting and entertaining, that's the hard part. It's a cliché, but only because it is true: Writing is one percent inspiration, and 99 percent perspiration.

Once you've come up with an idea or outline (try the exercise in Sample 1) that you think will make a good story, *don't stop there*. You mustn't be satisfied with the idea alone. You have to keep going and turn your idea into a story. It is only when you've finished something like a full story or novel that you can be truly satisfied.

If that doesn't convince you, consider it this way. Ideas are like foreplay, but completing a story is like orgasm. It's fun to have the former, but it doesn't truly mean anything until you've experienced the latter.

Sample 1
Rapid-Fire Story Ideas

Ideas are easy to come by, but turning them into stories is hard. If you don't believe it, try coming up with a bunch of story ideas in rapid succession. Write them all down, no matter what you think of them at the time, and stop when you've got five or so ideas. Of course, not all of them will be gems, but at least one of them might be worth turning into a full story, and perhaps even more than one. The point is that real writers don't suffer from writer's block. Instead, they find they never have enough time to write all the things they want to. There's no such thing as writer's block — and no room for it in a professional writer's life (if you don't write, you don't eat) — only a lack of will and determination.

Now, let's see what we can come up with.

On our mark.

Get set.

Go!

1. A man and a woman play on the company softball team. In the middle of a game, it starts to pour rain, and everyone runs to their cars to keep dry. The man and the woman discover they are hot for each other and have sex. When the sun comes out, they don't return to the field.

2. A man sends love letters to a long-lost love, and they are answered. The letters get hotter and hotter until the two correspondents decide to meet. When they meet, the man discovers that the woman answering his letters is not the woman he thought he was writing to. She says he had the address wrong, but his letter were so good she wanted to read more of them, so she answered. She hopes he doesn't mind too much. He doesn't, since she's better looking than he remembered the other one being.

3. A woman is having coffee with her best friend, and they are talking about sex. She says her husband doesn't have much interest in sex, and when he does, he doesn't seem interested in doing it very well. The other woman says her husband's great in bed, especially after she's spent so much time training him. She offers to train her friend's husband.

4. A waitress spills some coffee in the lap of one of her customers. She bends down to wipe up the stain and notices that the man has an erection. She says she's sorry about the stain, but if he waits until she's off in half an hour, she'll wash his pants for him, at her apartment.

5. A woman is interested in her hairdresser — a man she's been going to for years — but he doesn't seem to notice her very much. She's heard from some of the woman at the shop that he's gay, but she's also heard that he's quite a good lover, and that he likes things to be a bit exciting. She decides to go for a trim, but when he asks her where she wants him to trim, she answers, "Down there!"

Exercise

Take a half-hour and jot down whatever ideas pop into your head, no matter how silly or bizarre. If you don't like the results, try combining the ideas from more than one story.

Keeping Track of Your Ideas

If you intend to make writing erotica or any other kind of writing a part of your life (even if it's just as a hobby), you should keep a notebook.

Ideas pop into writers' heads at the oddest of times. I've often awakened in the middle of the night, walked down to my office and scribbled a few lines in one of my notebooks, just to be sure that I wouldn't forget the idea come morning. Notebooks are also handy if you have an idea (and an idea can be anything from a few lines of dialogue, a phrase, or an image, to a complete outline of a story) but don't have the time at the moment to write the full story.

My notebooks are filled with page after page of story ideas. Often I'll write the story a few days after the idea is noted in the book. When that happens, I put a line through the story outline so I'll know it's been written. Other ideas might hang around for a few years waiting for a market to open up for them. I've often reread my notebooks looking for story ideas and quite often have found just what I'm looking for. It's almost like shopping in an idea store in which you personally stocked the shelves.

Don't give up on a good idea. I've written stories two or three years after the idea first came to me, and in the case of novels, it might have taken me upwards of five years to use an idea that's been bouncing around inside my head for all that time.

Although ideas are fairly easy to come up with, never let one slip through your fingers. You never know when one might come in handy, or be turned into the story that earns the check that pays the bills.

Knowing Where You're Headed: Outlining

Some authors say that they don't like to know how a story ends because that would take away their pleasure in writing it; they like to be surprised by their characters along the way. For these people, writing is a journey of discovery, and knowing how the journey ends is like going to see a mystery movie and knowing "who dunnit" before the curtain rises.

That's all well and good for writers who like to think they're writing "literature," but let's face it: if you're writing erotica, you know that your characters are going to end up having sex, and that's more than likely how the story itself is going to end. Knowing how the story will end is helpful during the writing process because you can more easily guide your characters toward the bedroom.

As I've said, I keep a notebook of story ideas in my office, and I write down all of the ideas that pop into my head. The notes can range from just a few lines that might be useful in some way in the future all the way up to an outline of a complete story. For example, here are a couple of notes from one of my notebooks:

— *She had so much cleavage, it had its own echo.*

— *Her vaginal lips were delicate, hot and slick, and she moaned again as he traced them with his tongue, first the outer, then the inner.*

Just a couple of lines that I came across while reading or listening to a conversation that I thought sounded interesting and which I thought I might use (paraphrased, of course, or in some other format) in one of my own stories. Either way, the lines will eventually make their way into something of mine, and the only reason they will is because I took the time to write them down in my notebook.

The other type of notes I make are full story outlines. These can be very rough outlines that suggest the gist of a story, or they can be complete outlines that tell the entire story in a hundred or more words.

Here's a brief outline for a story that might or might not end up being a tale of erotica:

> *A woman writes a letter to a man, telling him how much she enjoyed the few nights of passion they'd shared together several years before. She wants to be with him again.*
>
> *When they meet, he is surprised to find that it is a totally different woman than the one he remembered spending time with. She tells him that she came across the other woman's diary, and their time together sounded so wonderful she just had to contact him.*

Obviously there are many possibilities presented by this scenario. It could be the start of a suspense story or thriller novel. It could be the start of a romance novel or story, even a tale of erotica. The end result depends on the details I choose to insert into the basic storyline.

Here are a couple of examples of outlines that were intended to be erotic stories from the start — one short outline, the other a more detailed storyline.

First is the note for the story "Logan's Run," which appears in its entirety in this book in chapter 9. It might be interesting to read the outline and see how it compares to the completed story.

> *A woman has a hole in her stocking and a man wonders about all the different ways it could have gotten there.*
>
> *Finally he asks her about it, and she says she put it there for him.*

Short and sweet.

The next note is the outline for my story "Dressed for Success":

CLOTHES MAKE THE WOMAN

A woman is late for work, all her clothes are in the wash, and she has no clean bra, panties, or pantyhose to wear to work.

She does have a nice set of lingerie she had been given as a birthday gift though. She puts it on.

She likes the feel of it under her clothes and the way the bra makes the most of her chest.

At work, everyone looks at her in a different way, as if all they want is to have sex with her.

She likes the attention and does it with the mail-room clerk in the copyroom. After lunch she does it with an accounts executive.

On her way home, she stops by a lingerie shop to buy more stuff. She thinks of all the laundry she has to do, and thinks it may be easier just to throw all her old stuff out.

An outline, yes, but not exactly the way the story turned out in the end. In the published version, she was close to losing her job because although she'd been working hard, she hadn't been attracting new clients into the investment office. Her sexy lingerie attracts a wealthy pro-football player, and the sex she enjoys with him secures his business and subsequently the business of other members of his team.

In the end, her job is saved, and she's commended and told to keep up the good work. Not exactly the most politically correct story ever written, but erotica is most often about fantasies that are only reasonable facsimiles of our everyday lives.

So keep a notebook handy, either at home where you do your writing, or better yet, with you at all times. Since people tend to think about sex all the time, you never know when inspiration — not to mention a great story idea — will strike.

Turning an Idea into a Story

The Seven-Step Story

In my previous book in the Self-Counsel Press Writing Series, *Writing Horror*, I made use of a plotting method developed by Algis Budrys, which divides a story into three parts: Beginning, Middle, and End, and further into seven steps. Table 1 shows what the seven-step story looks like when drawn in a diagram:

```
┌─────────────────────────────────────────────────────────┐
│  Table 1                                                  │
│                                                           │
│  The Seven-Step Story                                     │
│                                                           │
│  1. BEGINNING          2. MIDDLE            3. END        │
│  ───────────────────────────────────────────────────     │
│  (1) A Character       (4) An Attempt to    (7) Validation│
│                            Solve the Problem.             │
│                                                           │
│  (2) In a Context      (5) Unexpected Failure.            │
│                            (Problem is more               │
│                            difficult than first           │
│                            perceived.)                    │
│                                                           │
│  (3) With a Problem    (6) Success or                     │
│                            Failure.                       │
│                                                           │
└─────────────────────────────────────────────────────────┘
```

This is a very general outline for story structure that can apply to every genre. What follows is a condensed version of the seven-step story explanation. I've included it here because I think it is of value to writers of any type of fiction. If you want a more detailed explanation of how the Seven-Step Story works, I suggest you look at a copy of *Writing Horror*.

1. The Beginning

The beginning is obviously a very important part of your story because, if it's doing its job, it will grab the reader's attention and make him or her want to read on.

(1) A Character

Stories are about characters. Your main character should generally be likable or sympathetic, so that when he or she is confronted by a problem, the reader will want to see the character overcome the problem.

(2) In a Context

Context is another word for setting. Setting is the place and time in which your story happens.

(3) With a Problem

Stories are about characters solving problems. Once there is a problem, a struggle, then a story really begins to take off.

Character. Context. Problem.

That's the end of the beginning.

2. The Middle

The middle is the heart of all stories. This is where all of the good stuff takes place. In a horror story, it's where you'll find most of the frights. In an erotic story, it's where you'll find a lot of the sexual tension, building up to the story's climax.

(4) An Attempt to Solve the Problem

When confronted by a problem, your main character must try to rectify the situation. The character must try to do it himself or herself, not wait for the cavalry to appear.

(5) Unexpected Failure

(Problem is more difficult than first perceived.)

Nobody wants to read about problems that are solved the first time out. Characters in stories must struggle and fail; that's what makes them interesting. As a result, this is the part of the story in which all the real action takes place.

(6) Success or Failure

This is an obvious next step. In the end, your character either wins or loses.

3. The End

The end of the story usually wraps things up, sometimes very neatly, sometimes not.

(7) Validation

This is usually some indication to the reader that the story is indeed over, and the last failure or success was not just the latest piece of the middle.

The Six-Step Sex Story

Now that you're a bit familiar with the idea behind the Seven-Step Story, here is an erotic variation that I've come up with on the idea: the Six-Step Sex Story (see Table 2). This is a guide to the type of story that you'll find in most mass-market magazines and even a few erotic anthologies. But while it is a helpful guideline for stories geared to those markets, it might not suit a story intended for a more literary market. Just remember that this is a rough guideline that has worked for me in the past, not a sure-fire formula for success in the future.

Erotic stories differ from other kinds in one crucial way: the stories almost always climax with sex, and everything that comes before the sex in the story is there in order to guide the characters toward the successful completion of the sex act. Knowing this makes writing erotic stories easier because all that's left to figure out is simply how to get to the sex. Because the Six-Step Sex Story is a general guide to writing the sorts of stories you might find in the men's (and women's) magazines at your local newsstand, don't be afraid to change things around a bit to suit your story ideas. As with sex, experimentation in erotic writing can make an already good thing even better.

Finally, one of the most important things to remember is that you've got to get your characters into bed in a relatively realistic way. And since most erotica is fantasy, if you attempt to make the story seem plausible, the sexual tension and the sexual climax of the story will be all the more satisfying.

A clever imitation of love. [Sex] has all the action, but none of the plot.

— *William Rotsler*

Table 2

The Six-Step Sex Story

1. BEGINNING	2. MIDDLE	3. END
(1) Boy Wants Girl	(3) Boy Makes His Move	(5) A Truth Is Revealed
(2) Girl Not Interested	(4) They Have Sex	(6) The Sex Goes On

1. The Beginning

The beginning is where you have to hook the reader's interest, so it's important to set the stage as quickly as possible. (Note that many men's magazine guidelines require that there be some sex in the first few pages.)

(1) Boy Wants Girl

Like the Seven-Step plan, you must present a character in a context, but in erotica the character's identity and the setting of the story are much less significant than the character's problem, which in this case is Boy Wants Girl. (And before I go any further, let me say that I use Boy Wants Girl merely for convenience. The story would work just as well, and perhaps even better, if the problem was Girl Wants Boy.) The starting point of erotic stories is the story's problem.

(2) Girl Not Interested

But Boy Wants Girl is only the first part of the problem. The other part of the problem is that the Girl's Not Interested. The reason for this is twofold. If the Girl was interested, then there would be no problem, and there would be no chance to create any sexual tension. Sexual tension is to erotica as blood is to sexual organs: it is the lifeblood that makes erotica hot and exciting. The sexual tension is immediately established between the characters, as one wants things to move one way and the other is resisting. The result is two opposing forces, a conflict, and the benefit is an interesting beginning to your story.

2. The Middle

(3) Boy Makes His Move

Sexual tension can't last forever, and sooner or later something has to give. That's when Boy Makes His Move. The Move doesn't have to be anything dramatic or overt like a character saying, "Would you like to have sex with me?" The Move can be as subtle as saying, "Hello," or the placing of the Boy's hand on that of the Girl.

The Move does not necessarily succeed at first. Indeed, if the Move fails, then the story is made all the more interesting, since Boy will have to figure out another approach, maybe even more than one, until he gets it right. If the Move does succeed, however, it will set up an interesting revelation in Step 5 that will explain why all went well in Step 3.

(4) They Have Sex

This is what your story has been leading up to all along. The problem has been overcome, and your two characters are having sex. No matter who your characters are, the sex should be hot, at least hot enough to turn the reader on. There's nothing worse in erotic fiction than sex that's boring and mundane. When your characters finally get down to it, don't be afraid to let them have some fun.

3. The End

(5) A Truth Is Revealed

While many sexual encounters in real life might end with one or both of the participants rolling over in bed and falling asleep, you can't let that happen in your erotic fiction. Your characters need to stay awake long enough to say something that gives your story an element of surprise. This can be revealed by either character and in several different ways. One: If the Boy's first Move is successful, Step 5 is where Girl reveals that she's been attracted to Boy for weeks and was wondering when he might Make His Move. Two: If Girl was at first resistant to Boy's Move, then Step 5 is where she reveals what's changed regarding her feelings for him. (For example, if she didn't like Boy because he looked like a computer geek, but he turned out to be a great lover, then she explains how she'll never again pass judgment on anyone based on appearance.) Three: If Girl was at first resistant to Boy's Move, then she can explain what finally won her over. This can also be explained by a character other than the two involved in the sex scene.

(6) The Sex Goes On

Erotic stories are about people having great sex that is not only satisfying, but also endless. Just as some of the best horror stories end with a hint that the evil will return, so do erotic stories, only instead of the evil, it's the sex that will be back. The sex doesn't have to happen again in the same story, but there should be some hint that your characters will be having a lot of satisfying sex in the future. Most erotic fiction tends to be sex-positive and upbeat, so the message is that good sex is something that's worth having often.

Keep in mind that this Six-Step Sex Story suits just one part of the erotic market: mass-market magazines. However, if you are able to work this model successfully, it will be easy for you to modify and adjust your story to fit other markets.

Writing What You Know

Whenever you hear authors talk about writing, you often hear the phrase "Write what you know." This simply means that you should write about things with which you are familiar. It doesn't mean that because you are a housewife you should only be writing about housewives, or if you're a factory worker you have to set all your stories in a factory. Certainly, if you decide to make the character in your story a housewife or a factory worker, you might be able to include details that bring these characters to life, but you don't have to limit yourself like this. If you have a friend who is a teacher, you might make your character a teacher because you know enough about your friend to create a character who walks, talks, and acts like a teacher.

A Few Words with...

Caro Soles (writing as Kyle Stone)

On Fetish Fiction

EDO VAN BELKOM: In terms of erotic writing, what kinds of fetish fiction are the most and least popular?

KYLE STONE: One of the interesting things about writing erotic fiction is the chance to eroticize anything at all. This makes the writing a constant challenge and process of discovery. In terms of popularity, there are certain objects, roles, scenarios that have a more universal appeal than others. Dog collars, underwear, piercings, corsets, almost anything leather are far more popular than gas masks or tight rubber suits, for instance. The role of slave, or dog on a leash, or other scenarios involving utter submission to a powerful master are popular fantasies.

EDO VAN BELKOM: Do fetish publications try to cover a broad range of special interests, or is there a magazine for just about every fetish going?

KYLE STONE: Remember that what I say applies only to the gay male market. Some magazines like *Drummer* are for a specific community and focus entirely on leather, with articles and stories involving master/slave relationships, heavy bondage/ dominance, how to look after your leather gear, and how to build your own dungeon. Others print stories which are arousing and involving, featuring any sort of fetish or fantasy, although most have restrictions. For instance, some magazines want only boy-next-door stories, and needless to say, I don't send them much of my stuff. One of the outfits I write for the most publishes several magazines, each one focused on a different area. That way, if all you want are light sexy romps, you don't run the risk of getting a story which will have quite the opposite effect. Even here, however, there are exceptions. I remember once getting a letter from an editor saying this was the first time they had ever published an erotic story where a character is killed.

EDO VAN BELKOM: I would assume that writing about a particular fetish requires that the author has an intimate knowledge, not only of the fetish, but of how and why it provides a sexual attraction to the reader. Is this true, or can any competent writer use his or her imagination to fill in the gaps?

KYLE STONE: This is a question more about the writing process itself than about the fetish. I think that with any kind of writing, there must be some connection between the writer and the material. If this connection is not there, there will be no passion for the reader to pick up on, and it is passion that makes good writing stand out. That said, however, research is certainly involved. The story will not work if the writer does not know how a piece of equipment is put together. Besides, this kind of research can be a lot of fun!

EDO VAN BELKOM: Are there any truly bizarre fetishes that even the most liberated or adventurous among us might find repugnant?

KYLE STONE: Enter the world of fetish with caution. It is not for the timid or squeamish. As a writer, my role is to discover what it is that is erotic about the truly bizarre. Can I get inside a character so totally that I, too, will see the exciting, pleasurable possibilities of a gas mask? To me, it's a matter of extension. Certain types of clothing are definitely arousing. A gas mask is merely a type of clothing. Therefore, it too can be arousing. This kind of reasoning usually works, and I find it quite an interesting, involving challenge to do this. Nevertheless, there have been a few areas that I have left alone.

EDO VAN BELKOM: As an editor, have you ever had to explain the appeal of a piece of erotic fetish fiction to a publisher who just didn't get it?

KYLE STONE: Since I usually deal with editors who specialize in the subject, the answer is no.

Kyle Stone has edited several anthologies and is the author of the novels The Initiation of PB 500, *its sequel,* The Citadel, *as well as* Rituals, Fantasy Board, Fire and Ice, The Hidden Slave *and* MENagerie, *a 1999 release from Back Room Books.*

Everyone has talent. What is rare is the courage to follow the talent to the dark place where it leads.

— *Erica Jong*

In terms of erotica, writing what you know takes on a whole new meaning. Say you're a straight housewife who would like to write something exotic and erotic. If you write what you know, does that mean you have to write about a straight housewife who is looking for some excitement in her life? Maybe. And if you did, you'd probably be able to create a truly convincing character. But how many stories about bored housewives can you write? Sooner or later you're going to have to expand your horizons to include rich heiresses, powerful executives, or any number of young people who are enjoying their newfound sexual freedom. That's where your imagination and fantasies come into play. Perhaps you've imagined yourself to be the successful female executive of a cosmetics company. You have money and power in this fantasy, but you want more out of life — namely sex. If you've fantasized about it, then you know enough about what the character would be feeling to convincingly write about it.

But you might run into trouble if you decide to write about things with which you're not very familiar. For example, if you're a straight housewife, you might want to think twice before writing a novel about gay male lovers in Spain because there are all sorts of reasons why you're likely to fail. Do you know the subtleties of gay male intimacy and seduction? Do you know the sexual language used by gay males? (Remember that each branch of erotic fiction might have its own slang and phrases.) Do you even know the mechanics of gay male sexual relations? If you've answered "no" to any or all of these questions, and you still want to write that novel set in Spain, don't despair.

There is a way to write about what you don't know. It's called research.

Writing What You Don't Know: Research

If you don't know about something, then find out about it. If you want to write erotica about gay men, read a few nonfiction books in which gay men talk about their lives and loves. If you want to know what it's like backstage at a major fashion show in Paris, there are books and articles on the subject. If you want to know more about sex in general, there are sections in your local library (and bookstore) devoted entirely to that very subject.

Again, go where the intensity is, go where the pleasure is. Go where the pain is. Go for the passion. Do that honestly, and the rest will fall into place.

—Anne Rice

A Few Words with . . .

Loren L. Barrett

On Writing Erotic Nonfiction

EDO VAN BELKOM: How much of your own personal experience do you use in your nonfiction articles? How much research do you have to do?

LOREN L. BARRETT: You've probably heard the phrase "write what you know," and that's exactly what I do. I rely heavily on using my own personal experience when writing my nonfiction articles. I can't tell you that it feels good unless I've tried it and am prepared to report on it. I only need to research topics that are a bit unfamiliar to me, so that would depend on what the article is about. I enjoy writing stuff based on what I know, but it's also fun researching a new topic. I welcome the challenge of reading about new sexual experiences and trying new pleasures.

EDO VAN BELKOM: When writing erotic nonfiction, do you set out to instruct or to entertain the reader?

LOREN L. BARRETT: I was definitely hoping on a bit of both, actually. Hopefully, no one is confusing how-to sex articles in any men's magazines with scholarly journals about sex and sexuality. (I recommend going to your local library to ask for those books, which can be quite entertaining in their own way.) I do read an awful lot on the subject of sex, as I would like to one day become a sexologist. But I do derive great pleasure in writing how-to articles for men's magazines. Not only does it give me an opportunity to tell others what I know and what I have learned along the way, but it may, in fact, give a bit of instruction to some people out there who might be shy or introverted. It's a lot of fun writing this stuff, and I hope my sense of fun comes through to the reader. I wouldn't mind hearing back from some of the readers to know whether they read them for entertainment or for instruction.

EDO VAN BELKOM: Do men treat you differently when they discover that you write "how-to" articles about sex?

LOREN L. BARRETT: Do they ever!

Whenever I'm talking to someone in person or on-line, I can always instantly change the mood of the conversation by saying something like, "Did I tell you I write how-to articles about sex for men's magazines?" Suddenly, they're more attentive than ever and are tripping all over themselves asking questions like, "What kind of articles?" "Can you write some about me?" "Wanna try it out with me before your next article?" "Do you sleep with all these men?" "Have you actually done everything you write about?" "Where do you get your ideas?"

Make no mistake about it, I'm fully aware that men react this way and I use it to my advantage. If I see that a conversation is going nowhere, or if I'd like to impress a certain gentleman, all I have to do is toss the fact into a conversation, and boom — instant interest. His eyes might have been on the waitress's ass, but as soon as I tell him I write about sex, his eyes are focused on me. I guess men are just fascinated by sex and women who can speak freely on the subject.

Freelance writer and poet Loren L. Barrett has written erotic nonfiction articles for such magazines as Gent, Leg Sex, Voluptuous, *and* PBW.

When I began writing erotic nonfiction, I did some general research into all matters sexual and made notes on a variety of subjects. When I had enough material for an article, I would sit down and write it. When it came time to insert quotes, I usually made those up, which is one of the reasons why you shouldn't rely on the nonfiction in any sex magazines (perhaps with the exception of publications like *Playboy, Penthouse,* and *Cosmopolitan*) for anything other than the most general of facts. If an article cites its source on a piece of information, it's best to go to that source yourself so there can be no chance of error.

Doing research can give your fiction added strength and aid in the suspension of disbelief; that is, your ability to make the reader believe that everything you've written about could actually happen. In terms of nonfiction work, research can turn you into a sex expert overnight. I was once asked to write an article on "Five Foot Pleasures," which included things like reflexology, pedicures, and foot adornments such as toe rings and tattoos. I knew little about toe rings and tattoos, even less about pedicures, and absolutely nothing about reflexology. But a day at the local library solved all that, and the article appeared in *Leg Sex* a few months later.

Finally, if you're not a bookish type, there's nothing better than firsthand research, and in erotica that could mean anything from having sex in order to learn how to make your fiction more realistic to talking to your friends about their most intimate sexual secrets. Even if it doesn't improve your writing, your research will be a lot fun!

5
ELEMENTS OF EROTIC FICTION

Story Openings: Getting It On

If you know anything at all about writing fiction, you're probably aware that it's important to grab the reader's attention as quickly as possible so that he or she will want to read on, all the way to the end of your story. Sounds simple enough, but too many writers tend to start their stories well before the story actually *should* begin, forcing readers to wade through two or three pages of drivel before reaching the real starting point.

I often tell my students not to start their stories with a character rolling out of bed, having a shave, drinking his or her morning coffee or whatever; just get to the crisis as quickly as possible. And if they can't get to the crisis immediately, they should at least get started on the trip that will lead the reader to it.

The beginning of an erotic story is in many ways even more important than the beginnings of stories of other genres. The reader of erotica is reading the material to be stimulated and will likely not be willing to wait very long for something sexy to happen. And, indeed, as mentioned earlier, many magazines require that a sex scene occur within the first few pages of a story.

Fortunately, because you're writing about sex and sexual things, it's not all that hard to capture a reader's attention. And, since there are in essence four ways of getting a story started — description, character, dialogue, action — there isn't a great deal to learn about creating effective story openings.

Description

Starting a story with description is both easy and hard. It is easy because describing something is a fairly routine task. Take a look out your window and describe what you see, and you'll have the start of a story set in the world outside your window. However, starting with description can also be difficult, because to be effective, the description has to be very well written, as it is the writing that captures the reader's interest more than what is being described.

Luckily, in erotic writing, what is being described is often as interesting as the way in which it is described. The following is the opening to my story "The Lucky Break," which first appeared in the December 1993 issue of *Gent*. The story is about a guy who is giving a ride to a co-ed, who answered a notice he placed on a campus bulletin board saying he was looking for someone to share gas expenses with him on a drive to Florida during spring break.

> *Jim Garrett had been looking at her all day.*
>
> *It hadn't been an easy thing to do, considering she'd been in the passenger seat and he'd been driving along I-78 the whole time. Check that; it hadn't been easy. What it had been was rewarding.*
>
> *The womanly vision was soft and curvy, pleasing to the eye, a welcome diversion from the seemingly neverending highway in front of him.*
>
> *Even now, as he looked over at her well-rounded young body, everything seemed firm, fresh and definitely arousing, as if he were looking at her now for the very first time.*

He started at her legs. She was wearing a super-tight pair of jeans that hugged the long, lean lines of her hips, thighs, and legs like a second skin. Further up, the crotch of her jeans was so tight, her pussy lips were clearly visible — full and puffy and parted by the denim.

Every so often she stretched, spread her legs, and ran a hand over her pussy as if to scratch. The sight had made his cock instantly jump two levels of hardness and into the diamond-cutter category.

Above her legs was her thin, almost athletic waist, left bare by her two-sizes-too-small T-shirt. Although it left her belly naked and the white cotton material was almost see-through, the T-shirt suited her to a tee. Or perhaps it suited Jim to a tee. The shirt was so thin, he could clearly see her dark-brown, pancake-sized nipples beneath it, rising and falling with each breath. Every few miles, Jim flipped the climate control switch to allow cool air to blow through the vent. He was rewarded by her nipples hardening into thick, brown, inch-long teats.

When he posted the notice on the college bulletin board saying he was driving to Florida for spring break and was looking for someone to share gas expenses, he never dreamed he'd be so lucky.

Obviously, when writing for a men's magazine, it doesn't hurt to be describing a beautiful woman, but the technique would work just as well if it had been a woman describing a handsome man. Also, notice that there is some sexual tension, even in the first few paragraphs, as Jim is supposed to keep his eyes on the road yet can't help but let them stray.

Character

In many ways, opening a story with a character is the same as opening with description. It's the same in that the writer is describing something to the reader, but it is also different because the description isn't a physical one. Instead, it is a picture of what the character is like, and this sometimes requires little or no physical description at all.

The following example of opening a story with character is taken from my story "By the Book" (*Gent*, February 1992), in which a young university student has his eye on a librarian who seems absolutely un-interested in him or any other man on campus. He eventually unlocks the woman's secret sexual self with — what else? — a book.

> *Aaron Rothman's eyes followed the librarian as she crossed the library lobby on her way to the circulation desk.*
>
> *He'd watched Diane Chandler closely since his freshman year, trying to determine whether a gorgeous woman hid be-hind her conservative gray suit or his imagination merely wished it were so.*
>
> *The question intrigued the third-year psychology student, so much so that he spent most of his free time in the library.*
>
> *Some days she looked plainer than a brown paper bag. But on other days . . .*
>
> *On other days she looked as if she had the body of a buxom centerfold model.*
>
> *The change wouldn't be apparent to anyone who hadn't been watching her closely over the years. Her drab gray suit was unchanged and her hair was tied up in the same old-fashioned bun, but something about her seemed different, alive . . . sensuous.*
>
> *On one of those days, Aaron noticed she had traded in her sensible black shoes for a pair of three-inch black heels. Then, after casually moving to a study table near the circ desk, he saw her cross her legs and caught a glimpse of a black garter hold-ing up her taupe-colored stockings.*
>
> *The episode put the thought into Aaron's head that Diane Chandler was really a she-wolf in sheep's clothing. But then months would pass in which she would be perfectly prim and proper, leaving him no choice but to conclude that the brief mo-ment he'd thought of her as sexy was nothing more than a fig-ment of his hormone-charged imagination.*

While there is a fairly good description of Diane the librarian, the description goes beyond the physical to include elements that suggest something about the woman's character. Some days she's prim and proper; some days she's quite sexy. In the end, the woman proves to be a bit of an enigma, which suits the storyline well because this uncertainty also sets up the story's problem. Aaron wants to know (as does the reader) if Diane is a prude who just happens to dress sexily every so often in spite of herself, or if there is some latent sexuality bubbling just beneath the grey-suited surface.

Once again, sexual tension arrives early in the story.

Dialogue

Have you ever been riding on the bus or on the subway and, for lack of anything better to do, started listening in on someone else's conversation? The problem is that you've begun listening in the middle of the conversation, and you've missed all the background information that would help you make sense of what's being said. As a result, you're wondering, "What are they talking about?" and you're almost tempted to stay on the bus past your stop, just to find out what's going on.

The same sort of hook works for story openings as well. Starting your story in the middle of a conversation is a great way to grab a reader's attention, making them want to read on and find out what happens next. In fact, dialogue is a doubly effective way to capture a reader's interest because of the ease in which it conveys information to the reader. A general rule in writing is that three lines of dialogue are worth three pages of exposition. That sounds somewhat simplistic, but it is an effective way of explaining how much information can be brought into the story through dialogue.

A general rule to help you remember that much more information can be conveyed through dialogue as opposed to pure description is —

3 lines of dialogue = 3 pages of exposition

This dialogue-style opening comes from my short story "Merry Christmas, Mary," which first saw print in the December 1994 issue of *Gent*. The story is about Mary, who hasn't had sex in a long, long while, and her friend Amanda, who decides to send Mary a unique gift at Christmas.

> *"You won't believe the incredible night I had Monday,"*
> *Amanda Brookner said as she poured a cup of tea for her friend,*
> *Mary Rogers.*
>
> *"Do tell, friend, do tell."*
>
> *"Well, Jim called me at work. When I picked up the phone,*
> *he said, 'Downtown Ramada. Room 1203. 7 p.m.' "*
>
> *"That's it."*

"Yeah. That's all he said. At first I didn't know what to make of it, but I decided to go to the hotel after work and check out room 1203." She poured herself a cup of coffee and continued talking as she stirred in the cream and sugar.

"When I opened the door, the room was dark and there was nothing inside but a gift-wrapped box on the bed. I went inside and read the card on the outside of the box."

"What did it say?" Mary said, excitedly.

" 'I've been thinking about you in this all day.' "

"That's it. What was inside the box?"

"That's the best part. There was lingerie in the box, really sexy stuff."

"What? What? I want details."

"There was a black teddy, for starters, with a push-up bra and a tanga-cut on the bottom, you know, like a g-string. There were a pair of black stockings and three-inch black heels and a see-through black robe to go overtop."

"Wow," Mary said, taking a sip of her coffee.

"After I got dressed, I was so turned on I couldn't wait for Jim to get there. It's hard to describe, but I felt sexy and slutty at the same time. Anyway, I picked up the box from the bed and noticed something rattling around inside. It was a vibrator."

"No!"

"Yes! And strapped around the outside of it was a note. It said, 'Feel free to start without me. I want you good and ready when I arrive.' "

"So what did you do?"

"I turned it on and started using it. It felt naughty, almost dirty. I nearly came twice by the time Jim got there."

"What happened then?"

"He was out of his clothes in about ten seconds, and we made love in every conceivable way for the next three hours."

"Oh, really," Mary said, a little out of breath.

"He even did it to me in the middle of the night, entered me from behind while I was asleep. I tried to pretend I was still sleeping but I just couldn't. I had to get up. We had sex twice before ordering breakfast . . . in bed."

"Is this something you two do often, sex in a hotel, I mean? Or was it for some special occasion?"

"Jim's nephew is coming from college tomorrow, and he's going to be staying with us over the Christmas holidays. Jim said last night might be the last chance we'd have together for a little while. We went to the hotel just to make it a little more special, erotic."

Mary stared into the bottom of her cup, and the two women fell silent a moment.

"I haven't had sex since Marty left me," she said at last.

Amanda looked at her close friend with surprise. "You're kidding, that's almost two years ago. How do you manage?"

"I have a vibrator or two of my own," she said softly. "They're nice, but it's not the same."

"Oh, you poor dear."

"Don't feel sorry for me," Mary said, straightening up in her chair. "It's my own fault. I just don't get out of the house much. I guess I've been a little insecure ever since Marty left."

"You have nothing to be insecure about. You're still a beautiful woman, Mary."

It was true. Although Mary was in her early forties, she was still a very attractive woman. Her figure was that of a buxom and well-rounded, mature woman. Her legs and hips were shapely, and her large, full breasts had sagged only slightly over the years. If she dressed right to flaunt her assets, she could probably have any man she wanted.

Mary took the compliment in silence. Finally, she looked across the kitchen table at her friend. "Tell me more about Monday night," she said, shifting to get more comfortable in her seat. "And I want details."

When Amanda starts off by saying, "You won't believe the incredible night I had Monday," the reader is hooked. Just like Mary, the reader is asking "Why, what happened?" And when that happens, you've got the reader interested, and the story is on its way. Of course, it doesn't hurt that the story Amanda tells is about this great sex she's had, but even without the sexual element, having a character begin a story by talking is a great way to cover a lot of ground and set the stage. Again, in this example, through dialogue, the story opening eventually gets to the problem, which is that Mary hasn't had sex in ages. And even though she hasn't had sex, she would like to, even pleasures herself from time to time, so we know that if the right situation arose, she'd be more than willing. Sexual tension.

Action

Action is probably the easiest and best way to start a story or novel. Action is exciting — especially in a work of erotic fiction — and characters in motion, doing things, are more interesting to the reader than a description, an interesting character, or a conversation. Obviously, the greater and more intense the action, the more interest it will generate, but even subtle actions are sometimes enough to capture a reader's interest.

This bit of action opens the story "Getting Hard," which was first published in the February 1995 issue of *Gent*. In it, a television executive checks out the exercise show his station produces. A few days earlier, he had asked the producer of the show to liven it up, and today is the debut of the new and improved show.

> *Ross Murdock checked his watch, leaned back in his chair, and clicked on the television set.*
>
> *It had been a week since he'd called Bill Datlow, the producer of the station's daily exercise show, and told him to do something to improve the ratings or the show would be axed for one of the many syndicated workout shows on the market.*
>
> *Today's show was supposed to mark both the beginning of the all-new* Daily Workout *and the debut of the new girl Daltow had hired to round out the cast.*
>
> *The new opening credits were good — quick, tight shots of hard young bodies in motion — and the new music was good,*

too — a throbbing drum beat that almost had Murdock tapping his feet.

After the commercial break, the show began with three young women dressed in coordinated outfits, matching shoes, leg warmers, and exercise suits that were cut high on the thigh and low down in front.

Murdock was a little uncomfortable with the show's new look. It was a little too sexy for his conservative little television station. His was a station that showed good, wholesome family sitcoms from the fifties, sixties, and seventies, cooking and game shows, and nonviolent cartoons.

This — this had the look of soft-core porn.

Still, he watched, his eyes glued to the screen.

Through the first few minutes, the girls all moved slowly, seductively doing the bump and grind as they warmed up for the more vigorous portion of the show.

When the music became faster, they all jumped around in place while the camera panned slowly over their slightly damp bodies.

As he watched, Murdock slowly realized something.

One of the girls on the screen had a huge pair of breasts. As she jumped up and down with the others, her breasts bounced and lolled beneath the thin, stretch fabric of her suit, threatening to break free of their confines at any moment.

This one had to be the new girl Datlow had hired to liven up the show.

Murdock moved closer to the screen.

"What the hell does Datlow think he's doing?"

The three girls bent over, and the cameras all swung low to get a good view of all three of their behinds, as well as the hanging whoppers of the big-chested woman.

"I can't believe he thinks he can get away with this," muttered Murdock. "I'll bet the farm that the switchboard is already lit up with calls from feminist groups in all three counties."

When the three women stood up straight again, their outfits had ridden up their behinds and now looked like tanga bottoms worn by sunbathers on some European beach. None of the girls bothered to straighten out their suits, and all went through the rest of the show with their bare ass cheeks exposed to the cameras.

"I can't broadcast this kind of thing on my station." Murdock backed away from the television without taking his eyes of the screen. When he bumped into his desk, he felt around on top of it for his intercom and pressed the last button on the left.

As always, it doesn't hurt that the action involves beautiful women dressed in sexy exercise wear, but the principle behind starting stories with action is the same whether you begin with an aerobics show or the walking of the family dog. Action is easy to read, and it helps move a story along. Three pages of action to start a story will more than likely hook a reader and start him or her on the way to the end.

Finally, and perhaps most important, the above action creates tension, as do all the other story-opening techniques. While Murdock is watching (and, one assumes, enjoying what he sees on the screen) he's also planning to confront Datlow about the changes to the show. So, while the action is going on, the problem is being set up and a confrontation is being foreshadowed, all of which makes for a very effective and engaging story opening.

There is another way: Epistolary

One last word about story openings. In my previous writing book for Self-Counsel Press, *Writing Horror*, I also outlined the epistolary technique of getting stories started. The epistolary format tells a story using letters and journal or diary entries.

One famous epistolary novel is Bram Stoker's *Dracula*, which is told completely through letters and journal entries. While it would be possible to start an erotic story with something like a letter, it is generally a weak device in this genre, unless you're planning on writing "literary" erotica. For example, if the last story, "Getting Hard," were to open using this technique, we might have read the office memo from Murdock to Datlow telling him to spice up the show. While effective, starting with the memo would only postpone the true beginning of the story, which is the action of the first new show. Postponing the beginning might be useful in some situations in which a lot of information has to be disseminated to the reader before the story can begin, but erotic fiction needs to get going in a hurry, so any delay to the story should be avoided.

See Sample 2 for another look at story openings.

Recognizable Characters: That Could Be Me

If you've ever watched any adult videos, you've probably noticed that most of the people in them — especially the women — are attractive. One might even call them gorgeous, and rightly so. That's because videos are about visual images, and there's nothing more stimulating than watching two beautiful people having sex.

Luckily for those of us who don't look like adult-video stars, erotic fiction doesn't necessarily have to be about beautiful people. In fact, some of the hottest erotic literature isn't about beauties, but about normal, everyday people, which makes it all the more powerful.

Here's the first page or so from a short story of mine called "The Pair," which appeared in the December 1995 issue of *Gent*. It takes place in a retirement community and is about a younger woman (40 or so) who sits in on the card games played by the older men and how she uses her youthful charms on them, which nobody seems to mind.

> *I moved to Fort Lauderdale a year ago to take it easy, sit on the beach, and enjoy the sun. I've spent a lot of time on the beach lately, but I haven't been getting much sun.*
>
> *Every afternoon around two there's a poker game under the big beach umbrella behind Sully's Bar and Grill. With the exception of one, all the players are older men who retired with more money than they knew what to do with, and nothing but time on their hands.*
>
> *The one exception?*
>
> *Marjorie Watts is a 40-year-old divorcée, who's as good a poker player as she is a looker. Some might consider her middle-aged, or even old, but to us she's practically a schoolgirl. You should see the way she thrives on the attention she gets from the oldtimers, who practically fawn all over her whenever she's around. And who could blame them? Marjorie has the biggest set of knockers any of us has ever seen, and when you combine all our years of woman-watching, that's saying quite a bit.*

I don't think there is erotica without people, and I think that is one of the big problems with a lot of erotica. It takes stock characters and stock situations, and gives no indication that sex is a sexual interaction between two people's minds.

— *Leigh W. Rutledge*

She loves to sit in on our poker games, usually coming to the table wearing a skimpy little halter top that barely contains them big tits of hers. It makes it hard to concentrate on the game, because whenever she gets real thoughtful about a hand, she takes a deep breath and studies her cards. When she does that, everyone else around the table holds their own breath just waiting for that halter top of hers to give way so they can see those magnificent tits spill out onto the table.

Of course, Marjorie usually wins more than she loses, but nobody seems to mind. Having her at the table gives practically everyone a tent pole between their legs, and what's the value of that to a bunch of old guys like us?

More important than making your characters attractive is making them real. If you can do that, the sexual tension and situations will be easier to write about, and in the end will be more effective. Just as a reader of romance novels reads to escape, to imagine himself or herself as the hero or heroine of the novel, so too do readers of erotic fiction read erotica to escape. If they can recognize a bit of themselves in the characters you've written about, then it's easy for them to imagine themselves as the protagonist of the story.

The exception to making your characters real is the stereotypical character. This is the one-dimensional character who doesn't do much in the story other than advance the plot — like the uniformed cop who arrives first on the crime scene, or the bartender who serves the intimate couple their drinks. These characters can be created with a single line explaining who and what they are. It is left to the reader to fill out the character, because everyone has their own image of what such people should look like.

Finally, students often ask me how many characters a story should have. One answer I use is, "How long is a piece of string?" By that I mean you should use only as many characters as you need, no more and no less. However, if you're writing short stories, you might want to keep the number of main characters down to about three or four, with two being best for an erotic story. Remember that I'm talking about main characters, the ones with names and a bit of description to them, and not the stock characters, like the cop who put the handcuffs on the burglar. Also, when naming characters, try to give them names that are distinct and say a little bit about the characters themselves. For example,

Sample 2

Story Openings

Here's another look at the four ways in which to begin a piece of erotic fiction. The following are examples of each of the four different techniques (description, character, action, and dialogue) of beginning a story about a man who is intrigued by the new secretary who has started working in the office.

Description

She sat behind her desk answering the telephones as if it were the easiest thing in the world. Her hose-covered legs were crossed, exposing them past the knee. They were shapely legs, thin but powerful, suggesting that there was a lithe, athletic body beneath her staid grey business suit. There was a bit of frill where the lapels met across her chest, and Jerry could only wonder if it were a part of her blouse or a frilly, see-through camisole. Jerry decided he would try to find out.

Character

Jerry Royal had had his fair share of women. Every time he thought he found one that seemed a good fit, some problem seemed to emerge. Like last week. He'd been dating Norma Jean for three weeks and everything had been going great, especially the sex, which was fantastic. But then he found out that she was married, and that took a lot of the shine off the relationship. And then the whole thing went sour one night when Norma Jean's husband showed up on his doorstep wanting his wife back. She seemed glad that the man had noticed she was gone and ran back to him like she was doing wind sprints. Somewhere, Jerry mused, there's a woman out there for me. There's got to be.

Just then the elevator door opened, and there at the reception desk was a new secretary.

Action

Jerry Royal checked his watch and pressed the elevator button again. He was going to be late, and for a meeting with a big client, too. He knew he shouldn't have spent the extra time in bed this morning, but Martha Walters whispering in his ear about how she needed it one more time before she left town was too much to resist. Sure, it had been great . . . and the things she could do with her tongue. But now he was late, and his job might even be on the line.

He pressed the button again, then decided to take the stairs. Hell, it was only five flights.

He began to tire after three, and by the time he reached the fifth floor, he was out of breath and his clothes were sticking to his body like he'd just gone for one more liaison with Martha.

He opened the door and stepped into the office, sweaty and out of breath.

"What were you doing this morning?" said the secretary.

Jerry had never seen her before, but the coy smile on her face was sexy as all hell. Man, she said it as if she knew.

Dialogue

He had never seen her before. He would have remembered a woman who looked that good. "You're new here aren't you?"

"Started yesterday."

"I'd have thought maybe a week, the way you seem to know your way around."

"I'm new here, but I've been around."

"As a receptionist."

"No, mostly as a personal secretary and executive assistant."

"So, I guess you could say you've been with quite a few men over the years." He waited to see if she'd be shocked by what he said, but she wasn't. Not even close. She just smiled coyly at him.

"I've been with my fair share of men, but I've found that women can be just as satisfying."

She crossed her legs then, and twirled her foot to show off her ankle, as if a little tingle of sexual energy had just coursed up the inside of her thigh.

Exercise

Take an erotic story you've written or an idea you have for a story and write several different beginnings for it. Chances are you'll find one you like, or one that gets the story moving better than the others, and you'll be well on your way to finishing a story with a great beginning.

Rick might be good for a rough and tumble he-man, while Richard would be more suited to an artistic type. However, don't use variations of the same name for different characters, and try not to give different characters names that begin with the same letter or sound. Too many similar-sounding names make it toilsome for the reader to keep track of who's who.

Point of View (POV)

One of the most important things to learn about the art of writing any kind of fiction is point of view, or POV, and it can be one of the most difficult things for new writers to master.

Simply stated, POV refers to the agent (usually a character in the story or novel) through whose eyes a piece of fiction is presented. It can also be the character whose thoughts are revealed directly to the reader. POV is generally limited to a single character in a short story, while several characters can provide the point of view at different times in a novel. Having said that, it must be noted that individual scenes should always be told by a single POV character in order to avoid confusing the reader. A novel that uses many different characters' points of view — and as many as a dozen or more viewpoints can be used — is called a multiple-viewpoint novel.

Point of view changes according to character. For example, what if an old woman, a young man, a teenager, and a little girl had to describe a couple kissing on a park bench? How would their points of view differ?

Old woman

She noticed a couple in an amorous embrace on the park bench to her right. They were so young and seemed not to care who saw them. Well, good for them. Life's too short to worry about who's looking anyway.

Young man

He noticed a couple necking on the park bench to his right. From what he could see she was rather pretty and seemed to be enjoying herself. As he walked by, doing his best not to stare, he wondered if Margaret was doing anything tonight.

I think erotica needs more heroes. I think we need more characters like the romantic Master in [John] Preston's books. And I think that we need to not only start writing about the sex and the emotions realistically, but stop creating our '90s archetypes and have people grappling with real issues, and winning over impossible odds.

— *Laura Antoniou*

Teenage boy

He was on his way to the skateboard park when he noticed a couple making out on the bench to his right. Man, she's really putting out, and out in public, too. Cool!

Little girl

As she walked along the path she noticed a mommy and a daddy kissing on the bench near the swings. Mommy kissed daddy like that when he brought her flowers on her birthday. I wonder how old that mommy is today?

These examples are somewhat simplistic and perhaps overwritten to illustrate a point, but they do show how different characters have different ways of looking at the world around them. Even the words that are used to describe the couple's action change with each POV, from "an amorous embrace" when seen by the old woman to simply "kissing" when seen by the young girl. This is why, *before* you begin writing a story or novel, you must give some thought to which of the characters should tell the story.

If you're still not sure what is meant by POV, pick up a novel or short story, open it up to a scene, and start reading. You'll soon become aware of the following:

1. When you read passages about a character's thoughts or feelings, you've found the POV character, the character through which the entire scene is being viewed.

2. When you read passages of straight description, that's what you might call the narrator talking, since what is being described is not being filtered through the POV character but simply reported by someone or something who describes what can be seen. (Science fiction writer Orson Scott Card, in his excellent book *Characters and Viewpoint*, describes the narrator as a camera fixed somewhere up in the corner of a scene, objectively reporting what's happening without comment or prejudice.)

3. When you read passages about other characters, look closely at how their emotions are described, for that's where you'll learn the most about how to use POV to your advantage — and how to avoid its pitfalls.

Writing from a gay male point of view makes me feel more free to pursue things in a different way than I could otherwise. I think that's the main idea.

— *Caro Soles*
(writing as Kyle Stone)

To illustrate the above points, here is a scene from my short story "Stroke of Luck" (*40-Plus*, April 1992), in which a young man is trying to sublet the house in which he's living because he can no longer afford the rent.

1. *"Does this hallway lead to the bedroom?"* (1)

2. *"Uh, what?" Gerry Brooks mumbled.* (1)

3. *"I said, does this hallway lead to the bedroom?"* (1)

4. *"Yes, yes, it does."* (1)

5. *Gerry watched the woman walk down the hall. He'd been trying not to stare at her breasts but hadn't been too successful — they looked so big and round that he just couldn't keep his eyes off them.* (2)

6. *Now, with her back to him, he found himself staring at her ass too. Like her tits, her ass cheeks looked fully rounded, womanly . . . mature.* (2)

7. *"Your ad said there were three bedrooms," she said, looking at him as if she were growing impatient with him.* (3)

8. *"Pardon me?" Again he was caught staring.* (1)

9. *The hard lines of her face seemed to soften. "Where are the other two bedrooms?"* (3)

10. *"Oh, uh, they're at the other end of the house, on either side of the bathroom. Let me show you."* (1)

11. *Gerry led the older woman on a tour through the rest of the house that he was trying to sublet. He was fond of the house and really didn't want to let it go, but he had no other choice. He'd been sharing the cost of the lease with his girlfriend for the last six months, and now that she'd left him for a professional ballplayer, he was stuck with a monthly expense he just couldn't afford on a bartender's salary.* (1)

(1) Paragraphs 1 to 4, 8, 10, and 11 are in no character's POV. They are simply reportage of what is going on in the scene as described by the narrator (or relayed to the reader through the camera positioned high up in one corner of the room).

(2) Paragraphs 5 and 6 are from Gerry's POV. We know this because we are told that Gerry hadn't been able to keep his eyes off the woman. The only way we could know such a thing is if we are in his POV. But paragraph 11 is quite detailed, and this is where the limited-omniscient narrator comes even further into play. Because the narrator is in Gerry's POV, the narrator also knows Gerry's personal history and, when appropriate, is able to inform the reader of it. Such a divulgence of information about the female character would be impossible. The best that could be done would be to guess why she's there based on her looks, the way she's dressed, her mannerisms, and her speech patterns.

(3) Paragraphs 7 and 9 would appear to be in the woman's POV but they are not. We are able to get an inkling about what she might be thinking by having our POV character make an assumption about what's going on inside her mind. In paragraph 7, the phrase "as if" allows Gerry to make a judgment about what the look on her face might mean. Likewise, in paragraph 9, the hard lines "seemed" to soften, suggesting that she might be warming up to him. This is all conjecture, however, because we are in Gerry's POV and these things about the female character are guesses at best.

Once you know what to look for in terms of POV, you'll be able to recognize the techniques your favorite erotic authors use to maintain a scene's POV. And now that we've reviewed the basics of POV, here are some common POV variations to keep in mind.

First person

In a first-person narrative, the character telling the story refers to himself or herself as "I":

> *I moved my hands further up her leg and was now touching the middle of her inner thigh where the tops of her stay-up stockings gave way to naked flesh. As my hand moved over her skin, she opened her legs slightly to allow me more freedom of movement. I moved my fingers closer to the hotspot beneath her panties, and she let out a slight moan.*

This POV can seem deceptively easy to write, but it is, in fact, very difficult to write well. The entire story — including the all-important

Writing for Black Lace, you should be aware of viewpoints. If you are writing a story with several viewpoint characters, it will be acceptable if one of them is a man. . . . If you are writing from only one viewpoint, however, especially in the first person, the viewpoint character should be a woman.

— *Black Lace guidelines*

sex scenes — must be filtered through the "I" character's mind, and that can sometimes be hard to do consistently. The first-person POV can also be used along with the present tense, which would make the above paragraph read —

> *I move my hands further up her leg and touch the middle of her inner thigh where the tops of her stay-up stockings give way to naked flesh. As my hand moves over her skin, she opens her legs slightly to allow me more freedom of movement. As I move closer to the hotspot beneath her panties, she lets out a slight moan.*

The first-person present tense (and present tense in general) is better suited to stories intended for small and literary magazines, while the past tense is better suited to mass-market magazines and other, more commercial publications. Be sure to make a conscious decision about which narrative POV would best suit the story before you begin.

Second person

The second-person POV is used very rarely, especially in the erotic genre. In a second-person narrative, the story is told with "you" as the POV character. Using this technique, our sample paragraph would read like this:

> *You moved your hands further up her leg and touched the middle of her inner thigh where the tops of her stay-up stockings gave way to naked flesh. As your hand moved over her skin, she opened her legs slightly to allow you more freedom of movement. As your fingers moved closer to the hotspot beneath her panties, she let out a slight moan.*

As seldom as the second person is used in a story intended for a mass market (like the present tense, it, too, is more suited to a literary effort), it is even more seldom used in novels. One exception, though not an erotic novel, is Jay McIrney's *Bright Lights, Big City*, which became the basis for a film starring Michael J. Fox.

Third person

Third person is the most widely used of all the narrative points of view, and with good reason. It is the most flexible for writers, most readable for readers, and is so familiar to both as to seem invisible on the page.

While first- and second-person points of view draw attention to themselves and sound more literary, third person has become the natural way — an almost default format — of telling a story. In third person, the sample paragraph reads —

> *Lance's hand moved further up her leg and was now on the middle of her inner thigh where the tops of her stay-up stockings gave way to naked flesh. As his hand moved over her skin, she opened her legs slightly to allow him more freedom of movement. As his fingers moved closer to the hotspot beneath her panties, she let out a slight moan.*

Use of the third person also makes it easier to incorporate flashbacks into your story (because they, too, are in the third person) and to use multiple viewpoints in a novel. Although the POV character changes, the narrative style does not, and this is less jarring to the reader than having one scene told by the "I" or the "you" and then another told by a totally different character with an actual name. Also, present tense is least obtrusive when used with the third person. Our sample paragraph in third-person present tense would read like this:

> *Lance's hand moves further up her leg and is now at the middle of her inner thigh where the tops of her stay-up stockings give way to naked flesh. As his hand moves over her skin, she opens her legs slightly to allow him more freedom of movement. As his fingers move closer to the hotspot beneath her panties, she lets out a slight moan.*

Omniscient/Limited omniscient/Objective

The final POV variations are the omniscient and limited omniscient points of view. It sounds difficult, especially when you might still be trying to get a handle on first person and present tense, but it's really not all that hard.

Omniscient

Omniscient refers to the narrator's abilities. It means "all-knowing," just as omnipotent means "all-powerful." Until now, I've identified the narrator as the objective observer who reports on what he or she sees without comment. The omniscient narrator is able to know exactly what is going on in every character's mind. With an omniscient narrator there is no POV character because every character's thoughts are known to the reader. Although a valid narrative technique, it's probably the poorest one in the writer's arsenal. Part of the appeal of fiction is that it allows us to get deep into a character's mind, to know his or her thoughts, and to discover the unusual way in which he or she looks upon the world. None of this is possible with an omniscient narrator. True, you get to see inside all the characters' thoughts, but the probe isn't very deep in any of them and the reading experience can be somewhat flat. In erotic fiction, it's an especially weak device because there can be no withheld information and, therefore, little sexual tension. It might be successful when used in the inevitable sex scene in which the sensations of both characters can be made known to the reader, but the benefits don't outweigh the drawbacks.

Limited omniscient

The limited-omniscient POV is the one most commonly used by writers and is most familiar to readers. Simply put, the limited-omniscient narrator can know everything that is going on inside the head of the POV character but can only guess at what is happening in the minds of the others. This technique allows the writer to explore a character's thoughts and motivations and paint the best portrait for the reader.

Objective

Objective is the opposite of omniscient.

While an omniscient narrator knows everything that's going on inside of every character's head, the objective narrator knows nothing. The objective narrator is the camera recording what is happening, but never commenting upon or judging any of it. To remember this one, think of a reporter or a police investigator who must be objective and interested only in the facts rather than conjecture.

For some practice in using POV, see Sample 3.

Showing versus Telling

Next to mastering the use of point of view, the most difficult thing for new writers to grasp about the craft of writing is the difference between showing and telling. Telling, which most aspiring writers are guilty of,

Sample 3
One Scene/Two Points of View

The following is two versions of the same scene (the build-up of sexual tension between a man and a woman), told first from the woman's point of view, and then from the man's. The scene is from my story "Dressed for Success," which first appeared in the November 1993 issue of *Gent*.

To set the stage, the story is about a woman who works in an office as a financial planner and investment counselor. She wakes up late for work one day and discovers that all her underwear is in the wash. She decides to wear some sexy lingerie (a gift from a girlfriend) under her clothes — since she really has few other options — and her sexy apparel is noticed by the client she meets that morning, a professional football player. The version on the left is from the POV of the woman; the version on the right is from the POV of the man.

1 He listened attentively to her presentation, nodding in agreement with each of her points. Then, all of a sudden, he smiled at her and raised one eyebrow.

2 That's when she first felt a hand on her thigh.

3 He had found the slit at the side of her skirt and was slowly sliding his hand up her leg, gently squeezing her stocking-covered thigh until he finally came in contact with bare flesh.

4 Rachel swallowed to moisten her suddenly dry throat. Her legs had spread slightly at his touch, but she was determined to continue making her presentation.

1 He listened attentively to her presentation, nodding in agreement with each of her points.

2 Then, with a smile, he raised one eyebrow and decided to make his move.

3 He found the slit at the side of her skirt and slowly slid his hand up her leg, gently squeezing her hose-covered thigh until he finally came in contact with bare flesh. So, she is wearing stockings, he thought.

4 He caressed her thigh, enjoying the feel of her skin against his hand. Her legs had spread slightly at his touch, but she was still trying to make her presentation as if nothing was happening between them. Dan

As she continued talking, her voice grew weaker and weaker. Dan's hand slid across the naked flesh of her thigh until his fingers came into contact with the damp strip of material covering her now very moist slit.

Beneath the table, his touch felt like fire on her pussy. She spread her legs even wider to give him even better access.

Above the table, he placed his other hand on her shoulder, slowly moving it down her arm until it was on her chest. Gently, he squeezed her breasts as if to entice them from their confines.

5 Rachel finally gave up trying to make her presentation. If she was going to lose her job, she might as well get fucked doing it. She reached behind her, unzipped her dress, then pulled it down from her shoulders and away from her heaving chest.

wondered how long she could keep going, but figured it couldn't be long. Her voice was starting to get breathy.

He pressed on, and her voice seemed to get weaker as he touched the damp strip of material covering her sex. She was warm down there, probably just as turned on as he was. He let his fingers linger there a moment, and she responded by spreading her legs even wider for him so he could touch her more easily. It made him even harder, and he knew he had to have her.

He reached out with his other hand and gently felt her left breast through the material of her blouse. It felt full and round in his hand.

5 Finally, she stopped trying to make her presentation, and starting getting out of her dress.

Section 1: In both pieces in section one, the story is being told by the narrator since no specific point of view is being utilized. The events are simply being reported as if viewed by an unbiased party (or camera) set up at the table where they are sitting.

Section 2: In section two things start to change. In both versions we get the first indication of from whose POV the scene is being told. On the left, the phrase "That's when she felt a hand on her thigh" lets us know it's from her POV because she "felt" a hand on her. On the right, "That's when he decided to make his move" lets us know it's from his POV because he "decided" to make his move.

Section 3: This section is similar in both versions because there are events that have to be reported upon. His hand is moving up her leg. But while that is straightforward enough, the POV diverges toward the end of the paragraph. In the version on the left, she remarks that his hand is on her "stocking-covered" thigh, but in the version on the right he has his hand on her "hose-covered" thigh. She knows she is wearing stockings; he does not know. And so when he finally discovers what she's really wearing, we learn it, too, because the scene is being told from his POV.

Section 4: Section 4 is where the two POVS really become quite different. Not only is the action told in a different sort of way, but more important, each character's motivation is quite different. In her version, she feels his touch but is determined to keep doing her job, even though her body wants her to yield to his advances. In his version, he's making his move, but he's not absolutely sure it's working. It seems to be, but because we're in his POV we can't be sure until he's sure, and he won't be sure until she gives up the charade of trying to continue with her presentation.

Section 5: This section is pretty much the same in each version since each reports on the fact that she's given up on making her presentation and is slipping out of her dress. However, in her version, she thinks about what she's about to do and how it will likely cost her her job. None of that is in his version, since he's more concerned about getting laid than anything else.

Which character tells the more interesting story? Well, considering that the story begins with the woman, and that we are with her when she decides to put on the sexy lingerie to go to work (and early on she realizes she hasn't had sex in a while), the payoff when she finally does have sex would be so much greater than if we told the whole story from the male character's POV, which would be about a professional football player going to see his investment counselor and having sex with her.

This is the sort of thing you'll want to think about when selecting your POV character: Which character would tell the story best? Which would be most entertaining to the reader? Which would be the most fun to write about? There's no rule that says magazines like their stories to be told from a female POV instead of a male POV. It all depends on the story.

Exercise

A good writing exercise to practice handling POV is to write several scenes from the two different POVS. For example, you might want to explore the differing POVs between a man and a woman on their first date. Or perhaps the differing POVs between an exotic dancer and the customer she's doing a lap dance for, or perhaps an experienced older woman and her 20-something virgin lover.

is the stuff of poor writing and leaves fiction flat and lifeless. Showing, which most professional writers do with ease, is the mark of good fiction and makes stories ring true with a crispness that engages the reader and makes reading a joy.

In the previous paragraph, I've shown you the difference between showing and telling. If I had simply told you the difference, it would have read something like *Showing: good; Telling: bad.* Not very engaging, not very descriptive, and downright boring.

But how do showing and telling work in erotic fiction?

Well, say you wanted to create a female character who was young, beautiful, and sexy. How might you go about doing it? Here's how, in both telling and showing modes:

> **Telling:** *She was young, beautiful, and sexy.*

> **Showing:** *The skin on her face was smooth and unblemished, not a wrinkle in sight. Her long black hair hung in curly locks down to her shoulders, with plenty of hairs out of place, like she'd just spent the morning in bed making love.*

The telling example gives us only a little simple information. The showing example, however, gives us both that simple bit of information and a vivid picture of the woman. We see not only that she's young and beautiful, but also that she looks as if she has sex often and enjoys it.

Showing versus telling. Get the idea now?

Not, "He was well-hung," but, "There was a bulge in his pants that looked like he was carrying a cucumber in his pocket."

Not, "Her lips looked full and moist," but, "She ran her tongue from one corner of her mouth to the other, leaving a sheen of moisture across her plump scarlet lips."

Not, "They had wild passionate sex," but, "He entered her with an urgency that she hadn't felt in a man for years. His hands were all over her as he slid in and out of her sex. She could feel him approaching orgasm and wanted to climax with him, but his fingers found her clitoris and she came immediately upon his delicate touch."

Exposition

Exposition is factual writing that provides necessary background information that the reader must have in order to understand a story, and without which a story will not work. Exposition also provides information directly, as opposed to through thoughts and dialogue.

Exposition is something to be wary of. Too much, and your story will seem to stop dead in its tracks. Too little, and your readers won't have the information they need to make the story a success.

In most of my erotic stories, passages of exposition almost always occur in the first five pages so that I can get the information out of the way and won't have to stop the story later on — when things are getting hot — in order to explain something to the reader. I also want to avoid planting information into the story that the reader will need to know just a half-page later — that's too much of a coincidence.

Here's an example of a story that begins with a lot of exposition. The story, called "The Sales Call," appeared in the May 1991 issue of *Gent,* and as it was only my sixth story sale, it is perhaps a little rough around the edges. If I were to write this story today, I would likely ease up on the exposition in favor of more action, but as an example of exposition, it does the job well.

> *Jack Morton got out of the elevator and stopped in front of the mirrored wall across the hall. He put down his sample case, straightened his tie and ran his fingers through his hair. He glanced at his watch, realized he was running a bit late and quickly picked up his case. As he walked briskly down the hall,*

he read the names on each of the doors he passed, looking for the right one.

Jack was a salesman for the Ace in the Hole Plastic and Rubber Company of Rockford, Illinois. He was usually on the road, traveling through the Midwest, trying to sell marital aids to salt-of-the-earth, God-fearing conservatives. Needless to say, his sales figures weren't tops in the company.

But all that was about to change — he hoped. After months of writing letters and making phone calls, he'd finally managed to get a meeting with Bernice L. Custard, head buyer for J.M. Peterson and Company, the third largest department store chain in the Midwest. Jack had been warned about Custard — or "Ballbuster" — as she was called by most of the salesmen who'd tried dealing with her before. She was a terrifyingly big woman who knew how to throw her weight around. She'd started with the company as a sales clerk and worked her way up the hard way, never marrying and devoting herself totally to the company. As a result, she was a bit old-fashioned, extremely thorough in her market research, and expected only top quality and value for her money.

Jack knew the products he was pushing wouldn't make his job any easier, especially when sex toys and marital aids were traditionally sold in specialty shops rather than department stores. Even so, he didn't really have anything to lose by trying.

The name Custard was written on the fifth door he passed. Seeing the name, Jack smoothed out his lapels with his free hand, took a deep breath and knocked on the door.

"Come in," called out a feminine voice from the other side.

When I used to participate in a weekly writer's group, we'd call long passages of exposition "Horking Chunks of Exposition." It was an apt description, mostly because it gave a derogatory connotation to exposition and kept me on my toes whenever I began writing purely informational prose. Later, as I read other writers more closely (and writers are always analyzing while they read), I realized that the best writers rarely use more than two purely expositional paragraphs in a row without breaking them up with a line of action or dialogue. It's a handy rule to go by and will prevent your fiction from slowing to a snail's pace.

A Few Words with...

Nancy Kilpatrick

On Writing S/M Fiction

EDO VAN BELKOM: Is it more in fashion to have women in the dominant role — or that of the sadist in S/M fiction — or has the PC pendulum stopped somewhere in the middle and made it acceptable for men and women to play both roles equally?

NANCY KILPATRICK: I'd say that it's more fashionable to have women in the dominant role, both in fiction and in real-life play. Most extreme erotica is bought by men and, as with any product, it's the consumer's taste that dominates what sells, and that means what writing is purchased. With few exceptions (and I hope my books are among them), porn has never been artistic.

EDO VAN BELKOM: In your work, is S/M and dominance/submission a form of foreplay or is it an integral part of the sex act?

NANCY KILPATRICK: It's both foreplay and a part of the sex act, depending on the characters.

EDO VAN BELKOM: Since S/M and dominance/submission fiction has a very specific attitude about it, not to mention a fetishistic style of dress, how into the lifestyle do you have to be in order to write about it successfully? Or does it even matter?

NANCY KILPATRICK: Most human beings have fantasies, and writers are no exception. Writers can write from their fantasies. Still, the S/M and fetish world has some specific ways of being and some ritualistic elements. To successfully write about this realm, I think it's important to know what's what, and not everything can be gleaned by reading a nonfiction book on the subject.

Visiting a fetish club is often an eye-opener for people, whether they write or not. The reality of things is quite different than what the imagination creates. Still, fiction is not reality; it is imaginative, which is what metaphor is all about. In my

Amarantha Knight books, people could not do what my characters do. Real people would die trying. Of course, I'm also working with the supernatural, which puts another spin on things. My books are fiction, good to stimulate and twig the imagination. They are not how-to manuals.

EDO VAN BELKOM: What are the essential ingredients to making S/M and dominance/submission fiction hot?

NANCY KILPATRICK: Again, it's working with fantasies. I was once on a panel with about seven women who write erotic horror. Someone in the audience asked if we got off on what we wrote. It was curious to me that as we moved down the row from the very young women to the more mature women, the responses changed. The young women all reacted with horror. No! Of course not! How dare anyone think such a thing? As if this were an embarrassment. The older women were more open to admitting that yes, we have sexual fantasies, and they filter into our fiction.

I think that to make this type of fiction work, at least for me, I need to believe that the characters are real people, not stereotypes, or cardboard, generic-porn men and women. To me, hot fiction is real people reacting to a situation which frightens them, titillates them, pushes their boundaries. It is also consensual, and I find that within the consensual realm you can have quite a bit of room for say, terror, yet still have characters want to participate in the scene. Infusing the paradox of conflicting emotions into a character is the trick. Otherwise, for me, it becomes rape, and rape isn't pretty in real life or in fiction. Consensual rape is different. A woman or man might have a strong fantasy about being raped, taken against her/his will, and that can be acted out with a lover that is trusted, where closeness exists. My characters must trust one another in some way or the extremes they go through could not take place.

EDO VAN BELKOM: Is there anything that is still taboo in regards to S/M, or are today's readers ready for anything?

NANCY KILPATRICK: I think sadistic man/masochistic woman is what is most difficult to sell. It is still a PC era. I guess a lot of women still feel unequal to men in some way, and to have that balance in a sexual realm — where they are most vulnerable — or in a sexual fantasy, well, maybe it is too hard. Consequently, apart from some of the men's magazines, that is the fiction that is more difficult to sell in the erotic publishing arena.

I've been lucky in that my books are pansexual (different combinations and sexual orientations), and also characters often switch roles. I also traverse the range of extreme erotica, from heavy-duty S/M, to bondage and submission, to verbal dominance and submission, to coy little titillations, to simple fetishistic dress. And since the erotica I write is usually set in the Victorian era, I get to play with the mores of that time while infusing blatant erotica and, hopefully, tongue-in-cheek humor.

Nancy Kilpatrick writes in the dark fantasy, crime, and erotica genres. She is the author of 13 novels, 125 short stories, and has edited seven anthologies. Her erotic novels are all in The Darker Passions *series, and were written for Masquerade Books under the pen name Amarantha Knight:* Dracula, Frankenstein, Dr. Jekyll & Mr. Hyde, The Fall of the House of Usher, The Picture of Dorian Gray, Carmilla, The Pit and the Pendulum. *Her erotic anthologies are* Love Bites, Flesh Fantastic, Sex Macabre, Seductive Spectres, *and* Demon Sex. *More recent works include* The Vampire Stories of Nancy Kilpatrick, Bloodlover, *and* Graven Images *(edited with Thomas Roche). Her Web site address is* <www.sff.net/people/nancyk>.

Scenes

Scenes are dramatic representations of what is happening in a story, and they should be used as often as possible, since a story or novel is, in reality, a collection of scenes linked by a single narrative.

In erotic fiction, stories are broken up into scenes, such as the scene in which boy meets girl, the scene in which boy makes his move, the sex scene, and the scene in which they decide they will be having sex a lot more often. The number of scenes in a story can vary, but a 3,000-word story would not be likely to have more than four or five scenes. A 60,000-word novel, however, can have upwards of 60 or 80 scenes. One way to learn how to block out a novel in terms of scenes is to write an outline with brief descriptions explaining what happens in each scene. By the time you finish the outline, you'll know how your novel will end, and it will be that much easier to write since all you'll have to do is flesh out the scenes.

Dialogue

Dialogue between characters has to sound real. If your characters talk in language that is stilted or strained, your dialogue will draw attention to itself and the story will fail.

The next time you go out, listen to the way people talk. If you hear an interesting pronouncement or phrasing, repeat it over and over in your mind so the next time you have to write a colorful character, his or her manner of speech will be there for you. Also pay attention to how people of different ethnic backgrounds speak English. There's no easier way to make supporting characters stand out than to give them an ethnicity that will automatically make their names, speech, dress, and gestures different from the other characters in your story.

Dialogue in erotic fiction can be very, very sexy, both in general storytelling and in the depiction of the sexual scenes themselves. To illustrate the first point, here is the opening to my story "Bawdy Stockings," which appeared in the April 1997 issue of *Nugget*:

> *She gazed nervously at the clock. It was nearly five. She glanced at the telephone on her desk. It hadn't rung all day.*
>
> *"I can't believe he hasn't called," she said under her breath.*
>
> *Just then the telephone rang.*

"Hello."

"Happy birthday, baby!"

"I'd thought you'd forgotten."

"Never. I just wanted to get everything arranged before I called. I want this night to be special. I've made reservations at our favorite restaurant —"

"The one where —"

"That's the one."

"You're in for a treat, then," she said, recalling the last time they'd eaten there.

"So are you."

"What do you mean?"

"I've got a surprise for you."

"Any hints?"

"Let's just say I'm going to give you something we're both going to enjoy."

"I'm getting wet already."

"Tell me about it. My cock's been stiff all day."

"Really?"

"Yeah, really. I've got to go now. I'll meet you there at eight."

"I'll be there."

Admittedly, not much happened in that scene, but the dialogue between the two characters is sexy and helps create sexual tension because there is an expectation created that tonight's sex is going to be hotter than usual.

To illustrate the second point about how dialogue can intensify the sexual act, I suggest that you refer to the section in Nancy Friday's book, *My Secret Garden*, which is devoted to sound. Several different women comment on how words and noises (yes, grunts and groans) intensify their sexual intercourse. I'll also offer a scene from my own short story "Teacher's Pet" (*Gent*, September 1995), in which a shy man is taught to take charge of his life by an older, more assertive woman.

Barney opened his mouth to speak, but barely managed to mumble a few words.

"Speak up. Speak your mind."

"I get," Barney stammered, unable to believe he was going to say it. "I get turned on by your breasts. E-every time I see you, I want to know what they look like, what they feel like. I just wish I could touch them." Barney gave his head a shake, finding it hard to imagine that he was saying these things.

"Is that all?" Christine said, her voice level and calm.

"No," said Barney. "I want to kiss them too."

"And?"

"Suck on them."

Barney looked up for the first time and saw that, as they'd been talking, Christine had undone the bow of her blouse and unbuttoned several buttons down the front. Now her black lace bra was clearly visible as it pushed her big tits together, giving her a magnificent amount of cleavage. "Barney, you have beautiful eyes," she said. "I've never even seen them before."

Barney's eyes were locked on her tits as she ran a finger across the sheer fabric along the top of the cup, turning it down to expose her large pink nipples.

"That's what you want, isn't it?" she said.

Barney nodded.

"Go ahead, then. You might bite, but they won't."

Barney felt himself hesitate. This wasn't like him. Normally he'd be running away at top speed, but here he was getting up from the desk and moving closer to those gorgeous puffed-up nipples. It was an exhilarating feeling, this asserting yourself.

"Come, come," she said with open arms.

He nestled his head between her breasts and began licking at one of her swollen areolae and nipples. In seconds it puckered, forming a long, stiff teat.

"That's it," moaned Christine. "See what happens when you know what you want and go for it."

Barney nodded, but kept his lips and tongue on her nipples.

After a few minutes, Christine spoke. "What else do you think about when you see me in class? Tell me!"

"Your legs," he said, a little breathless.

"Yes, what about them?"

"I always want to touch them, feel them."

Christine undid a few buttons along her skirt, showing even more of her creamy thighs. "And what else?"

"I want to know if you're wearing pantyhose or garters and stockings."

"Which one do you hope I'm wearing?"

Barney's mouth was getting dry, but he managed to get the word out. "Stockings."

"Would you like to find out?"

The answer came without hesitation. "Yes."

"Speak up!" she said. "I can't hear you."

"Fuck, yes!"

Christine let out a little laugh as he placed a hand on her thigh. He resumed kissing her tits as he ran his hand up and down her leg. The hosiery was silky and smooth, but he couldn't tell whether they were pantyhose or stockings. There was only one way to find out. He moved his hand higher and higher up her leg until he felt the thicker band of material and then flesh, glorious flesh.

As he felt the inside of her thigh and the fleshy side of her buttocks, Christine took hold of his head and pulled it harder against her breasts. "Now that you know," she said, parting her legs slightly "what else do you want to tell me?"

Barney tried to answer but his mouth was too full of tit.

"Don't you want to tell me something about my pussy?"

"Yes."

"Well, what about it?"

"I've always wanted to pull aside your panties and lick you."

"Lick my what?"

Barney was going to say pussy, but he felt compelled to be more assertive, maybe even a little aggressive. "I want to lick your cunt."

Christine let out a moan of pleasure, then raised her skirt to expose the slip of black panty covering her cunt. "Show me that you're a man of your word," she pleaded.

Dialogue — before, during, and after sex — can add another element to your erotica, turning on the reader not only with the action depicted on the page, but with the sound depicted there as well.

For some practice in handling dialogue, see Sample 4.

Grammar

The use of proper grammar is, of course, as important in erotica as it is in any other genre. Certainly an author can get away with using improper grammar when trying to convey a certain character's POV, such as an uneducated narrator, or perhaps one from the deep south or a rural area, whose word construction and phrasing are unique to the area. It is also possible to get away with poor grammar when writing dialogue. Contrary to the quotes you read in newspaper and magazine articles, the dialogue you hear in movies and on television, and the dialogue you read in fiction, people do not speak in grammatically correct sentences. Their speech is usually quite choppy, fragmented, and interspersed with plenty of "uh-uhs," and "you knows." Writers are also able to get away with ungrammatical sentences when they are trying to achieve a certain rhythm or effect with the words on the page.

Now, while I've made the case for the periodic use of ungrammatical sentences, it's essential that every new writer have a grounding in the basics of proper grammar. To explain them all here would take more room than I can afford, and besides that, good grammar isn't something specific to erotic literature; it is a universal requirement of good writing. If you're still unconvinced, just remember that Picasso could render realistic paintings as well as Norman Rockwell could, but decided to use his brushes and canvases differently. You have to know what the rules are and how to follow them before you can break them.

Sample 4

"Dialogue," he said.

When it comes to dialogue, there is only one word you need to know: *said.*

Many aspiring writers feel it's a writer's job to use as many different words for "said" as there are in the English language. In fact, books and pamphlets listing these words can be purchased through magazines such as *Writers Digest*. (If you can believe it, the word "ejaculated" at one time enjoyed common usage instead of "said," but thankfully it has fallen out of favor.) Frankly, these pamphlets are a waste of time and money because when you use those other words you draw attention to them, distracting the reader from the story. Said is an invisible word and can be used over and over again without getting in the way. If you don't believe me, pay attention to how many times the word said is used the next time you crack open a novel or read a short story.

Of course, you can use other words such as "asked" when a question's being asked, or "cried" when a character is crying or shouting out with joy, but any more than that and a reader's eye will get bogged down in verbosity.

Remember also that each line of dialogue gets its own paragraph. This helps the reader know who is speaking and will allow for paragraph after paragraph without a single said getting in the way. Also, it is possible to do without said if you use other ways to identify who is speaking.

For example —

Mary noticed him next to her at the bar and smiled. "I knew you'd be here."

"You did?" His smile was warm and sexy.

"Yes. In fact, I was counting on it."

He let out a little laugh. "That's me, a guy you can always count on."

"I was also counting on spending some time with you." Her hand slid across the bar and came to rest on top of his, her slim fingers intertwining with his thicker, stronger ones.

He raised his eyebrows. "How much time?"

"The night . . . all night."

His fingers curled around her hand, leading her away. "Let's go!"

Exercise 1

Write a conversation between two characters, using said as often as you like. Then go through the conversation again, taking out a few saids, and see whether or not the conversation has lost any of its clarity. Then try different ways to identify who is speaking, remembering that the goal is to make the scene as clear to the reader as possible.

Exercise 2

Write a conversation between three or more characters, using what you've learned in the previous exercise, making it clear to the reader who is speaking at all times without interrupting the flow of normal conversation.

Exercise 3

Take one of the previous conversations and interject some body language into it. Then add some mention of scenery to help dramatize the scene.

The best book on the subject of grammar is *The Elements of Style*, by William Strunk Jr. and E.B. White. It's usually referred to simply as Strunk and White, and is available in just about every bookstore on the planet.

Humor: No Laughing Matter

Plenty of people will say that when it comes to being sexy, a person's sense of humor is just as important as anything else about him or her, but the truth is that humor really doesn't have a place in erotic fiction. Sex is serious business in erotica, and the appearance of humor in a steamy sex scene would turn things cold in a hurry. Humor and sex work best in bedroom farces or satirical pieces. Erotica is about getting turned on and getting off. If you're determined to include some humor in your erotica, a humorous minor character in an erotic novel might work well as comic relief, but all your main characters need to be serious about their sex.

I don't think everyone conceives of sex the way I do — surrealistic and rich with humor.

— *Woody Allen*

Themes: More Than Just a Sexy Story

Simply stated, theme is the primary statement, suggestion, or implication of a literary work. It describes that portion of the work that comments on the human condition.

Sounds simple enough, but what exactly does it mean?

Science fiction author Robert J. Sawyer explains theme in this way: If you can tell what a story is about without referring to the plot (the events of the story), then you've found its theme.

This explanation works very well with countless sex novels featuring female heroines, which are almost always about a young woman's journey into womanhood.

Of course, not all stories and novels have themes, and not all authors start writing with an actual theme in mind. Quite often, a theme is unconsciously incorporated into a novel during its creation (suggested by its subject matter or storyline) and is discovered only after the piece is finished — and sometimes not even by the author. A piece of fiction's theme is a nebulous entity that is open to debate, discussion, and interpretation. It is something that a new writer should be aware of but not obsessed with. After all, there are plenty of other aspects to writing erotica to be mastered before one worries about including a theme in one's story or novel.

They can mount a picket line around a 7-Eleven store that carries *Playboy*, and they can take things off the market because of the pictorial content, but so far they haven't been able to do in any of us for the written word.

— *Larry Townsend*

6
HOW DOES EROTICA WORK?

Turning the Reader On

Erotica is all about turning the reader on. And if the reader isn't turned on by reading erotica, then at least he or she is thinking about sex a little more than usual after reading it. Since erotica is about stimulating the human libido, it's not surprising that erotica and pornography are often euphemistically referred to as "one-handed reading."

If you think that's silly, think again.

"For men, erotica is often used to enhance self-pleasure," says Dr. Ruth Westheimer in her book, *Dr. Ruth's Encyclopedia of Sex.* "While women who do not have a partner can certainly masturbate while reading such novels, women with a partner often use such literature to lead up to a genuine sexual encounter."

What Turns Women On in Erotica

In the past, women's erotica had been written by men — albeit from a woman's point of view — and was usually about some innocent young woman who'd been turned into a whore by some ogre of a man, and who ends up having sexual desires and needs similar to those of men. Today, women's erotica is written by women, and as a result, the female characters women write about have gained control of their lives — financially, emotionally, and sexually. Furthermore, the women in women's erotica are no longer simply poor whores or bored heiresses, but can be anything and everything real women are and aspire to be in their everyday lives.

Now that women's erotica is competing on a level playing field with men's erotica, what exactly do women want to read about?

Well, it turns out they want a lot of the things that men want to read about. According to the guidelines of erotica publisher Black Lace, "Men and women seem to want the same things; they just like them dressed up differently."

So what's the right way to dress up women's erotica?

Generally speaking, women are more attracted to sensual (emotional) stimuli rather than physical (sexual) stimuli. That means that while a man might be turned on by the physical description of a woman's body and the sexual act, a woman might be more turned on by the sexual tension that leads to sex. If you were to write a sexual scene that takes place in a motel room above a market square in Morocco from a woman's perspective, you would spend time describing the smells that wafted up from the street, the feel of the warm breeze on her skin as it blows gently under the door, the sounds of vendors plying their trade on the street below.

On a more basic level, women's erotica tends to be about making love and experiencing erotic and sensual pleasure, while men's mass-market erotica is about fucking and coming.

What Turns Men On in Erotica

If you were to write that very same sex scene taking place in the hotel room above a market square in Morocco from a man's perspective, there may well be mention of what was going on in the street below, but that mention would be simply a matter of context. The main event would be

It's fun for couples to read stories to each other. It's a way of enhancing their relationship. It's a way to play with fantasy for some couples, to try new things with it. . . . For individuals who don't have a partner, it's a way to give them a sexual life so they can feel turned on and add to their own fantasy life. . . .

— *Sex therapist Lonnie Barbach*

The purpose of a Black Lace book is to arouse the reader sexually.

— *Black Lace guidelines*

A Few Words with . . .

Lynda Simmons

On Erotica in Romance Novels

EDO VAN BELKOM: How have the descriptions and depictions of sexual situations changed in the romance genre over the last 30 years?

LYNDA SIMMONS: While the basic premise of romance novels remains the same (monogamous, heterosexual relationships) the biggest change has been the level of sensuality and the inclusion of explicit sex scenes. Prior to the 1970s, sex in romance was limited to a heated touch, a lingering glance, and a kiss that usually took place on the last page — and no tongues, please. The heroine was always a virgin, and while it was understood that the hero would be wonderful in bed, it was also understood that he would get to prove this only after a wedding ring was firmly planted on the third finger of the heroine's left hand. Sex was all about longing back then.

But with the women's movement in the early 1970s came writers like Rosemary Rogers and Kathleen Woodiwiss who introduced historical romances with long, detailed sex scenes and heroines who actually enjoyed the act. Sex in print was finally available to women who wouldn't be caught dead reading Erica Jong but were ready for more than a chaste kiss, and they couldn't get enough of these books.

Publishers responded to the demand, giving birth to what has became known as the "bodice ripper" (a term best used out of earshot of most historical romance writers, by the way). Covers became increasingly bolder, featuring young women with flowing hair and heaving breasts clutching the iron thighs of a tall, bare-chested hero, a man who embodies all things male — six-pack abs, great teeth and bronzed, hairless skin. Judging by the expressions on their faces, both hero and heroine are obviously on the brink of orgasm, offering the reader a glimpse of what they'll find on the 400 or more pages inside. But even though sex was obviously what the reader was buying, the act itself was cloaked in euphemisms — "quivering thighs," "rising manhood," and my personal favourite, "the damp crevasse of her desire."

Sex was largely rape fantasy, where the heroine, still a virgin, resisted the advances of the dark knight at first, but was overcome by her own blossoming passion and desire. Reasons for the readers' acceptance of these near-rape scenes has been discussed over the years, but the one most widely touted is that women in the 1970s were still sexually inhibited, making it impossible for them to submit to the act willingly. The rape fantasy took away the heroine's responsibility for the act itself, leaving her free to finally enjoy herself. Personally, I think it had more to do with the fact that women bought the early books because they were new and daring, and marketing did what it always does — gave us more of the same. But the die had been cast and the inclusion of sex in romance novels was here to stay.

EDO VAN BELKOM: Which imprints are the steamiest in terms of sexual explicitness, and are there any authors who have reputations for writing great sex scenes?

LYNDA SIMMONS: While the level of sensuality in category romance (which includes everything by Harlequin and Silhouette as well as Zebra Bouquets and Precious Gems) can vary from book to book even within an imprint, Temptation Blaze is probably the hottest line on the Harlequin side, and Silhouette Desire and Intimate Moments are the sexiest on the other. Zebra doesn't break their imprints down into further sub-categories but usually like their books to be steamy. Avalon does not include detailed sex in their books, and neither do Inspirational or Christian romances.

But in even the hottest category romance, the sex is still monogamous and heterosexual, and you won't find anything kinky. No serious bondage, no voyeurs, no groups, no pets, and no special equipment. Oral sex is eluded to, but anal sex has never, to my knowledge, appeared on the pages of a category romance. If the hero and heroine talk dirty to each other, it's never in graphic terms. Ever heard George Carlin's "Seven Words You Can't Say on Television"? Well, you can't say them in romance novels either. It's just not what the readers are looking for.

On the other hand, longer, mainstream romance novels, both contemporary and historical, can be quite explicit. The language is not limited the way it is in category, and I have read some books where the authors are taking risks with multiple partners, bondage, and anal sex. Bertrice Small and Thea Devine are good examples of the bolder, sexier historicals.

EDO VAN BELKOM: In romance novels, is sex possible without romance, or are the books always romantic first and sensual second?

LYNDA SIMMONS: Romance novels are heterosexual love stories, first and last. The heroines in contemporaries are no longer virgins, but their list of past lovers are not the stuff of legend either. They don't have sex just to scratch an itch and they believe themselves to be in love when they do lie down with the hero.

For his part, the hero in a romance novel is not a casual-sex type of guy. He has experience and he is hell in bed, but he's not careless and he's definitely not stupid.

In category romance, neither the hero nor the heroine are the type of person who will ever wake up in bed and not know the name of the person next to them.

EDO VAN BELKOM: Is there anything that's still taboo, or are there enough different imprints from the various publishers to accommodate everyone's tastes?

LYNDA SIMMONS: Gay or lesbian secondary characters do appear in romance novels, usually portrayed positively, but not sexually, to the best of my knowledge.

Incest, pedophilia, heavy S/M, bestiality, and sexual humiliation of the main characters, as far as I know, have also never appeared in a romance novel. These are not stories that set out to shock the reader or revel in the baser side of human nature. Whether it's romantic suspense or light-hearted comedy, family sagas or swashbuckling adventure, when you're talking romance, you're talking great sex, men who can commit to a long-term relationship, and happy endings. Female fantasy at its finest? You bet.

When Lynda Simmons is not hunched over a keyboard writing fast-paced romantic comedies such as Perfect Fit, Charmed and Dangerous *and* That Devil Moon, *she teaches Crafting a Novel at Sheridan College in Oakville, Ontario. Visit her Web site at <http://www.getset.com/lyndasimmons>.*

the description of exactly what is happening on the bed between the man and the woman, or perhaps even more precisely, what's happening to the man while he's having sex with the woman.

While the above example is somewhat simplified for the sake of argument, it's generally accepted that men are attracted by visual stimuli. For men, erotica is often about female bodies — breasts, legs, vaginas — and that's why men's magazines are so explicit and successful.

Men and women tend to differ in the aspects of sex they put most emphasis on: men like anatomy, women like environment.

— *NEXUS guidelines*

In the simplest terms, women's erotica is usually about nuance, sensuality, and subtleness; men's erotica is commonly about tits, asses, and fucking.

So, if erotica — for both men and women — is about turning the reader on, either during sex or leading up to it, how does an erotic writer go about achieving that goal?

Sexual Tension: Fiction Foreplay

Walk into any adult video store and you'll see walls full of videotapes neatly separated into sections that appeal to different customers' tastes. On one wall, there might be new releases, and on another, you might find special-interest videos that focus on a particular subject matter. Elsewhere, there are shelves featuring "Stag" films, and other shelves containing videos with "Couples Appeal." The stag films are usually four-hour videos that feature one sex scene after another and are geared toward a male viewer. The couples' films are similar to regular movies in that they have actors, dialogue, and most important, a storyline. These films are meant to be watched by men and women, so not only do they have explicit sexual scenes, but also a story that gives a reason for the characters to have sex.

A storyline creates sexual tension, and sexual tension in erotic fiction is like foreplay. It makes the sex all the more satisfying when it happens.

As an example of how to create sexual tension, here is the beginning of my story "Don't Look Now," which was published in *Gent* magazine in 2000:

The home team called for a timeout and the roar that had been thundering through the stadium the past 15 minutes slowly died down.

"You seeing anybody these days?"

Darren looked over at his friend Jack curiously. "I didn't think I was your type."

"Very funny," said Jack, biting into a pretzel. "But I'm serious. You seeing anybody?"

"Not right now. Why?"

"There's a woman at work named Beth who thinks you're cute."

"You sure it's me she's talking about?"

"The one and only. She saw you when you picked me up for last Friday's game and she mentioned it Monday morning. She asked if you were unattached, so now I'm asking you."

"Is she pretty?"

"She's beautiful."

"Then what's wrong with her?"

"Nothing," said Jack. "Well, not really."

"What do you mean — not really?"

He sighed. "She's pretty and sexy and everything, it's just that . . . "

"Yeah, what is it?"

"Well, when you go out with her, just don't look at her tits."

"What!"

"Just what I said. Don't look at her tits. She's sort of sensitive about them."

"What are they, small?"

Jack shook his head. "No, they're big. Real big . . . so big you can't help but stare at them whenever she's around."

"Oh."

"She's always complaining about the guys she dates being in a hurry to get their hands down her top. To be fair, I don't blame these guys. I mean, I just work with her, and she's caught me staring more than a few times."

"You're putting me on, right?"

"Nope, just giving you a bit of friendly advice. She's sweet and good looking, and she's already interested in you, so you're halfway there. I just don't want you to give her a reason to think you're like all the rest. That's all."

Darren thought about it a moment. "Okay."

"Okay what? You'll go out with her?"

"Sure, why not?"

"Great, I'll get her number for you tomorrow."

"I mean, how hard can it be? Not looking at her tits."

Jack grinned widely. "Believe me, I've looked at them every chance I've had, and it gets hard, very hard." He laughed loudly at the joke.

This opening creates sexual tension because a) we're informed that the woman, Beth, likes Darren, and b) he's not to act too interested in her physically, although her attributes are such that he can't help but notice them, even ogle them.

As with all erotic stories, we know that the characters will be having sex. It's just a matter of when and how. But the story above has a storyline that prolongs the tension, as Beth shows up for her date dressed in revealing clothes that show off, rather than hide, the things he's not supposed to notice.

To make a long story short, they do indeed have sex, but it turns out she was all dressed up because Darren's friend Jack, who set up the date, told her that Darren was a breast man, so she decided to dress to make sure he didn't overlook what she had. Of course, Jack had been having fun with both of them, and the result is a story that is light-hearted, loaded with sexual tension, and (perhaps most important of all) fun to read.

Story: The Slow, Sensuous Build-up

Aspiring writers who have tried and failed at writing in other genres ask me — often over the phone — about writing erotica. They want to know how one goes about it, as if there were simply some trick to know that, once learned, would make writing erotica easy. What I tell them is that writing erotica is no different from writing science fiction or mysteries or whatever else they've been working on. Although erotic stories feature sexual scenes, they also have characters and storylines that have to be every bit as believable as the storylines in other genres.

For some reason, this comes as a surprise to them. It shouldn't. Writing fiction means telling stories, and if your characters happen to end up having sex, then it's your job to tell the story of how they got to that point in their lives. And you have to make the story believable. There is some room to maneuver here, though. In our everyday lives, we don't usually have sex at the drop of a hat, but you must present a storyline in which sex at the drop of a hat is *possible*. Genres such as science fiction, fantasy, and horror work on the notion of "suspension of disbelief," which is the ability to make the reader believe that what is happening in the story could happen. This is just as important in erotic writing. Character, setting, and plot all have to contribute to the reader believing that the sex was inevitable, rather than inserted because a sex scene was required.

Although many magazines prefer that the stories they publish have sex scenes early on to grab the reader's attention, it's my opinion that the longer the sex is put off, the greater the sexual tension. The more time you spend on story (remembering to keep that somewhat sexy as well), the more satisfying the sex — when your characters finally get around to doing it.

Good Sex: A Satisfying Climax

Since you're writing about sex, the sex you write about has to be good. Your characters need to enjoy it, and that sex has to actually be possible. The sex in erotica *is* often incredible, but not every story is about circus acrobats and gymnasts. The majority of stories are about regular people, and regular people can have great sex without having to do flips and twists. When you're writing a sex scene, it's all right to put your characters under some physical strain, but keep a mental image of them in your mind while you're writing to keep track of where all the body parts are at any given moment. As well, make certain you know where all the body parts are located. Here's an excerpt from the guidelines that publisher Nexus has created for their erotic novels:

> *Take care with anatomical descriptions — it is quite astounding how many men are confused about the relative positions of the female genitalia. Female orgasm is triggered in most instances by clitoral stimulation. This clitoris is not situated inside or adjacent to the vagina. If a penis (or anything else, for that matter) has penetrated the cervix, something very unusual is going on.*

It's also a good idea to keep in mind what things might feel like during sex so you can give accurate descriptions of the action. If you want to describe a scene involving anal sex, you don't want to have your male character ramming his cock into the female character's anus. You might want to mention the use of lubrication (natural or otherwise), or a gentle insertion followed by a slow increase in pressure. If you're writing from the woman's point of view, you might want to mention that she feels spread wide, stretched apart, but that it is a good feeling (remember that erotica should always be sex positive).

Safe Sex: Keep It Fun

Another thing to keep in mind is to not have your characters do anything that might hurt them. For example, you wouldn't want your characters to go straight from anal sex to vaginal sex without a break to clean up or otherwise reduce the risk of infection. Having said that, it's your choice whether or not you want to mention safe sex in your erotica. The sex in erotica is often fantasy, so the mention of condoms, safe sex, and the risk of pregnancy is typically not welcome. Breaks in the action for public service messages tend to be a bit of a turn-off. Publishers give the reader credit for knowing that erotic fiction is not real life, and that in real life, precautions need to be taken. Some publishers have even gone a step further, putting a note at the front of erotic books to explain that what the reader is about to enjoy is fiction, and that in real life, practicing safe sex is encouraged. It's almost like a warning label on cigarette packages.

The Language of Erotica

Much in the same way as an orgasm can have a different level of intensity, so too can erotic writing. But, unlike orgasms, it's not the intensity

I'm not an authority on sex. I'm more of a fan.

— *George Burns*

of the climax that changes. What changes is the way in which the climax is described.

A December 1991 *Penthouse Letters* article entitled "My Life as a Pornographer," by acclaimed science fiction writer Robert Silverberg, began with Silverberg writing a sex scene in the style of 1991, and then revealing how he had originally written the same scene in 1959, when he was making a very good living writing sex novels for a Chicago publisher.

The difference in the two pieces is startling. In the updated version, cocks spring up into aching rigidity, mouths are as soft and as sweet as velvet cunts, and characters have no problem giving instructions like, "Go on, suck it! Oh, Jesus, suck it, babe!" In the earlier, original version, a man and a woman roll off the couch onto a carpeted floor, where they remain side-by-side for an hour, lips glued together and hands roaming each other's bodies until the woman says, "Now, darling! Take me now!" When the couple finally experiences orgasm, the woman gasps, breathlessly uttering "Oh" four times (the last one in italics), and then he feels a hot explosion in his loins. And then it's over.

Censorship is an excuse to talk about sex.

— *Fran Lebowitz*

Even though the 1959 version doesn't delve into body parts and graphic depiction of sexual acts, it's still quite erotic and even hot, "in its quaint fashion," as Silverberg says.

The difference between the erotica of 1959 sex novels and the sex fiction you're able to read today (whether it be in magazines or in novels) is the difference between soft-core and hard-core erotica.

Going Soft and Getting Hard

The market for which you're writing will determine whether a story's sexual scenes should be written as soft core or hard core. If, on one hand, you're writing for *Playgirl*, you'd definitely be doing soft core, as the readers of that magazine don't go for anything too hard. On the other hand, if you're writing for *Hustler*, it's hard core all the way, preferably right from the first page.

The following is a scene from a short story of mine called "After Hours Deposit," which first appeared in the July 1999 issue of *Petite*. It's about a male writer of sexy stories (where do these writers get their ideas from?) who is attracted to a sexy young female teller in his bank. He asks her out on a date, and she, interested in him and what he does for a living, says yes.

Soft

It's largely a contextual thing but the verb "fuck" is okay and certainly preferred to "screw." It's better used in dialogue, though, and shouldn't be overused.

— *Black Lace guidelines*

"Where do you get your ideas?"

"Well, sometimes I'm in a situation and find myself fantasizing about a certain woman, and that leads to the creation of a story."

"Really?"

He nodded.

"Have you written a story about me?"

Greg wondered what he should say. He'd just started a new story that afternoon, one that featured a sexy bank teller. If he lied, Brenda might read the story later and catch him in the lie. "As a matter of fact, I am working on one right now called 'After Hours Deposit.' "

"Is it about me?"

"Well, it's about a woman like you."

She settled down onto the couch and moved closer to him. "Tell me all about her."

"Well, she's beautiful and sexy, and has got a terrific figure . . ."

Brenda moved closer, snuggling up against him.

" . . . and when the guy comes to the bank, he's so turned on by her that all he does is imagine what she might be like in bed."

"And how is she in bed?" She placed a hand on his thigh and began caressing it.

"Well, I haven't got that far in the story yet. You see, he's only fantasizing about her at this point. And the thing that has his attention is the bra that she's wearing."

"Oh really," said Brenda, moving her free hand over her sweater and through the V between her breasts.

"Yes, because he can see it through her sweater and likes the way her breasts move when she walks. He fantasizes about making a deposit between those breasts after the bank has closed. See? 'After Hours Deposit.' "

"That sounds hot," she said, climbing over him, so that she was straddling his legs. "How does the story end?"

"I don't know," Greg said, finding himself short of breath. "Like I said before, I haven't got that far yet."

"Would you like to find out?" Her hands were roaming freely over her breasts and pushing them together to make an even deeper line of cleavage between them.

"I'd love to."

He reached out and took her in his arms. Their lips met, hot and wet, and their tongues darted in and out of each other's mouths. And then her hands were roaming his body, moving downward until she had a hand between his legs.

This is going to be a great ending, thought Greg.

She was fumbling with his belt now, and undoing his pants. There seemed to be an urgency to what she was doing, as if she wanted him — now!

Greg obliged, following her lead.

Minutes later, they were both naked. She straddled him and began lowering herself down onto his hardened shaft. Greg helped out by using a hand to guide his manhood inside her, but that was all the help she needed. In seconds she was moving up and down on him, her head arched back in pleasure and her breasts jutting out before her with her hardened nipples rubbing teasingly against his lips.

He thrust up to meet her, and each time he did she let out a satisfied moan. Her breath was getting short, and her body seemed to be trembling in anticipation of something wonderful.

She let herself down more forcefully onto him and then she stopped and let out a shrill cry of ecstasy.

Greg joined her in a long satisfying climax that left them both out of breath and damp with sweat.

"Have you got an ending now?" she said.

"Yes," he nodded. "An ending — " he kissed her breasts and neck, knowing he'd be hard again in no time, "— and a beginning."

Harder

"That's sounds hot," she said, climbing over him so that she was straddling his legs. "How does the story end?"

"I don't know," Greg said, finding himself short of breath. "Like I said before, I haven't got that far yet."

"Would you like to find out?" Her hands were roaming freely over her breasts and pushing them together to make an even deeper line of cleavage between them.

"I'd love to."

"I know I'm aching to find out."

She lifted her sweater over her head, and Greg was suddenly staring at the full cups of her black lace bra. He reached up and took one of the bra cups in his hand, while he worked his other hand under her skirt. To his surprise, she had removed her pantyhose at some point in the evening. He moved his hand higher and found she had removed her panties as well. Perhaps she'd been thinking about a situation like this, just as he had.

"Tell me more about her," she said, undoing the front clasp of her bra.

"She has beautiful tits, with big nipples that are always aching to be sucked."

"Yes," she moaned, directing one of her breasts toward his mouth. He sucked on the nipple for a long time before Brenda pulled back to offer him the other.

"What else?"

"Well," he said, his throat suddenly quite dry. "Although she's gorgeously slim and petite, she has a very big appetite. . . ."

"Appetite for what?" she whispered into his ear, giving his lobe a lick.

Greg wondered if he should be bold enough to say it, but he'd already gotten this far, so why the hell not. "A very big appetite for hard cock."

She moaned at the mention of the word and moments later was on her knees before him, working at his belt and the waistband of his pants. In seconds she had them both undone and she was stroking his hard cock with what felt like an expert hand. And then she slid her lips over the bulbous tip and sucked him deep into her mouth. Greg moaned with pleasure, and began thrusting slightly against the exquisite touch of her lips and tongue. The longer it went on, the more eagerly she took him deep into her throat. After several minutes, she looked up at him and flicked her tongue over the tip of his dick. "Anything else she likes to do?"

"Yes. She likes to have her pussy licked until she comes in a loud shuddering orgasm."

In seconds, Brenda was lying back with one foot on the floor, the other draped over the back of the couch. She was stroking her clit with the fingers of her right hand and tweaking her erect nipples with her left.

Greg knelt on the floor and rested his upper body on the couch. Then he lowered his head and tickled her swollen clit with the tip of his tongue. She responded to his touch by letting out a loud moan. She massaged her breasts and fingered her nipples.

After a few minutes, Greg began using his tongue on her like a cock, thrusting it in and out of her hot, wet pussy. Soon she began bucking against his mouth as she neared orgasm. Her legs closed tightly around his head and would not let go.

Greg pulled his tongue from inside her and kissed her swollen clit, gently sucking on it for a while and sending her over the edge into an explosive orgasm.

"Oh, yeah," she cried, her voice trailing off into a series of long, drawn-out moans. "Yeah. . . that was. . . great."

It sure was, thought Greg, even though he was still rock hard and unsure about what was going to happen next. He decided he'd fuck her. If he was lucky, maybe he could make her come again. He began moving into position.

"What about the after hours deposit?" she said, stopping him. "That's a much better ending."

Greg had forgotten all about the story he'd been telling, but if that's how she thought the story should end, then who was he to argue with an appreciative reader?

"Sit up straight."

He sat up on the couch.

She knelt down before him and wrapped her breasts around his cock. Her breasts weren't big enough to completely envelop his cock, but the sight of her titfucking him and the occasional licks of her tongue she was giving to the head of his prick were more than enough to make him climax.

"That was a great story," Brenda said when it was over. "Want to tell it to me again?"

Hardest

"Where do you get your ideas?"

"You really want to know?"

"Yeah, I do."

"Mostly from the cunts I fuck."

"Really?"

He nodded.

"Are you going to write one about my cunt?"

"Are you a good fuck?"

"Never had any complaints."

Greg smiled. She didn't look like the kind who would leave a man with a sackful of cum. In fact she looked like she was born to fuck. "I bet you haven't."

She ran her tongue over her upper lip. "So, are you going to write about my cunt or not?"

"I haven't even seen it yet."

She let out a little laugh and got up off the couch. Then she took off her sweater and slipped out of her skirt, revealing a pair of big tits and a cleanly shaved slit. "Better get your big fat pencil ready," she said, looking at the bulge in his pants. " 'Cause I'm gonna give you something to write home about."

Then she dropped to her knees. In seconds her expert hands had freed his cock and were jerking it, making it big and hard for her hungry mouth. First she licked his cock, then took the bulbous head between her lips and sucked on it.

After a while she looked up at him, smiled and said, "Your turn now." Then she lay down on the couch and spread her legs and cunt lips for him. Greg used his tongue like a cock, fucking her with it until she wrapped her legs around his head and rammed her wet cunt hard against his mouth.

Greg tried to move but she wouldn't let him, holding him tightly against her swollen lips until she came, spurting her love juices into his mouth.

"You enjoy that?" he said, when she finally let him go.

"It was good," she answered, spreading her legs and lazily fingering her glistening cunt. "But that was just the first chapter."

"What do you mean?"

She reached forward and grabbed his still hard cock and guided it between her legs. "Now it's time for chapter two."

"Chapter two?"

"The one where you fuck me til I scream."

If you're wondering, the scene classified "Harder" was the version that appeared in print. It seems the best fit of the three, because it works on the soft-core level as the sexual tension is being built up, then delves into hard-core waters. The soft-core version seems to go to extreme lengths to avoid using a four-letter word, while the hard-core version concentrates on the sex act so much that the reason behind it happening seems to have been lost.

Of course, these shortcomings are more a result of the way the scene was originally written. Had it been written to be part of a soft-core story, then an even harder version of it would seem out of sync; and if it was originally hard core, softening it up would have seemed wrong for the piece. This is a long way of saying that soft core is no better and no worse than hard core, and vice versa, but rather each has its place, depending on the type of story you are writing.

Four-Letter Words

Some words are charged with sexual energy. You can't see the words fuck, cock, or cunt on a page without immediately thinking sexual thoughts. Still, you don't have to use those words every chance you get. In fact, in terms of explicit words, less is more. The more often someone uses the word "fuck" in their everyday speech, the less impact it has when they are angry. On the other hand, if a man never swears or says an improper thing, and then shouts out "Fuck!" when he's angered, the use of the word is fairly significant. Be aware that there are plenty of words that have sexual impact, but choose them wisely. Use them sparingly and for effect.

Whether a story is soft core or hard core depends on the language used to tell the story, and all three levels of explicitness can be effectively used over the course of a single story. As you build sexual tension, you might be inclined to use soft-core terms. As the tension heats up, a harder reference might be in order. And finally, when the characters are getting it on, the four-letter words your mother warned you never to say suddenly seem appropriate. Table 3 gives some examples of language that can be varied from soft to hard core.

Is erotic fiction dirty?
Only if it's done right.

— *Woody Allen*

Table 3

Soft- to Hard-Core Language

Soft	Harder	Hardest
Make love	Have sex	Fuck
Manhood	Penis	Cock
Sex	Pussy	Cunt
Kiss	Lick	Suck
Chest	Breasts	Tits
Climax	Orgasm	Come
Love juice	Load	Cum, jism
Love button	Clitoris	Clit

How Erotica Doesn't Work

There are a number of things you should avoid in creating an erotic story, but the major ones to watch out for are listed below:

1. *Pain:* The sex in erotic fiction is enjoyable and positive. If your character is in pain, the reader will be turned off (unless of course, he or she is a sadist, which would limit your fiction to a very, very small number of readers).

2. *Children:* Sex might produce them, but there's nothing that turns off readers more than mention of the consequences of the sexual act. Similarly, publishers and editors avoid all mention of kids in the stories they print because a mention of a child in their pages could close them down in a hurry. Even a mention of a schoolyard would be enough for a story to receive an automatic rejection. It's called adult material for a reason.

3. *Incest:* Sex between family members is a no-no. I once wrote a story about twin sisters having sex with one of their boyfriends, a sort of contest to see who was the better lover. The story was immediately rejected, and I couldn't figure out why. Months later, the story was bought by the same magazine to which I'd first submitted it, but the twin sisters had been changed to college roommates. Just as a hint of children or underage participants merits a sure-fire rejection, so too does mention of sex between or with family members. Publishers of erotic novels are a little freer, sometimes allowing relations between close family if one of the participants isn't much younger than the other. (So now you know why there are so many stepmothers and stepfathers in erotica.)

4. *Non-consensual Sex:* Portrayals of non-consensual sex should generally be avoided in writing erotica. It might, however, be okay to portray a scene in which a character is at first held against his or her will, only to eventually be overcome with desire and end up enjoying the sex. (Keep in mind, nonetheless, that any deviation from this sequence of events will bring on rejection from a publisher.)

For example, take the Christina books written by Blakely St. James and published by Playboy Press in the 1970s. Here's the back-cover blurb from *Christina's Torment*, published in 1979:

> *Tauntingly beautiful, achingly desirable, the wealthy Christina van Bell is lavishly seduced — and then kidnapped by a cult of sexual psychopaths. As the ransom negotiations drag on, her life turns into an eternity of lust, passion, and orgies. And what will the outcome be, nobody knows. But for Christina, the waiting is sheer pleasure.*

So while Christina is being held against her will and much of the sex in the book is forced, she considers herself to be a sexual artist and enjoys every sexual encounter she has.

5. *Degradation:* Sex scenes that clearly degrade women or men are not advised. People aren't reading erotica to feel guilty or otherwise bad about themselves or their lives.

Other things to be avoided (according to the Nexus guidelines) include sexual acts that cause bloodshed or other permanent physical damage; sex acts that would cause genuine tragedy or anguish; bondage that involves constriction around the neck; and sex with corpses. Nexus states, "Watersports are fine. It's often the tone of a piece rather than the actual content which is offensive."

7
REVISION AND POLISHING

Unlike the subject matter you're writing about, there's no urgency to writing erotic fiction. You can spend as much time as you like making sure everything is right before you slide the envelope containing your manuscript into the mail slot.

Revising and polishing what you've written to make it the absolute best it can possibly be is one of the easiest ways to become a better writer of erotica. It is also one of the most difficult things to get a new writer to do. After all, once you've completed a story, checked it for spelling and grammar, and made sure all the sex is right and that it's as hot as you know how to make it, how much more can there be to do?

The answer is: Plenty.

Have you used the best words and phrases to describe things, or were you satisfied with merely good words? Is there a slight glitch in your story that you think no one will notice? Are bodies contorted in a way that's physically impossible? Is there a detail you've left out because you didn't want to make a trip to the library to do the research to get it right?

All this is part of doing revisions and polishing your work to make it the best that it can be.

Revising

Revising your work can be difficult if you're a new writer, especially if you're writing erotica. After all, you've spent so much time on your story or novel, how could you possibly change any of it, or even worse, cut something out? And though your subject matter is exciting, even the hottest sex can become boring after you've read the same passage more than a dozen times.

The truth is, even novels written by the best writers of the day can be improved by revision and cutting. But if you're at the point where you're still learning how to write an erotic story, how and where are you going to learn to revise it?

It used to be that magazine editors would be good people from whom to get advice on how to revise your story and make it saleable. As well, book editors used to have more input into a book before they published it, asking for revisions and changes several times before ushering it into print. Today, if a book isn't close to being publishable as is, an editor won't be likely to spend the time working with an author to fix it. That job seems to now rest solely on the author's shoulders.

And most magazine editors are too busy these days to offer more than a scribbled note along with a rejection slip — if you're lucky. After all, why should an editor spend time trying to get you to fix your manuscript when there's probably one that's usable as is further down the slush pile? It's easier to use that one than waste time on something that *may* be publishable somewhere down the road.

Still, if magazine editors and the editors at publishing houses aren't about to provide you with suggestions, who is?

Getting second and third opinions

It never hurts to get a second opinion about your work, but if you're asking the wrong person for advice, it might hurt you more than you think. I've always said that you should never ask your husband, wife, mother, father, brother, lover, or close personal friend what they think of your work. Furthermore, you shouldn't ask anyone who has an interest in your personal well-being. What you don't want is someone

When I was writing the soft-core sex novels, economic considerations largely ruled out rewriting. Who could afford it? Who had time for it?

— *Lawrence Block*

telling you something you wrote is good because he or she doesn't want to hurt your feelings (husband, wife), or because his or her eyes are clouded by affection and pride in your effort (mother, father).

The person to give you advice is someone who can be absolutely honest, who doesn't care if the truth hurts your feelings, who has read in the field in which you're writing, and who knows how to articulate his or her thoughts. A tall order, certainly, but not an impossible one. If you work in an office, find out who reads books on breaks or during lunch hours and ask if he or she might like to give you feedback on your story. Because you'll be asking someone to read erotica, be certain you choose someone who has an open mind about such things. You don't want your co-worker or acquaintance to suddenly have a lesser opinion of you because he or she knows you write what he or she would call "porno." You want to find the person who can read some of your work and say, "Cool."

Getting this kind of feedback is an important part of writing and selling fiction because the time you want to hear criticism of your work is *before* you've sent it to an editor. Once it's in the editor's hands, you can't make any more changes to it until the editor has made a decision on it. And if you think that at some point you won't need the advice of others, think again. I know a writer who has published 12 novels to date and won countless major awards, but who still gets a dozen or so people to read each of his novels before he turns them in to his editor.

My own first critique came at the hands of respected science fiction author Judith Merril, who absolutely savaged my attempts at writing a novel and left me walking around with my tail between my legs for days. But I bounced back, wrote more crap, and eventually produced something saleable. Years later, she told me that she'd thought I had talent (although I couldn't write very good science fiction), but she wasn't about to tell me that at the time and watch me get a swelled head. Nevertheless, she was at the launch party for my first novel and was proud to have played a part in my education as a writer. (I also remember showing Judith some of the erotic stories I'd published in men's magazines. She acknowledged the importance of the sales, and didn't turn her nose up at the work. To her, a sale was a sale. She even went as far as to say, "Not everyone can write that stuff.")

This all refers back to one of the underlying messages of this book: Writing is hard work. If you're not prepared to receive honest criticism and rejection of your work, perhaps you'd be better suited to some other profession.

Letting a story simmer for a while

Once you've finished your erotic story, you'll probably be proud of it and eager to show it around or send it off to a magazine. A word of advice: *Don't.*

Instead, pat yourself on the back for a job well done, put the story in a drawer, and let it sit for a few days (if you're in a hurry), or a few weeks or months (if you have the time), while you work on your next masterpiece. When you read the story over again several weeks later, you'll be looking at it with fresh eyes, and you'll be able to notice things that you couldn't see before because you were all too familiar with the story after having worked on it steadily for so long.

Things such as spelling mistakes and bad grammar become more apparent after a break, because you're not as familiar with the text as you were while you were working on it. Awkward and run-on sentences will also be more obvious to you, as will gaps in logic, flat characterization, poor dialogue, and the need for more detail. If you let a story sit long enough, it will be almost as if you're reading it for the first time, just like one of your readers.

Tightening

Aspiring writers often have trouble cutting parts from their own work. It took so much effort to write in the first place that it's painful to see it go. But every single word you write doesn't necessarily belong in the story you're working on at the moment. If you cut something from a novel (say a scene or a chapter), you can always save it and, later, turn it into a short story or part of another novel.

When I was an aspiring writer, a moment in which I thought that I might someday be a real writer came when I discarded a large section of a story I was working on and tried a completely different tack. At that moment, what was important to me was the quality of the work, not just doing the work, and I felt as if I was that much better a writer (all right, aspiring writer) because of it.

Some writers and editors say you have to be ruthless with your own work, cutting and slashing until the work is as taut as a drumhead. Realistically speaking, things aren't so bad. Just remember that sometimes things must be cut from a work in order for it to be improved.

Here's an example of the kind of tightening stories often need. The following is an early story of mine called "Teddy and the Merry Widow." It was my 23rd short-story sale and was originally published in *40-Plus* as "The Merry Widow" in June 1992, and then reprinted as "Lingerie Party" in *Gent* in July 1993.

Originally published version

Elizabeth Evans hesitated a moment before knocking on the door.

It wasn't as if she'd never done in-home lingerie parties before; that was how she made her living. What was different about this particular Friday night was that it was the first party that was exclusively for men.

She wasn't exactly sure what was making her nervous. Lingerie parties for men seemed to be natural. After all, it was men who got the most enjoyment from push-up bras, garter belts, and stockings.

But while men liked lingerie, they hardly ever bought any. Some of Liz's men friends had told her they felt embarrassed about going to the lingerie store at the local mall. Going to the store wasn't a problem — they liked walking through the racks of teddies, merry widows, and French maids. Their problem was with having to ask the store's salesperson — usually some blue-haired pensioner who was old enough to be their grandmother — if crotchless panties were any good.

With a bit of tightening

Elizabeth Evans hesitated before knocking on the door.

It wasn't as if she'd never done in-home lingerie parties before — that was how she made her living — but this was the first party that would be exclusively for men.

She wasn't sure what was making her nervous. Lingerie parties for men seemed to be natural. After all, they were the ones who got the most pleasure from push-up bras, garter belts, and stockings.

But while men liked lingerie, they hardly ever bought any. Some of Liz's men friends had told her they felt uncomfortable

inside lingerie stores. Going to the store wasn't a problem —
they liked walking through the racks of teddies, merry widows,
and French maids. But having to ask a salesperson (usually
some blue-haired pensioner old enough to be their grandmother)
if crotchless panties were any good was something to be avoided
at all costs.

Admittedly, the changes to the piece are subtle, but still enough to cut 15 words, making it tighter and easier to read. However, although the story has never been published under the longer title, "Teddy and the Merry Widow," that's the title I most prefer. It's probably the only place where there's been expansion rather than tightening over the years.

Writing to length: Size matters

When it comes to erotica, size matters. In guidelines put out by magazines and book publishers, one of the most important bits of information is the word limit for stories and novels. For stories in mass-market men's magazines, the usual range is from 2,500 words to about 4,000 words. If you intend to sell to such markets, your story must fall somewhere between these two numbers. If it's too short or too long, it will be automatically rejected. An editor slots only so many pages for fiction in each issue of a magazine and reads the slush pile with the intention of filling that space. If the story is too short, the editor will have to fill up white space with call-outs (quotes taken from the story and blown up to fill space) or extra stock photos of naked men and women. This might be okay once in a while, but it's far easier just to buy stories that fit the space.

Book publishers also have word limits, but they are a bit less stringent, because it's easier to save space or make room with different-size fonts and leadings over the course of the 200-plus pages in a book than it is to do so in two or three pages in a magazine. However, when you're writing for a specific market, keep in mind that market's stated word requirements. If the editor has had a bad day and wants to clear his or her desk of submissions, it's easier to get rid of a bunch of manuscripts because they were too short or too long than it is to read them all and judge them upon their merits.

Luckily, erotica is a genre in which the prose is rather elastic. By that I mean that it is easy to make a piece longer or shorter just by adding or subtracting from the descriptions of sexual activity.

To illustrate the point, here are a few paragraphs from the sex scene of my short story "After Hours Deposit," originally published in the July 1999 issue of *Petite*.

Original version

In seconds, Brenda was lying back with one foot on the floor, the other draped over the back of the couch. She was stroking her clit with the fingers of her right hand, and tweaking her erect nipples with her left.

Greg kneeled on the floor and rested his upper body on the couch. Then he lowered his head and tickled her swollen clit with the tip of his tongue. She responded to his touch by letting out a loud moan while massaging her breasts and fingering her nipples.

Shorter version

In seconds, Brenda was lying on her back, stroking her clit with her fingers. Greg got onto the floor beside her and tickled her clit with the tip of his tongue. She let out a moan.

Longer version

In seconds, Brenda was lying back with one foot on the floor, the other draped over the back of the couch. She looked to be enjoying herself, slowly stroking her delicate clit with the fingers of her right hand, and tweaking her darkly swollen and erect nipples with her left.

Greg took a moment to appreciate the vision of sexual beauty lying before him, then kneeled down on the floor. He rested his upper body on the couch and lowered his head so that it was positioned directly between her legs. Then he opened his mouth and tickled her swollen clit with the tip of his tongue. She responded to his touch by spreading her legs slightly and letting out a loud moan. She continued to massage her breasts and finger her nipples, but there seemed to be an urgency to her movements now...as if she might come at any moment.

Polishing

When you've spent some six months or maybe even six years working on a novel, it can become a burden to look at the same words yet again. But polishing a piece of prose until you've worked out all the kinks is probably one of the best things you can do for yourself. After all, once you've sent your story off, you can't fix it any more.

But when you've got the story or novel working as well as you possibly can and you don't know what's left to fix, pick scenes or chapters at random and read them over. Skip from front to back, reading a few pages here and there, and see if it's all as good as you remember. Or read a section out loud and see how it *sounds* as opposed to how it *looks* on the page. Mistakes are frequently more apparent when heard rather than read. If you catch just a single mistake, the entire exercise will have been worth it.

Proofreading

Proofreading is one of the easiest ways to polish your manuscript. The spell checkers on computers are good tools for catching some misspelled words, but they should never, under any circumstances, be used as the only or final check of your spelling.

Most spell checkers aren't loaded with words like fuck, cunt, clit, or cum, so you'll have to pay extra attention to a lot of the erotic and sexually explicit words in your manuscript. That's a good reason for you to distrust your spell checker, but it's not the best.

Everyone else on the planet will tell you that you shouldn't trust spell checkers because they can't tell the difference between "their," "there," and "they're," but I have a more dramatic example. Don't trust your computer's spell checker because it can't tell the difference between the following:

therapist

the rapist

The distinction between the two can make a world of difference in your manuscript, especially if it's a work of erotica. And proofreading is just a plain good idea if you want to submit to professional markets and look like a pro. For years I had a sign in front of my computer screen that read **PROOFREAD** in big black letters. It was a reminder to me that as much as I didn't want to read through a story yet again, it was something that had to be done. If I were competing against ten other writers for a spot in a magazine, I figured that I could easily improve the quality of my story just by reading it for typos one more time. Nothing reflects more poorly on a writer than a typo that could have easily been caught, if only the writer had been more careful.

I took the sign down several years ago, but the proofreading habit has stuck with me, and I've often been complimented on how clean and well prepared my manuscripts are.

One last read through

Now that you've got everything polished and clean, take one last look at the manuscript — much as it might pain you to do so. Read it over in hard copy (as opposed to on the computer screen), where words and phrases can look very different from the way they do on-screen. You might find something you didn't see before — a typo, the wrong word, or a comma out of place.

This is, after all, your very last chance to make a correction, and you'd better take advantage of it. There's nothing more disconcerting to a writer than seeing a typo in a manuscript just as he or she is putting it in the envelope. It makes you wonder, "If I just saw that one, how many others might there be?" You'll sleep better, and have a better chance of making a sale, if the issue never comes up and you're unable to find any problems at all.

Part Three
SELLING EROTICA

Writing is like prostitution. First you do it for love. Then you do it for a few friends. Finally you do it for money.

— Jean-Baptiste Molière

Almost anyone can be an author; the business is to collect money and fame from this state of being.

— A.A. Milne

8
WHAT TO WRITE? WHERE TO SELL?

Sex for Sale

Once you've written a piece of erotica, your next logical desire will be to send it to some anthology or magazine editor who will pay you for the right to publish your work on his or her pages.

And now is not the time to play the role of shrinking violet and claim that you never intended to sell your work for money and you would be happy just to see it in print. None of the editors who are in a position to buy something you've written will have that attitude, so you shouldn't either. Of all the genres out there, erotica is the one that pays the best, especially for works of short fiction. Even lesser-name men's magazines will pay upwards of ten cents a word for fiction and nonfiction, which is more than three times the minimum professional payment of three cents per word, which is acknowledged by such organizations as the Science Fiction and Fantasy Writers of America and the Horror Writers Association.

So you're more than likely writing erotica for the money — and isn't everyone who works in the sex industry doing it for the money? Even if you're writing erotica simply because you enjoy it or want to entertain your friends, just imagine how much more you'd enjoy it if there were a few paychecks in your mailbox with your name on them. But how do you find out where to send your stories once they're written?

Firsthand Market Research

To learn the answer to that question, you must begin at the end. By at the end, I mean with the end result, which means the finished books and magazines sitting on the newsstand and bookstore shelves.

Again, this is no time to be shy about what you're doing. If you don't have the courage to go into your local convenience store with pen and paper to check out the magazines for fiction, perhaps erotica isn't your genre. I've gone into countless stores and spent time flipping through magazines to find the ones that publish fiction and take down the editorial address and editor's name. Whenever I got a curious look from the store clerk, I simply told him or her what I was doing. They were usually so dumbfounded by my explanation that they left me alone to finish my business.

(When you do this sort of drive-by market research, be sure you copy down the editorial address and not the address for the company that circulates the magazine. If you make that mistake, your query will eventually get to the right place, but it will take forever to be forwarded, and it might reflect poorly on you that you couldn't even get the magazine's address right.)

If you're not interested in slick, mass-market magazines, or don't like the thought of your work appearing on the same page as naked bodies in explicitly sexual poses, try the "Erotica" section of your local bookstore. There you'll find publishers that produce erotic anthologies (books that feature stories by many different authors) and novels. Inside the books, usually on the copyright page, you'll find an address for the publisher to which you can write to request writer's guidelines or request to be put in touch with an anthology editor so you can submit to their next project. This sounds like a long, drawn-out process that may or may not bear fruit, and that's exactly what it is. But if you want to write erotica and have it published, and you know nothing about the genre or any of the people working within it, this is a way to start.

It sold very well. The Master books have generally done very well. For a gay book. A gay male book that does very well is 10,000 to 15,000 copies.

— *John Preston*

We recommend studying sample copies of the magazines to gain insights into each one's unique style.

— *Score Group guidelines*

A Few Words with . . .

Cecilia Tan

About Circlet Press

EDO VAN BELKOM: First of all, what is Circlet Press and what were your reasons for starting it?

CECILIA TAN: I started Circlet for very personal reasons at first. I was working in book publishing and had always considered myself a writer, but had really not written anything I felt was worth sending out for publication. I had always been an avid science fiction reader and had thought I wanted to be an SF writer like Roger Zelazny or Marion Zimmer Bradley. It had never occurred to me to write erotic fiction at that point. But when I realized what my most vivid fantasies were, what the characters and situations that really captivated my imagination were, I realized they were scenarios that combined the erotic with fantasy and science fiction. The first story I wrote that I felt was really "all there" was "Telepaths Don't Need Safewords." I posted it on the Internet in 1990 or 1991, and the response was phenomenal.

I thought, okay, I want to write it, people want to read it, but who is going to publish it? At the time there was no magazine or book publisher that would touch the story. So I thought, well, I am a book-publishing professional, why don't I start a publishing house? I wrote a few more stories, then published them as a chapbook (entitled *Telepaths Don't Need Safewords*) and started selling them. That little book is what launched Circlet Press. As soon as it got around in science fiction circles, I started to get manuscripts in the mail, many from professional science fiction writers who would complain to me that they couldn't find a market for erotic SF/F work and ask if I wanted to publish theirs as well. I started collecting them into themed anthologies (vampires, technosex, erotic fairy tales, etc.) and Circlet Press took off from there. We quickly gained a reputation after that with both erotica writers and readers, and, as they say, the rest is history. We've now got over 30 titles in print, with more on the way. [Details at <www.circlet.com>.]

EDO VAN BELKOM: What types of erotica have proven most popular with book-buyers and readers?

CECILIA TAN: Our most popular series is the *Erotic Vampire* series, which is up to four volumes now. It began with *Blood Kiss* in 1994, and we have since added *Erotica Vampirica, Cherished Blood,* and *A Taste of Midnight*. I think a lot of vampire fans were getting frustrated with how little actual sex tends to be in mainstream vampire novels (Poppy Z. Brite's *Lost Souls* being a big exception). I wanted to explore the vampire mythos in an explicitly erotic way. The other thing is that vampire fiction is often classified as horror, whereas I wanted to publish erotic vampire stories that were much more in the erotica vein than the horror vein. There's still plenty of blood and sometimes terror, but the sex itself is used to arouse, and not to shock or horrify.

Our S/M-themed books come in a close second. *S/M Futures, S/M Pasts,* and *Fetish Fantastic* are hard to keep in stock, actually. I think it's partly because there's so little really good "scene-aware" S/M erotica out there for people who are into the S/M and bondage lifestyle to enjoy. A lot of the novels out there are more about non-consensual situations, women getting kidnapped and then falling in love with their captors, etc. It rubs people who support the "safe, sane, consensual" lifestyle of S/M wrong. It's very exciting and validating for people to read erotica that acknowledges their own particular fetish or desire. So we have a big following in the bondage-S/M community.

EDO VAN BELKOM: In addition to editing books for Circlet Press, you yourself are a writer of erotica. How did running Circlet help or hinder your own writing career?

CECILIA TAN: At first, Circlet was a way to really kickstart my own career. It put some of my stories out where people could read them and created enough of a sensation that I quickly became known in many circles, especially among science fiction writers and publishers. I got my first agent as a result of that first chapbook. And it gave me something to focus on besides exclusively my own writing while I was honing my craft. As I honed my editorial instincts, I also improved my own writing. (Getting a masters degree in writing at the same time also helped.)

Now, in some ways running Circlet detracts from my writing career, mostly because of the time it takes to keep the company going. Right now, I've reached the point where if I had more time to write, I would earn better and my career would be in better shape! I end up passing on a lot of anthology invitations because Circlet's deadlines take precedence.

EDO VAN BELKOM: Even though Circlet Press is a fairly progressive publisher, there are still some things that are taboo even for you. How much attention do you find authors pay to your guidelines?

CECILIA TAN: Well, we have a commitment to celebrating the sexual and the erotic, which for me means I'm looking to publish stories that promote a positive view of sex and sexuality. The guidelines have a pretty strict list of stuff we don't want to see: murder, necrophilia, castration, dismemberment. . . . Part of the reason for the stringent guidelines is because in the early years we just got so much stuff in submissions that was like that, where sex was equated with death or with something horrible and disgusting. I know that's the underlying assumption of puritan society, but that's exactly what we're trying to fight!

This isn't to say that every Circlet story is all happy-go-lucky with no conflict or trouble — the stories would get boring if that were true. But a positive and celebratory image of sex is a must. These days I think authors are much better at sticking with that theme than they were when we first began.

Surprisingly, one of the main reasons still, to this day, that I have to reject manuscripts is because they don't have enough sex in them. Fortunately, most authors who have erred on the side of caution can be coaxed to draw their sex scenes out a bit longer and give us a fuller picture of the characters and their interactions.

EDO VAN BELKOM: What's in store for Circlet in the future?

CECILIA TAN: Having been publishing since 1992, and having established a reputation for high-quality, cutting-edge erotic literature, we are seeing the opportunity to publish much better known authors. For example, in 2000 we have *Nymph* by Francesca Lia Block, and last year we reprinted Delia Sherman's

Through a Brazen Mirror. I'd like to continue to do what I did for myself — publish material that more mainstream publishers would not — for other, better-known authors. We are launching a line of nonfiction books, called Circumflex, which will begin with a book called *The Erotic Writer's Market Guide,* which will be a market listing and reference for erotica markets, magazines, book publishers, and Web sites.

Cecilia Tan is the author of Black Feathers: Erotic Dreams *(Harper-Collins), and founder/editor of Circlet Press, Inc. She bears the distinction of being the only writer to have erotic fiction published in both* Ms. Magazine *and* Penthouse. *Her stories appear regularly in* Best American Erotica, Best Lesbian Erotica, *and many other anthologies. She is at work on her next erotic book, a novel mosaic entitled* The Book of Want. *To find out more about Cecilia or Circlet Press, to read full writer's guidelines, or to order books, visit* <www.circlet.com>.

An even better way of researching markets is to actually buy a few books and magazines and read the kind of work that's currently being published. Admittedly, at $8 to $10 for a single copy, any in-depth research into even a segment of the marketplace could quickly become quite expensive, so choose wisely. A cost-effective alternative might be an adult store that sells secondhand magazines. As long as you stick to recent issues, you should be able to get a feel for a magazine's content without going broke. But even if you spend a few dollars, think of it as an investment, since a single sale will earn you enough money to buy a dozen or more magazines. Also, if you're serious about becoming a writer, the purchase of magazines to educate yourself about the market is a legitimate tax-deductible expense.

If you really are too shy to do firsthand research or perhaps find it a little expensive, there are some other resources that list erotic markets and their needs. *Writer's Digest* is one magazine that lists a few markets each month, and Writer's Digest Books produces annual volumes listing most of the major fiction and nonfiction markets in America. The yearly *Novel and Short Story Writer's Market* is the best guide for fiction writers, while the simply named *Writer's Market* has far fewer fiction markets and is geared toward an all-around freelance writer working in both the fiction and nonfiction fields. In addition, there are market magazines like the *Gila Queen's Guide to Markets* and books devoted solely to erotic markets. Finally, there is everyone's new research tool, the Internet, which not only has sites that report on markets, but which is also teeming with markets for erotica. (For more on these information sources, see chapter 13.)

Writer's Guidelines

If you've found a publisher or magazine to which you'd like to submit and you're still unsure if what you've written is a good fit with them, try writing to them (including a self-addressed stamped envelope — SASE for short — because you want them to send you something back in the mail) for a set of writer's guidelines.

Writer's guidelines can run anywhere from a single page (for magazines) up to a dozen pages (for books). For the publisher, guidelines are a way of weeding out inappropriate submissions before they arrive in the mailbox. For writers, guidelines can be invaluable: they can help you fine-tune a submission to make it a better fit or help you realize that your submission isn't what the publisher wants at all.

Guidelines: The specifics

What follows here are a few examples of things that can be listed in guidelines, which will result in an immediate rejection if the writer ignores them.

The Score Group

> *The Score Group publishes five men's magazines:* Score, Voluptuous, Naughty Neighbors, Leg Sex, *and* BabyFace.
>
> **Fiction:** *Stories should be written in a professional and erotic manner. Fiction stories should contain at least two sex scenes, the first scene beginning within the first four pages. They should be written in a first- or third-person style narrative and slanted toward the particular focus of one of our publications.*

A Few Words with . . .

Kathryn Ptacek

On Erotic Fiction Markets

EDO VAN BELKOM: What are the erotic short fiction markets like compared to some of the other genres?

KATHRYN PTACEK: Well, first off, when you say "erotic" I am thinking of anything that has to do with sex — whether it's graphic or not. Many of these markets fall into the category that some folks deem "porn"; I like to call them "smut" markets. You have two basic groups: magazines that want graphic sex fiction (mostly oriented toward men, whether gay or straight) and magazines that want more erotic (read: "literary") fiction. Some of the markets look for sex fiction with actual plots and genres (adventure, mystery, horror, etc.) — *Hustler* is a good example of this.

Many of the magazines (*Hustler, Gallery, Genesis, Penthouse,* etc.) have been around for decades now. A number of the magazines have come and gone within a few years — much like what's happened in the horror genre.

A number of erotica e-zines are cropping up, too — *Clean Sheets* and *All in Your Mind* are two that come to mind. Also, many of the erotic markets encourage different orientations — hetero, bi, lesbian, gay, transgendered, etcetera. This is something you see more in the newer markets; less in the older, more established markets.

EDO VAN BELKOM: Almost in contrast to short fiction markets, the market for erotic novels virtually disappeared several years back. What's the market like for erotic novels these days? And what about other book-length erotica?

KATHRYN PTACEK: The outlook for erotic novels on paper doesn't look good. Years ago there were a number of publishers. Now . . . maybe one or two. Masquerade Books, which used to publish dozens and dozens of paperbacks and had a number of imprints as well, cut back drastically.

There are one or two other places that publish "alternate lifestyle" type books — bondage, S/M, spanking stuff — very

Victorian, etcetera. Beyond that . . . forget it. However, with the Internet, we now have e-books, and I think it's there that erotic novels will once again flourish.

EDO VAN BELKOM: While there might be plenty of erotica markets out there, keeping track of them all must be quite a task. How often do erotica publishers change addresses, or otherwise vanish and reappear from the publishing scene? How does this compare with other fiction markets?

KATHRYN PTACEK: I think nothing can compare to SF/F/H markets for popping up on the scene and then disappearing after an issue or two (or even before the first issue hits the stands!). The erotica markets tend to last longer — most of these are print publications and many are "slick" magazines or digests, and they're largely funded by the advertising in the back. I really haven't noticed the erotica publishers changing addresses a lot. I think people have a notion that this is all some sort of "back street" publishing operation that moves furtively from one sleazy building to another. It could well be, but erotica/sex writing is in many cases big business.

EDO VAN BELKOM: What is the largest erotica market? Where would a new writer have the best chance of publication?

KATHRYN PTACEK: That's a tough one. I don't know that any one market dominates, as it were, the field. As for a new writer's best chance, I would say, start with the letters published by digests. They're short — 500 to 1000 words. It's a good way to hone your writing — you get in and say what has to be said, then get out, all in under four pages.

Kathryn Ptacek, also known as the Gila Queen, is the publisher of The Gila Queen's Guide to Markets, *a guide to markets and all sorts of publishing information and tips for writers and artists. She prints a special issue for erotica markets every other year or so. She is also the author of 18 books, among them the erotic horror novels* Blood Autumn *and* In Silence Sealed; *she has also published numerous short stories, reviews, and articles, many of them in the erotica field. Visit her Web site at <www.gilaqueen.com>.*

So if you have just one sex scene and it doesn't start until page five, your story will be automatically rejected.

> *Subject Needs for* **Leg Sex**: Leg Sex *focuses on hips, heels, and all points in between. Fiction stories should focus on fetishes (author should have a strong understanding of leg and foot fetishes) and/or light female domination. Non-fiction stories can focus on such topics as leg/foot fashion, foot-binding, performance art, etc.*

So if you're not into women's legs, this magazine probably isn't a market for your fiction. However, if you've got a story that features women's legs prominently — and has a sex scene in the first four pages — *Leg Sex* just might be for you.

Nexus

> *Nexus is a long-established imprint of erotic fiction with more than 100 titles on its list.*

> **Introduction:** *We do not as a rule, publish "vanilla" erotica books — books about either "bonking" or "making love." We are in favor of proposals dealing with bondage, S/M, fem dom, or anything experimental — our favorite books are written (and read) by enthusiastic pervs. Have a look at one of our recent anthologies, such as* New Erotica 4, *to see the kind of material we're looking for.*

So if you've written an erotic novel about two peole in love, Nexus isn't the market for you. But if you've written a novel about a bored housewife who runs away from her life to experiment with the dark sexual undercurrent of the city in which she lives, you're already one up on the other aspiring Nexus authors.

> **The Limits:** *What we want is as much varied and exciting sex as possible. But — please — no sex with children (i.e. people under 16) or flashbacks to childhood "experiments"; in fact, we'd rather all participants in sex acts were 18 and over.*

So if you've got any characters under 18, your book is automatically a tough sell. If you've got any much younger than that, it's an automatic reject.

Black Lace

> Black Lace is the leading imprint for erotic fiction for women, selling over a million and a half copies in the first two years of publishing.

> **Introduction:** We accept submissions only from female authors, with no exceptions. We have found that, in this genre, authors tend to write better for their own gender. The fact that all our authors are guaranteed to be women is a valuable part of our marketing strategy.

So if you're not a woman, forget it. And don't think you can fool them, because they'll know or find out one way or another. Besides, if you're male and want to write erotica, there are plenty of gender-neutral imprints out there.

> **The Plot:** One bonk after another is not enough. A Black Lace book should be a real novel. It should have a story: a beginning, a middle and an end. The story gives the reader another reason for turning the pages. She wants to find the next dirty bit, of course, but she should also be intrigued about what happens to the characters. . . . One plot line that we don't favor is the life story. The biography or autobiography of a fictional character is not enough to sustain the reader's attention.

So make certain you've got all the elements of a good novel rather than just a string of sexual encounters, or you'll be quickly rejected. Figure out a problem for your characters to face and then a way in which sex helps them solve that problem. If you can do that, then at the very least, you will have avoided automatic rejection.

Guidelines vary from publication to publication, and obtaining them before you submit is wise. It's a bit of extra work when all you want to do is start writing, but it will save you time and needless aggravation (in the form of rejection) over the long term.

Marketing Your Fiction

Once you have a rough idea of which publications might be interested in your work, you need to figure out a submission strategy. Since your intention is to be paid for your work, it makes good sense to adopt a plan for how you intend to conduct your business.

If your story isn't geared toward a specific market, adopt the top-down method. Make a list of ten markets that publish the kind of story you've written. Place the magazine that pays best in the number one spot, and the magazine that pays least at number ten. Then submit to markets one through ten until the story sells. If you make it to the tenth market without a sale, create a second list, this time of magazines numbered 11 through 20. Eventually the story will find its own market, meaning that the story will find a market whose quality is the same as that of the story. It may take time, and you may end up spending more on postage than you'd earn from the eventual sale, but it always pays to keep your work in circulation.

If your story is geared toward a special market, it might still be possible to make up a list of three or four similar magazines and start at the top, working your way down. It might also be possible to cross over to other specialty magazines by slightly rewriting your story for a different special market. For example, a story written for a magazine like *Plumpers,* which publishes fiction featuring full-figured women, can easily be rewritten to fit a magazine featuring mature women, like *40-Plus.* In fact, a story that combines both these specialties could be marketed to either magazine without any changes at all.

9
MANUSCRIPT
FORMAT

You've written a hot tale of erotica, done some market research, and found a couple of magazines that publish the type of story you've just written. Now you're ready to print up the story and send it off to a magazine so you can find out what an honest-to-goodness editor thinks of it. Great. But there's just one more thing to do before you send the story to the printer: Make sure the story is in proper manuscript format.

Looking Like a Pro in Print

How important can formatting be? I mean, it's the story that counts, right?

Absolutely, but to have the editor read the story and judge it solely on its own merits, you need to present it in the proper format so the editor isn't distracted by the form and can concentrate solely on the content.

It can sometimes be difficult to get this concept across to a new writer. Once, when I was teaching a college creative writing course and explaining that each new paragraph has to be indented, a student called me on it, saying that in business letters, paragraphs are never indented. In another class, a student's word processor had printed the last line of each page twice, once at the bottom of the page and again at the top of the next. The student blamed her computer and refused to believe that an editor would reject a story simply because of this one mistake.

Maybe; maybe not. But be aware that editors spend much more of their time rejecting stories than accepting them, and anything that makes the job of rejecting a story easier means one less manuscript the editor has to read all the way to the end. Chances are that a writer who hasn't bothered to learn something as easy as how to properly format a manuscript also hasn't learned how to do all those other neat things like tell a good story, create fleshed-out characters, and build sexual tension or suspense.

The Basics of Manuscript Format

Manuscript format is easy to learn, however, and once learned it is never forgotten. Many books on writing explain what proper manuscript format is, but few explain the reasons behind all the quirks of the format. Sample 5 is a short story of mine called "Logan's Run," which was published in the August 1999 issue of *Leg Show* magazine. Admittedly, the story might never be confused with a work of great literature, but at least its format is exemplary.

1. The first page of the manuscript should include your name, address, and phone number, and any other means through which an editor might get in touch with you. In the case of "Logan's Run," I've added lines for a fax number and an e-mail address. E-mail correspondence between editors and writers has become more common in recent years, so include an e-mail address if you have one.

    It's important to include all this information because an editor might need to contact you in a hurry, and the more options he or she has to do so, the more likely he or she is to connect with you. I include all my contact information on every manuscript I send out, even to editors with whom I've been dealing for years. Even if an editor already has your phone number in a file, why send him or her looking for the number if he or she wants to ask you something about your manuscript? If the number is printed right on the first page, the editor can call you immediately. Why make an editor's dealings with you more difficult than necessary?

Sample 5
Manuscript Format

```
Edo van Belkom
69 Erotica Writer Avenue
City, Province/State
Country W3L W7T            ①        ②  2,300 words
Phone: 905 555-3208
Fax: 905 555-3207
E-mail: edress@emailaddress.com
```

③

⑤　　LOGAN'S RUN
　　by Evan Hollander

⑥ John Logan sat idly at his desk, his morning's tasks completed and an hour to go until lunch. There were a few reports he could read over, files in his computer that could be updated, and a letter to a customer in New Mexico to write, but those things could wait.

④ Right now there was something on his mind that took precedence over everything else. It was a problem of such magnitude that it consumed him totally. He would ④ give it his complete concentration and hopefully at some point today he'd arrive at an answer.

The problem?

Sheila, the attractive executive assistant who sat at the desk across from him, had a run in her pantyhose.

A common enough occurrence, but this was no ordinary run. It was a magnificent streak of torn nylon-spandex that began at the top of her foot and ran all the way up her leg, curving slightly at her knee before disappearing beneath her skirt along the ⑦

④

inside of her thigh.

Such a run. It took his breath away.

Did she know it was there? Where did it lead to? And how on earth did it get there?

The answer to the first question was obvious. Of course she knew it was there. It was so long and so wide there was no way Sheila could not know of its existence. She was probably waiting til noon so she could go out and buy a new pair of pantyhose during her lunch hour.

Which led to the second question. Where did the run lead to? Well, if you followed the line up her leg, and continued it up under her skirt, it clearly led to her pussy. Sort of like an arrow, thought Logan. Might as well put a sign on her lap saying, "This way to Paradise!" And maybe, just maybe the run ended somewhere between her legs with a hole big enough to. . . ⑪

Logan closed his eyes and let himself dream.

⑩ He and Sheila take a table at the back of the restaurant where it is dark. He slides into the seat and expects her to sit across the table from him. But instead of taking the seat facing him, Sheila slides in next to him, pressing her thigh tightly up against his leg.

They order some wine and make small talk.

"I need to unwind," she says, moving her leg up and down so it rubs against him. "I've been way too stressed out lately."

"I know what you mean," he answers. "I could use a good workout myself. You know, work up a sweat."

She smiles at him.

Their drinks arrive, they order their meal. Logan unfolds his napkin, puts it on his lap, then, on a lark, leaves his hand under the table. Slowly, he moves his hand to the right, placing it on her thigh, just below the hem of her skirt.

The material of her pantyhose is soft and silky. It glides easily under his fingers as he begins to slide them over her leg.

He proceeds slowly at first, unsure whether or not she approves of what he's doing. But she does not move, does not stop him. It's as if nothing at all is going on under the table.

Manuscript format   145

Encouraged by this, Logan squeezes her thigh gently and moves his hand upward and inward, toward her inner thigh. This brings about a response.

She spreads her legs slightly so that he can move his hand more easily up and down the inside of her legs.

Just then his ring catches on the fabric of her pantyhose. He pulls his hand away, but instead of letting go, the ring tears her pantyhose. There is a ripping sound, and Sheila lets out an exhilarated gasp.

"Sorry," he says.

"Whatever for?"

"For ruining your pantyhose."

"Oh, that," she says. "Not to worry, I think you've improved them." She opens her legs wider for him.

"What do you mean?"

"Now you've got easier access."

He doesn't ask her what she means by that. Instead, he slides a finger through the hole he made in her pantyhose and moves his fingertip up her thigh until he can feel the lacy trim of her panty.

The waiter arrives with dinner. Logan eats with one hand, never taking the other from its place under the table.

The run grows wider, longer. It now stretches from the middle of her left thigh, down past her knee and halfway down her calf. Higher up, it has widened into a gaping hole just below the edge of her panty.

Logan traces the length of the run with his middle finger, up the calf, over the knee, along the thigh to the large hole at the end of the run. There he slips his hand through the hole and slides his fingers under the lace trim of her panties until he can feel the slick warmth of Sheila's neatly trimmed pussy.

As he explores her sex, she drinks a mouthful of wine, throws her head back and lets out a moan of pleasure.

Logan pushes his hand further through the hole, forcing his fingers deeper inside her. The penetration causes Sheila to shriek with delight.

<u>"How would you like to do the same thing . . . with your tongue?"</u> <u>she asks, almost out of breath.</u> ⑪

"Huh?"

"How'd you like to go for a burger?"

"Huh? What?"

Logan opened his eyes and blinked a few times to orient himself. He was still in the office. Sheila was gone. Standing in front of him was Eddie Fleck from accounting.

"You all right?" asked Eddie.

Logan rubbed his fists against his eyes. "Yeah, sure."

"You want to go for a burger?"

"Uh, yeah, okay."

Logan got up from his chair, straightened the hard-on straining against his crotch, and got out from behind his desk.

"Did you see where Sheila went?"

Eddie shook his head. "Probably on her lunch."

"Too bad."

"Girl's gotta eat," said Eddie.

"I guess," said Logan, deciding not to explain how he'd been looking forward to seeing her stand up and seeing if it made the run even longer.

⑨#

When he got back to his desk shortly after one, Logan found Sheila already at her desk and working. The first thing he did after seeing her there was check her legs, or more specifically her pantyhose.

One look, and Logan felt his crotch tightening again. She still had the same pair of pantyhose on and they still had the gloriously long tear running up her left leg. If anything the run had gotten bigger over lunch and seemed to be much wider near the crotch.

Why on earth didn't she change them? Logan wondered. Maybe she liked the feeling of the cool office air blowing up her skirt and against her leg through the run. Or maybe, he mused, she liked having a run in her pantyhose because it made her feel a little bit naughty and wild. Maybe she continued to wear them because the run reminded her of something hot, like the moment the run got started. . . .

Logan thought about what could have put the run there. . . . ⑪

They are sitting in Sheila's car. The car is parked in a dark corner of the office's underground parking garage. It is 8:30 a.m.

"It's bad enough I have to spend eight hours in there, now I'm half an hour early," she says, shaking her head in disgust.

"We don't have to go in yet," says Logan. "We can wait here in the car until nine."

"A half-hour would pass like a day just sitting here waiting."

"Well, we could always do something to pass the time."

"Like what?"

"I dunno. Maybe we could, uh . . . fuck."

She looks over at him, and a sly smile spreads across her face. She runs her tongue over her lips and says, "That would be nice."

He moves toward her, but she stops him.

"You stay there," she says. "I'll come to you."

He sits back and relaxes, and watches as she moves toward him, crawling over top of him until she is comfortably straddling his crotch. Her chest is inches away from his face. Through her red silk blouse he can see her full round tits held in place by a lacy black demi-bra. He reaches out to touch them but her lips are suddenly in front of him, kissing him. Her tongue darts in and out of his mouth and her breathing grows heavy and more rapid.

He moves his hands from her chest to her ass. He feels the tightness of her buttocks and runs his hands down her thighs. Her pantyhose feel smooth and soft. He wonders for a moment how he is going to fuck her, but the thought is gone in an instant as she unbuttons her blouse and opens it up to him.

Her tits are even bigger than he imagined. When she undoes the front clasp of her bra, her breasts spill forward against his face and he frantically searches for the nipple. It is thick and long and pops into his mouth as if it were always meant to be there.

He sucks on her nipples and kisses her breasts. She moans with pleasure in response to his touch and soon is grinding her crotch against the bulge in his pants.

"Fuck me!" she whispers in his ear. "Fuck me with that gorgeous prick of yours!"

He fumbles with his zipper, then his belt, then his waistband. Eventually he gets them all undone and manages to pull his pants down around his knees.

She has more obstacles to overcome. Her skirt comes first and is easily pulled up and out of the way. Next are her pantyhose. They are sheer to her waist and he marvels at how smooth her cleanly shaven pussy is. It is then that he realizes she isn't wearing panties.

His throbbing cock rubs against the crotch of her pantyhose as her moist cunt grinds against him through the sheer fabric. "I want you inside me!" she says.

He pushes harder, but can't get through the nylon spandex of her pantyhose. It might as well be a brick wall.

But instead of ending the encounter, she reaches down between her legs and uses one of her sharp fingernails to poke a hole in the crotch of her pantyhose. The sound of tearing lycra fills the car, then is replaced by the sound of her satisfaction as he slides his cock through the hole in her pantyhose and up into her cunt.

"Yes," she says, grabbing his head and pressing his mouth to her breasts. "Fuck me!"

He thrusts his cock upward, feeling the kiss of her pussy lips on his shaft and the delicious rub of her pantyhose against his balls. She spreads her legs further and every time he lifts her off the seat her moans are accented by the sound of the hole in her pantyhose growing bigger.

Three more thrusts and she's screaming at the top of her voice. "Oh, yes . . . Yes! Yes!"

They come together in a mass of thrusting, churning bodies all dappled with sweat and covered in provocatively torn and wrinkled clothing.

"What time is it?" she asks, buttoning up her blouse.

He looks at his watch. "Quarter after nine."

"We're late!" she shrieks, scrambling out of the car.

He follows her. "Time flies when you're having fun."

#

It was just before five.

After a long, hard day on the job, Logan was about ready to pop. Having to sit at his desk for eight hours with nothing to look at except Sheila's torn pantyhose had been a delicious form of torture. He didn't want it to end, but it had to for the sake of his mental and physical well being.

Going home would bring him relief in more ways than one. But before he left work, there was something he needed to know, something he had to ask Sheila.

He walked casually over to her desk, knowing he should try to conceal the bulge in his pants, but not really caring if Sheila noticed he had a hard on. She was to blame for it, he thought, might as well let her see what she's done to me.

"Hi Sheila," he said.

"Hey there!" she answered with a warm smile.

"Um, there's something I've got to ask you. . . . " ⑪

"Yes?"

"But I don't want you to think me too forward for asking—" ⑪

"I wouldn't think that," she said quickly, cutting him off. "Go ahead and ask me."

"You've got a run in your pantyhose."

"I know."

"You do? Well, I've been wondering all day, uh . . . how did it get there?"

"I put it there this morning," she said.

"You put it there? What for?"

"For you."

"Me?"

"Yes," she laughed. "The last time I had a run in my pantyhose, you couldn't keep your eyes off my legs all day. I liked the feeling, so I thought, why not try it again? It seems to have worked beautifully."

Logan laughed. "I'd imagined you'd torn it in some wild sexual encounter or something."

"It's been known to happen."

"Really?"

She nodded. "In fact, this stocking — " she put her right leg on her desk and lifted the hem of her skirt to show the top of her stocking and the garter holding it up " — is still in one piece. How'd you like to come home with me tonight and help me put a run in it? A big long one?"

Logan stood there silent and still. She hadn't been wearing panty-hose at all, but stockings and garters. The sight of it thrilled him, made him even harder. He swallowed and found his mouth had gone dry.

"I'd love to," he said at last.

"I thought you might." She took his hand and they ran to the ele-vator, heading for home.

⑫ ######

2. Placing the word count on a manuscript serves a number of purposes. First of all, it tells the publisher how much it would cost for the right to publish your story. For example, "Logan's Run" is roughly 2,500 words long, and if it sold to a magazine paying three cents per word, payment for the story would be $75. (Nevertheless, be aware that most men's magazines pay a flat rate for fiction, and the amount is the same for any story they accept in their word range. A 2,500-word story will sell for the same amount as a 3,300-word story. But don't be tempted to write less. Use as many words as your story needs, and if it is too short or long when completed, deal with it then.)

Another reason for putting the word count on the first page is that it indicates the story's length at a glance. Say an editor has a few pages left in the current issue of his or her magazine. A story of between 800 to 1,000 words is needed. He or she takes a quick look through the slush pile and pulls out all the stories of that length, including yours. As a result, your story gets some additional attention that it wouldn't have otherwise received.

"Logan's Run" didn't, in fact, work out to exactly 2,300 words. According to the program on which the story was written, the word count came to 2,344, a number easily rounded off to 2,300. For longer stories, it's a good idea to always round down from 50 and under, and up from 50 and over. A word count done by your computer of 3,242 would be shown as 3,200 words on the first page of your manuscript, and 3,258 words would become 3,300 words. You could, of course, use the exact count provided by your word-processing program, but editors aren't concerned with whether or not your computer can count words; they want a general idea of how much space your story will take up in their magazine. Also, different word processors count words differently (some count actual words, some count the number of characters and divide by four or five, etc.), so the number you provide on the manuscript might vary from the publisher's own program once the story is typeset. For that reason, and the others mentioned, it's best to round off the count.

3. Empty white space is a useful thing for editors, and that is why manuscripts should always start halfway down the first page. Doing so leaves a large blank space at the start of the story on which an editor can write notes: notes intended as personal reminders ("Check with publisher on subject matter"), messages to another editor or typesetter ("Do you think this will work in the upcoming *Luscious Legs* theme issue?"), or a comment on the manuscript intended for the author ("If you change it to black pantyhose, I'll buy it").

4. Proper manuscript format requires that you leave an inch of white space all the way around the type, which will serve the same purpose as the white space at the top half of the page: it gives the editor room to make notes in the margins.

5. The title of your story doesn't have to be set in capital letters, but it should be given some special distinction from the story's text so that it can be quickly identified and easily read. Instead of using capitals, you might underline the title, wrap it in quotation marks, or use a different typeface — one of the few times that a different font might be desirable.

   Including your name on the byline is optional if the name under which you want the article or story to appear is the same one as you've placed on the address in the upper left-hand corner of the page. However, sometimes editors will put a name to an article if the author hasn't clearly stated what name is to be used on it. I've had articles published under the names Vance Edom and Eric Hollis, and the first I ever heard of it was when I received the magazine in the mail. So if you want your own name to be used, it doesn't hurt to put it in the byline. A lot of magazines prefer that their authors use pseudonyms or pen names — names other than their own; in the erotic genre, most authors use them anyway. If you want to use a pseudonym, you don't have to do anything more than list it in the byline.

In this instance, I have used my pseudonym, Evan Hollander (more on pseudonyms and my use of the name Evan Hollander later in this chapter), so the story's title reads —

LOGAN'S RUN
by Evan Hollander

Doing this causes the pseudonym to become part of the title and will ensure that the story is published under the name the author prefers. This is the only change required when using a pseudonym. Just make sure your real name appears along with your address so the magazine's accounting department will know who to make the check out to and where to send it.

6. You should begin each new paragraph with an indentation. Most word processors allow you to indent with a tab key. If you're still working on a typewriter (and there is nothing wrong with that; many writers still use typewriters), the typical indent is five spaces. Do not indicate breaks by inserting blank spaces between paragraphs.

The text should be double-spaced, which will leave an editor enough space to make notes or corrections (of typos, imprecise words, or awkward phrases or sentences) on your manuscript between the lines of text. (In Sample 5, the spacing of "Logan's Run" is less than double-spaced in order to better fit this book's pages.)

Finally, the font you should be using is a 10- or 12-point Courier. Many writing guides and manuals will tell you that it is okay to use serif fonts such as Times Roman because they are easier to read. That may be true, but there is a very specific reason for using Courier.

If you've used Courier, double-spaced the manuscript, and left a one-inch margin around your text, each one of your lines will be 60 to 65 characters long and have roughly 10 to 12 words to it, and each page will have roughly 250 words on it. That makes it easy for an editor to estimate the length of your story, even if you haven't put the word count on the top right-hand corner of the first page. The use of 10- or 12-point Courier will also make it easier for an editor to know how much has been cut from your manuscript after he or she has edited a few paragraphs.

One thing all writing manuals agree on is that you should not use any sans serif fonts, such as Helvetica. It's terrific that your word processor can produce all those wonderful fonts, but they're not for manuscripts, as over the course of a few pages they will strain an editor's eyes.

7. While the left-hand margin of your manuscript is justified (meaning that, except for indents, all the lines start at the same point), the right-hand margin must remain ragged. This ragged edge is called ragged right, and it ensures that all the letters and words are equally spaced across the line. If you use a right-justified setup, your computer's word processor will squeeze some words together and stretch others apart in order to make each line begin and end at the same point. The compressing and expanding of words makes them more difficult to read, which will hinder an editor's ability to judge the work on its own merits.

Another thing to avoid on the right-hand side of the page is the use of hyphens. When words are printed in newspapers, magazines, and books, hyphens are often used to break up longer words so that at least part of the word can be used to fill out a line. That's fine for typeset text; in manuscripts, hyphens just make things more difficult for an editor to read, which is precisely what you want to avoid.

8. After your name, address, and contact information appear on the first page of the manuscript, each following page should have a header that includes your name, your story's name, and a page number. This might seem like a bit much, but imagine a young editorial assistant picking up a pile of manuscripts from one editor's desk and carrying it across the office to deliver it to the desk of another editor. The assistant trips on an extension cord halfway across the room, and the manuscripts all go flying. Having your name, story title, and page number on each page will make the job of putting your manuscript back together that much easier.

If you've written a piece for a particular publication, you can also include the publication's name in the header. If I had done this, the header for my story would have read —

Edo van Belkom/ WRITING EROTICA: Logan's Run/ 2

Doing this helps editors who work on more than one magazine or anthology at a time, letting them know at a glance (or serving as a reminder about) the publication for which the manuscript is intended.

9. Line breaks are used to signify a change of scene, the passage of time, or a change in point of view. Some books on writing will tell you that leaving a blank line to signify a line break is acceptable, but this is not so. When the blank line appears as the first or last line on a page, it is invisible and will cause a moment or two of confusion in the reader's mind.

Some publishers' guidelines ask that you use three asterisks to signify a section break. If the guidelines ask for something specific, then do it. If not, it's best just to use a number sign.

10. Although computers make the printing of italics easy, their use in manuscripts is still not advised. Instead, indicate the use of italics by underlining the words or phrases to be italicized. Underlining is the clearest, most easily discernible method for differentiating regular type from its italicized brethren. In fact, it is the best way to indicate any font other than the standard one. For example, if you have the words from a lawn sign in your story, or the headline of a newspaper article, indicate it by underlining the words. This is done because no matter what font you'd like to see used, the ultimate decision on which typeface is used will be made by the copy editor or book designer, who will use the fonts that are standard for his or her magazine or publishing house.

Sometimes a character's thoughts are set in italics, which sets them apart from the rest of the text. This tactic can become unwieldy if italics are also used throughout the text for other purposes, such as for emphasis. In "Logan's Run," I've avoided using italics to show the point-of-view character's thoughts because I'm using italics to indicate the dream sequences. If I had used italics once to show a character's thoughts, I would have had to do it consistently throughout the story, which, with so much inner dialogue included, would have been awkward.

I chose to underline the dream sequences so that when the story appeared in print, these sections would have a different typeface (italics or some other font), making it obvious to the reader that they were set apart from the rest of the story.

11. Correct format not only makes an editor's job easier, it also helps a reader get the most enjoyment out of his or her reading experience. When used properly, ellipses and em-dashes can help convey the tone or pace of your work.

    An ellipsis can be used to signify a trailing off or fading away of either a character's voice, a character's thoughts, or the narrative itself. In "Logan's Run," an ellipsis is first used as a sort of transitional device to let the reader know that the narrative is fading away as Logan's thoughts move into a dream sequence. Later, one is used to space out Sheila's words in the dream sequence, giving pace to her words as she hesitates before suggesting that her lover utilize his tongue instead of his fingers.

    Finally, one is used to show Logan's shyness when asking Sheila about the run in her pantyhose. He can't quite bring himself to say it, so the question first goes unasked as he gathers up his confidence. The ellipsis here also contrasts the use of the em-dash two lines later. While an ellipsis is used to show a trailing off, an em-dash is used to show an abrupt break in thought, or words cut off in mid-sentence. Em-dashes are used again a little later to cut a sentence in half in order to insert a motion (or thought) that is happening simultaneously while the character is speaking. The em-dashes at either end of the action let the reader know that there is no pause in the dialogue, and that the action and dialogue happened at the same time.

12. In nonfiction work, especially articles and magazines, it is customary to place -30- at the end of the piece. There's no such tradition in fiction writing, and authors have used any number of ways to indicate the end of a story, from typing THE END at the bottom of the last page to placing a string of number signs after the last line. If your story ends on the last line of a page, it's useful to let the editor know the story's over so he or she won't go looking for the next page.

    If you've sold a story and have been asked to provide a disk version of it, remove whatever mark you've used to indicate the end of your story. Once, when I sent a disk with a story called

"Reaper vs. Reaper vs. Reaper" to White Wolf for their anthology *Death and Damnation*, I left the words THE END at the end of the story. The stories in the book were published almost untouched from their disk versions, and out of 12 stories, five had nothing at their ends, while four had END, and the other three had THE END, (mine), *Finis*, and *(end)*, respectively. In this instance, it would have been better to have left the end of the story blank.

Pseudonyms

Many authors of erotica write under a pseudonym; that is, a name other than the one that appears on one's driver's license. This pseudonym can also be called a pen name or a *nom de plume*. The reasons for using one can be as varied as the names themselves. For instance, you might want to use a pseudonym if —

- you're a member of the church choir and you don't want anyone in the congregation to know that you write *filth*;

- you are building a career in another genre — say, the mystery field — and you don't want to confuse your readers by using your own name when publishing material outside that genre. (This is especially true if you are writing at book length. If sales of your past four mystery novels have been good, you don't want the fact that you're publishing a book of erotica with a smaller press, or with a press with smaller distribution, to suggest to bookstore owners that your last book didn't do so well. In this case, your publisher might even suggest that you use a pseudonym.)

- you're a writer of some stature in a particular field, and even though you enjoy writing erotica and you've produced quality — even literary — work, you don't want to risk harming your reputation by publishing in a genre some might look down upon. (Science fiction writer Robert Silverberg wrote some 150 sex novels between 1959 and 1964 for Nightstand Books of Chicago under a variety of pseudonyms. Mystery writer Lawrence Block also wrote close to 100 erotic novels on the side, as did other writers who went on to become bestselling authors or Hollywood screenwriters. Some of the pseudonyms used at the time included Andrew Shaw, Don Holliday, J.X. Williams, Don Bellmore, and Clyde Allison.)

- you're a male writer, but the story needs to be written from a female point of view and won't have the same effect if the reader knows it's written by a man;

- you're writing about a particularly perverse fetish, and even though you're just writing a piece of fiction/nonfiction, you know that readers often have a hard time distinguishing between the author and the author's work, and you don't want to be thought of as a pervert/weirdo/psychopath by those who don't understand erotica and never will;

- your real name is Herbert Crumple or Mildred Sickley, and that just doesn't instill the same sort of excitement in your work as the names Jake Torrence or Jessica Cardinale might;

- your name is Jack Dawes and there is already someone who is well established in the erotic genre writing under the name Jake Dawes;

- you're being published by a publishing house that doesn't use any writer's real name on anything in their magazine, so you either provide a pseudonym or they will make one up for you without even asking; or

- you're just writing the stuff for the money and you don't want anyone to know about it.

Why I am Evan Hollander

Of the dozens of erotic short stories I've written over the years, less than ten carry my real name. The rest appear under my pseudonym, Evan Hollander, and that will likely continue for all of my future appearances in men's magazines.

Why? you ask. The whole point of writing stories and getting them published (aside from being paid for your work) is to see your name — your real name — appear in print. Isn't it?

That's true for the most part, but there comes a point at which seeing your name in print isn't as important as it once was, and there are plenty of other things to consider regarding an author's good name.

Let me explain.

My very first short story, "Baseball Memories," appeared in a literary magazine called *Aethlon*, published by East Tennessee State University.

The story was subsequently reprinted in an anthology called *The Year's Best Horror Stories 20*. To borrow a metaphor, it was as if I'd hit a home run my very first time at the plate. Obviously, I was proud of the accomplishment, but I wasn't the type to sit around and gloat over my success. I was writing stories at a furious pace at the time, and in addition to "literary" stories, I was also writing erotica for men's magazines. So though my first sale was to a literary magazine, my second was to the men's magazine *Gent*. My third story was accepted by a small-press horror magazine, and my fourth story also went to *Gent*.

Soon I was selling stories regularly, a couple to horror magazines and anthologies, a couple to *Gent*. At the time, I really didn't care where I was selling stories and under what name they were being published; I was happy just to be selling stories. To me, the stories were all my creations, and there was no real difference between them, so I was using my own name for everything. Hey — I'd been working to get to this point for several years and I wanted everyone to know I'd made it.

My mother sure was proud. She'd go looking for my men's-magazine stories, combing the racks and telling the curious store clerk, "My son has a story in there!"

But other people didn't see things quite the same way as dear old mom. When people asked me about my writing, I told them that my first short story was in *Year's Best* and I'd show them the book . . .

"Yeah, uh-huh, that's nice."

. . . and then I'd tell them that I also wrote for men's magazines, and I'd show them a copy of one . . .

"Oh baby, would you look at that!"

People are far more fascinated (perhaps even impressed, in a strange sort of way) by erotica and the people who write it than they are by any other form of literature. Once people knew that I wrote porn, they didn't really care about anything else I'd done. And so my accomplishments in the other genres were being overlooked, or perhaps overshadowed, by this one small part of my total output.

It was time for a pseudonym.

My wife and I thought about it for a few days (we even wrote up a bio for this new writer) and we finally came up with the name Evan Hollander. The Evan comes from the initial "E" and the first part of my last name, "van." The last name, Hollander, was chosen because I'm

Go to a party and mention that you're a lawyer, a marketing rep, or a lobbyist, and no one will give a damn about your day-to-day routine. The interest level goes up a little for a fiction writer of the mainstram variety. But tell people you write porn for paychecks and it's a different story. Their curiosity meter goes off the scale.

— *Daltrey St. James*
"Lust in My Art," Hot *Talk*, October 1992

half Dutch (the other half is Italian, if you're curious) and the name "Hollander" has a special ring to it in erotic circles, thanks to the exploits of the Happy Hooker, Xaviera Hollander.

Since then, most of my men's magazine fiction has appeared under the Hollander name, and in 1995, Circlet Press even published a chapbook, *Virtual Girls: The Erotic Gems of Evan Hollander,* consisting of five Evan Hollander science fiction stories. The chapbook also spawned an audiobook from Sexxxy Audio entitled *Amber,* which features three Hollander stories read by swimsuit/lingerie model Amber Smith.

I have had two other pseudonyms foisted upon me by editors who changed my name without consulting me. One of my stories appeared under the name "Vance Edom" (sounds very much like a piece of cheese, doesn't it?), and a nonfiction article of mine was given the name "Eric Hollis" because I also had an Evan Hollander short story in the same issue of the magazine.

Looking back, if I had to choose a pseudonym today, I probably would have gone with a simple contraction of my own name, using my first initial with the rest of my name to create "Evan Belkom." That way, my name would have been only slightly disguised, and if someone had cared to do so, he or she would have been able to make the connection between me and my *nom de plume* fairly easily.

One final note about pseudonyms. A few years ago, I got an e-mail from someone whose real name is Evan Hollander. He'd been searching Amazon.com and plugged in his own name to see what came up. My book *Virtual Girls* appeared on his screen. He ordered a copy to see what it was all about, then asked me to stop using his name when I published erotica. It seemed that he was thinking he might one day write a book, and he didn't want readers to be confused.

Of course I refused.

First of all, Evan Hollander is hardly a household name. Besides, this is just the sort of situation middle names and initials were invented for. Furthermore, someone who is *thinking* about writing a book one day is someone who will likely never *write* one. In addition, I've spent years establishing the name Evan Hollander in the erotic genre and am not about to have that effort wasted by dropping the name and starting all over again.

And so — Evan Hollander lives.

> When you use a pseudonym, even if everybody comes to know who you really are and the pseudonym is totally transparent, you play a psychological trick where you let yourself be totally uninhibited. It's sort of like wearing a costume.
>
> — *Steven Saylor/ "Aaron Travis"*

Types of Books

A *chapbook* usually runs to less than 100 pages and will contain a single novella or a collection of a few stories. Most often, chapbooks are saddle stapled (i.e., stapled in the middle like a magazine) but can also be perfect bound (i.e., with a stiff spine).

Mass market paperbacks are also known as pocket books. "Mass market" is used to describe them because print runs commonly begin with 20,000 or 30,000 copies and the books reach the widest possible audience.

A *trade paperback* is the size of a hardcover book, but has a paper cover and is priced midway between a mass-market paperback and a hardcover. Although more prestigious a format for an author's work than mass market paperbacks, print runs are usually low, starting at 1,000 copies; 5,000 is a respectable number at the upper end.

Hardcovers are the usual first printings of major books by the likes of Danielle Steele, Anne Rice, and Erica Jong. They are expensive, well made, and are as much for collecting and cherishing as for reading.

Omnibus editions collect two or more books into one volume, such as *The Sleeping Beauty Trilogy* by Anne Rice, which combines all three of the "Beauty" books Rice wrote under the name A.N. Roquelaure: *The Claiming of Sleeping Beauty, Beauty's Punishment,* and *Beauty's Release.*

An *anthology* is a collection of stories by multiple authors, as opposed to a single-author collection, which is — as the term might suggest — several stories by the same author.

Other Things to Note about Manuscript Format

Listing rights

Some books on writing suggest that you list which rights you are offering in the top right-hand corner of the first page (something like first North American serial rights, or reprint rights, or whatever). However, this is unnecessary, since your cover letter will clarify whether the story is original or, if a reprint, where it was originally published. As an editor of three anthologies of both new and reprint material, I've yet to see a professional writer list rights on his or her manuscript. Listing rights seems to me to be a flag to an editor that the writer is still a neophyte.

Paper quality

It would seem to be a matter of common sense rather than something that must be stated, but you should use a decent-quality bond paper (20 lbs. bond is the norm) in sheets measuring 8½" x 11". And, of course, it should be white. This last suggestion might make you laugh, but I've heard stories of manuscripts printed on yellow paper in orange ink, and even one about a writer who inserted the carbon the wrong way in his typewriter and had the text come out reversed. Instead of retyping the story, he asked the editor to hold the manuscript up to a mirror to read it. There is nothing so obvious that it can go unsaid.

Print quality

Years ago, when computers first became a writer's tool, many guidelines specified no dot-matrix printouts, because these early printers produced type that was difficult to read. These days, most printers do a great job, so there's no longer a need to specify a preferred type of printout. If you're still using a dot-matrix printer, however, make certain the ribbon is fresh and that you set your printer on "near-letter quality." If you're using a bubble-jet or laser printer, don't let the ink or toner cartridge run too low before replacing it. A manuscript that's difficult to read will make an editor less inclined to buy it.

It used to be common practice to include a large-size self-addressed stamped envelope (SASE) with your submission so that the entire manuscript could be returned to you, allowing you to send it out again to the next market. These days, with high-tech printers and copiers, it's easier (and cheaper) just to include a letter-sized SASE so the editor can send you a rejection letter (along with the first page of your manuscript so you know what's been rejected) or contract. Since the whole point of manuscript format is to give an editor an easily readable, professional-looking manuscript, it's best to produce a new manuscript each time you make a submission.

Staples and paper clips

It's a definite no-no to staple your story together at the top left-hand corner, much as it might make sense to do so. Editors like to be able to shuffle pages during the editing process.

Paper clips are a good alternative, but some editors — Marion Zimmer Bradley (who edited her own fantasy magazine for many years) comes to mind — have stated in their guidelines that they want nothing at all binding manuscript pages together.

Contest format

Sometimes magazines ask that you submit your story in contest or competition format. This means that you type all the information about who you are and how you can be contacted on the first page of the manuscript, along with the title of the story. Your story begins on page two *with* the title of your story but *without* your name on it, while each of the page headers on the following pages show only the story title and a page number. This format ensures that the judges in a contest won't be swayed by a writer's name or past works, and will judge each story on its own merits.

I am not aware of any erotica markets that require writers to submit their work in contest format, since there are really no BIG names in erotica, and if a magazine were to receive a submission from a known writer, they would want to know about it. But while you'll probably never have to use contest format when writing erotica, it's still good to know what it is.

Manuscript Format for Novels

Title page

Manuscript format for novels doesn't differ much from that used for short stories. The biggest difference is that your novel will begin with a title page that will have your name and address in the top left-hand corner, as well as the name and contact information of your agent, should you happen to have one.

The word count (this time a number over 40,000) should appear in the top right-hand corner. Place the novel's title in the middle of the page, perhaps along with a line situating the novel in a particular genre.

Include your name or, should you choose to use one, your pseudonym. The rest of the manuscript follows the rules previously outlined in this chapter.

Chapter headings

Novels are broken into chapters, so you'll have to identify the start of each chapter. Begin chapters on a new page, with the chapter heading (Chapter One; ONE; 1) on a line by itself about halfway down the page. As before, this will give an editor space to make notes about specific chapters as he or she reads through the novel.

Manuscript Format for Adult Film Scripts

The format for erotic scripts is the same as for any other film or teleplay.

Your script must set up the overall situation, giving each actor a hint as to who his or her character is and what his or her motivations are. You must also set the scene, whether it be in an apartment or office, and include any particular needs the scene might have. You also have to list any establishing shots that are required to set up things such as where and at what time of day a scene is taking place.

For example:

WORKING HARD

by Evan Hollander

1. Ext. — day — Cox and Moore Law Offices — Establishing Shot.

2. Int. — day — Cox and Moore Reception Desk.

The office is neat and tidy, suggesting that Cox and Moore is a very successful law firm. Marion Kind is the attractive receptionist behind the front desk. She's dressed conservatively for the office, but her blouse is undone, revealing a bit of her bra and a little cleavage. She took this job hoping to land a lawyer for a husband, and while she's made a play for every eligible man who's come through the door, she is still very much a single and sexually active woman.

Dialogue is attributed to each character as he or she speaks, much in the same way a play is written. You can give directions to the actors in your script, such as *(runs a tongue over her lips)*, or *(shakes his head in disbelief)*, but one would hope that these things would be done by the actors during the course of the action in the scene.

As the scene unfolds, give the actors their cues as to how quickly the scene moves toward a sexual encounter (and let's face it, just about every scene in an adult film leads to sex). Let's say a young man has come into the law office for an interview with Mr. Cox. Our secretary, Marion Kind, shows the young man her moves, so while the dialogue is happening between the two characters, you might want to use a cue like —

> *Marion places a hand over her chest as if she's startled, but her hand lingers there, eventually caressing one of her breasts as she speaks.*

This will ensure that the scene keeps to its proper pace and that when the characters eventually do get down to having sex, there has been a proper set-up and adequate build-up of sexual tension.

Once you've got the characters into a sexual encounter, you need not detail every sexual act between the actors. Much of what they do will depend on the mood they're in on the day of shooting, their chemistry on the set, and the guidance and suggestions made by the director. It's all right to step back and let them take over:

> *Marion gets up from her desk and sits on its edge, crossing her legs to show a bit of thigh.*

> MARION: Mr. Cox will see you in a few minutes. He asked that I look after your needs until he's ready for you.

> *She begins to slip his jacket off his shoulders, then undoes his belt. When they're suitably undressed, they have sex on Marion's desk. Afterward, she buzzes the intercom to Mr. Cox's office.*

> MARION: He's ready to see you now, Mr. Cox.

An exception to this would be an instance in which you require the actors to do something important to the story while they're having sex. This could be a key to the plot, a character quirk, or a joke that might set the tone for the rest of the film. For example, if we gave our script a slightly humorous tone, then the sex scene could read like this:

> *Marion is leaning over her desk while the young man is doing her from behind. They've been having sex for some time now*

and are both very close to climax. At this point, the intercom on Marion's desk buzzes.

MR.COX: (Through the intercom) I'm ready to see him now.

MARION: (Trying to hold back her cries of ecstasy) He'll be coming in a minute, sir!

Keep in mind that this is a cursory explanation of script format. If you want to write an entire script, I recommend that you seek out a book on the subject such as Katherine Atwell Herbert's *Selling Scripts to Hollywood* (Allworth Press, New York, 1999). Although it doesn't deal specifically with the adult film industry, there is enough about the movie business in this book to provide you with an understanding of how to prepare and sell a script. Don't skimp on research. The last thing you want is some producer to think that your script won't be any good because you haven't even bothered to learn the proper format.

10 SENDING OFF YOUR MANUSCRIPT

You've written a tale of erotica that's pretty hot, you've let it sit a while, made some revisions, and polished it until there are no typos or awkward sentences. You've made sure all the sex is physically possible and that the action is clear to the reader. Now, finally, you can start thinking about sending it to a magazine editor. But before you go charging off to the mailbox, there are still a few things you need to do to make certain your story is truly ready to land on an editor's desk.

Cover Letters

A cover letter introduces you to an editor, and perhaps tells him or her a little about you or your story. But writing a cover letter can be difficult, especially if you're a new writer trying to break into the field of erotica. How much information should you include, and what should you leave out?

Well, here's what you should include:

- If you've ever sold a piece of your writing, mention that. Even if it's only a few "Letters to the Editor" of a men's magazine or a few articles to the local newspaper, it will still tell the editor who is considering your work that you have some writing ability.

- If your story is set in an interesting place — such as on the beaches of Cancun or on the set of an adult film shoot — and you have some particular knowledge about the setting, mention that. For example: "The story takes place on the set of an adult movie shoot, with which I am quite familiar after working as a camera and sound man in the adult film industry during the past nine years." This lets the editor know that anything incredible or peculiar about where the story is set, or about what happens in the story, is probably based — even if only loosely — on fact.

- Make reference to any particular knowledge you might have about the subject of your story. If your story is about a man or a woman who becomes aware of his or her body and decides to use it to experience the greatest amount of sexual pleasure possible, and you've worked as a sex therapist for the past ten years, then that just might pique an editor's interest.

- If a respected author or editor suggested that you send the story to a particular magazine, you might want to state this. Many editors know what is appropriate for other magazines, and an editor might look differently at a manuscript knowing that a peer thinks it might work in his or her magazine. If you sent a story to *Gallery* and received a rejection letter in which the editor said, "This is the sort of thing that Wally over at *Hustler* likes," say so in your cover letter.

- Be sure to mention any submissions you've made to the magazine in the past. Editors admire perseverance. Even if the editor doesn't remember your last submission, he or she might be impressed that you've sent another story. In addition, you'll be letting the editor know that you plan to write several stories for the magazine and that if he or she does take one, more will follow. This can help make a sale if your story is borderline. Editors like to encourage new writers and are always in need of good work.

- If you've met the editor at, say, a conference on erotic writing or sex in the media, or perhaps a sexual trade show, you can mention that as well. Again, the editor might not recall meeting you (they are usually introduced to countless people at these events), but mentioning it will help you make a connection, however tentative, with the editor.

Of course none of this will get your story accepted if it isn't right for the magazine you've sent it to, but dealing professionally with an editor could help you sell your fourth, fifth, or even twentieth submission. You might as well get the ball rolling now.

Just as there's a list of things you should include in a cover letter, there are also things you should leave out.

Here is a list of what *not* to include:

- Don't tell the editor what the story is about. If the editor is sharp (and editors usually are), he or she will want to personally discover what the story is about. Besides, if you're submitting a piece of erotic fiction, it's obviously about people getting turned on and having sex.

- Don't tell the editor that the story is good, or that your spouse/friend/lover thinks it's hot and got really turned on by it. First of all, the only opinion that counts is that of the editor, and he or she will be the one to decide if the story is good or not. It may well have done a great job of turning on your friends, but it is up to the editor to determine whether or not it will turn on the magazine's readers.

- Don't say anything about how hard you worked on the story, or how much time you've spent writing it. Editors aren't concerned with such things, and may reject a story that you spent a year writing or accept a story that you dashed off in a few hours. The only thing that matters is the quality of the work.

All this is common sense. Tell an editor the things that are relevant to the story (that is, things that might help him or her make a decision on it) and keep the other stuff to yourself.

Editors take their jobs seriously. So be a professional, and take your writing very seriously.

SASEs

SASE stands for self-addressed stamped envelope.

If you want to get a response to your submission, include an SASE with your manuscript. In fact, if you want a response to any sort of query (e.g., to request writer's guidelines, or to find out if a magazine accepts reprints) an SASE is a must. Some magazine editors receive up to 1,000 manuscripts per month, and book publishers can receive in the neighborhood of 100 proposals per month. If publishers had to pay for return postage on all of them, as well as on the various other queries that come in from authors and readers, there would be precious little money to pay contributors, or to print and distribute the magazine. SASES are also a good idea if you're writing to a fellow author to ask a question, or would just like to get a response for whatever reason.

If you live in Canada and are submitting a manuscript to the United States, your SASE must have American stamps on it. The same is true for an American writer submitting to a Canadian or other foreign market. When I edited anthologies in the past, about 30 percent of the submissions from American writers had American stamps on them. One writer didn't bother to include any postage at all (claiming, like some burned-out surfer dude, that he couldn't figure out the postage thing), only a self-addressed envelope (SAE). It's not only writers who fail to use international postage on an SASE; I've had publishers do it to me as well. Sometimes, when a magazine sends a contract, they'll include an SASE to ensure its safe return. More than a few times, I've received an SASE with a US stamp pasted onto it (and domestic postage at that), which, of course, can't be used in Canada. Luckily it's not a big problem, since I can always use the American postage for my own SASE, but it can be inconvenient. Be forewarned that improper postage on an SASE can also signal to an editor that you, the writer, don't pay much attention to details concerning your work.

What do you do, then, if you don't have the correct stamps? If you're submitting to a foreign publication, buy an International Reply Coupon (IRC) from your local post office (every post office in the world is supposed to have them) and include it with an SAE. The editor will then be able to exchange the coupon for postage so that he or she can respond to your submission. IRCs are more expensive than stamps, but they do the same job. The only drawback of IRCs is that not every post-office clerk knows what they are or how to process them. When I found several clerks in one postal outlet who could properly handle my IRCs, I made that location my regular post office even though it was slightly out of my way.

Perhaps a better alternative is to stock up on stamps whenever you visit Canada or the US, or have a friend do it for you. I have a small sewing box with numerous compartments for threads, and in each compartment I keep an assortment of US, Canadian, and British stamps, as well as one or two IRCs in case of emergency.

Response Times

When you do send off your story, choose the publication wisely. It might be a long time before you hear whether its been accepted or rejected.

When I first began submitting my stories to men's magazines, I often waited six months before receiving a response.

Table 4 is a chronology of a few of my early story submissions to *Gent*:

Table 4

Chronology of Submissions

Title	Submitted	Accepted/ Rejected	Published
"The Zero Gee Spot"	Feb 15, 1990	(A) June 11, 1990	Nov 1990
"Night Vision"	Aug 27, 1990	(A) Feb 11, 1991	July 1991
"The Sales Call"	Oct 31, 1990	(A) Jan 28, 1991	May 1991
"Chance Encounters Inc."	Dec 11, 1990	(A) Feb 11, 1991	Sept 1991
"The Lucky Break"	Apr 8, 1991	(R) Apr 19, 1991	--- ---
"Someday My Prince Will Come"	Jul 23, 1991	(R) Aug 2, 1991	--- ---
"By the Book"	Aug 21, 1991	(A) Sept 24, 1991	Feb 1992
"Shop at Home Service"	Oct 16, 1991	(A) Nov 1, 1991	Apr 1992

As you can see by the response times for my first two submissions, it took about six months to get an answer from the editor. (This chart begins with my second submission to the magazine, as I didn't record the date I sent my first submission, "Artistic License," and know only that it was accepted January 1990 and published in July of the same year.) After a few sales to the magazine, my response times suddenly dropped to three months. By then I had made a few sales. The editor knew that my work was more than likely publishable and so gave it a bit of priority over other manuscripts in the slush pile. My response times took another dramatic cut as I continued to submit to the same magazine. It took just over a week for both "The Lucky Break" and "Someday My Prince Will Come" to be rejected.

I remember that time clearly. After selling so many stories so quickly, I thought I had found a market that would take everything and anything I wrote. Getting rejected twice in a row was quite a blow, and I wondered if the previous sales had been flukes. Despite the setbacks, I continued to submit, and I got word of the next two sales, "By the Book" and "Shop at Home Service," in one month and two weeks, respectively.

Rejections tend to come more quickly than acceptances. If something is wrong with a piece of fiction or magazine article, it is often readily apparent to the editor. Work that is acceptable, however, requires a closer look. Note that I did not stop submitting to the magazine after a few failures, and this is where many new writers fall by the wayside. Rejection is never easy to take, even less so after it's become obvious that the person you're trying to sell to appreciates your work.

My perseverance was rewarded, which is evident not only in the story sales that followed the rejections, but also in the fact that both "The Lucky Break" and "Someday My Prince Will Come" were later accepted by the same editor. "The Lucky Break" was accepted in 1993 after a wait of two weeks, and "Someday My Prince Will Come" was accepted in 1994 after a wait of two months.

Simultaneous Submissions

The standard protocol is to send your story to one publication at a time, which can be a lengthy procedure.

As I mentioned before, when I first began submitting my stories for publication, the average response time was in the neighborhood of six months. After waiting for six months, I would sometimes send a polite follow-up letter as a reminder to the editor about how long he or she had had to look at the story, and shortly after that I'd get my story back.

Today it seems that six months is not much time at all to wait, and response times of eight or 10 months, or even more than a year, are not unheard of. Because of this, simultaneous submissions — submission of the same story to more than one magazine at the same time — have become more accepted among editors. Instead of your story going to one magazine for six months and then to another for a similarly long period of time, it goes out to ten magazines at once and has a chance of selling more quickly than it might otherwise have done.

Sounds great, but not all magazines are willing to look at simultaneous submissions. Why should an editor spend time considering a manuscript that might already be taken by another magazine? However, some editors don't mind that you've sent a story to more than one market, as long as you mention in your cover letter that you're simultaneously submitting the story elsewhere.

If in doubt, check the publication's guidelines, or query the editor first. Nothing will irritate an editor more than accepting a story, only to be told by the author that it has been accepted somewhere else.

Rolling Submissions

Because of the long waiting periods encountered by writers in recent years, many have opted for a strategy called a rolling submission.

Here's how it works: When you submit your story, you mention in your cover letter that you are allowing the editor an exclusive look at the story for a period of three months. If you haven't received a response in three months, you will assume the editor is not interested and you will then send it to another publication. And so on, and so on.

This seems to be a happy medium between making single and simultaneous submissions. It gives the editor a fair amount of time to consider the manuscript, but doesn't tie up a writer's work for an unreasonable period.

E-mail Submissions

Some magazines accept e-mail submissions, and, in fact, some even prefer it. Electronic magazines obviously lead the way in terms of e-mail submissions, but print magazines are slowly catching up. If you know the e-mail address of a magazine, but are unsure if they accept submissions through that account, send a query. Or check a magazine's guidelines for mention of electronic submissions. Many editors do all of their correspondence via e-mail, but prefer that submissions be made through snail mail.

If you're going to submit a story by e-mail, attach it in a plain-text format like ASCII or place it inside the body of your e-mail letter. You can send attached files in WordPerfect and MS Word over the Internet, but you can never be sure if your file can be read at the other end. For this reason, you should send the text in as simple a format as possible, and then in a preferred format after an editor requests it.

11
GETTING A RESPONSE

The Waiting Game

If you're sending an erotic story to a magazine for the first time, the best advice I can give you is to drop the envelope into the mail box and forget all about it. Go home, give yourself some comfort food or a pat on the back in recognition of a job well done, and get to work on your next story.

A response from a publisher could take anywhere from one week to forever: you might hear back from a magazine's editor in no time flat, or you might not hear back at all. Response time depends on the individual editor as well as the people running the company. If the company exists primarily to make a quick buck publishing skin magazines, you're not likely to get a response at all. Such a company may well go under in the time it would take to consider and comment on your submission. Another possibility is that even if the editor has decided to use your story, it might still be hung up for months, even years. Editors can sometimes be too busy to worry about an acceptance letter or contract and will often contact you as needed, which means about a week before the story is published.

This is why the rolling submission method (discussed in Chapter 10) can be of some value. The editor is given a reasonable amount of time to consider your manuscript, and if you haven't heard back after a given time period, you inform him or her that the work will be sent elsewhere for consideration.

Over the course of my career as a writer of erotica, I've experienced response times of just a few hours (even had stories accepted before I'd submitted them) as well as up to a year or more. Long response times are not always a matter for concern. An editor might let you know about a rejected a story in a few weeks but might hang on to acceptances until it's time to issue a contract.

Understand that no matter how much you know about the editor with whom you're working, or about the day-to-day operation of the magazine to which you've submitted, you'll never be able to figure out why you haven't heard back about your manuscript. Aspiring writers like to think that the longer a manuscript stays with a publisher, the more seriously it's being considered, or that it's being read by more than one editor. The truth is that your story could have been taken home by someone in the office and lost, or forgotten in a pile of other manuscripts, or recycled with all the other paper in the office. It could also have been tossed into the "to buy" pile, and you'll hear back only when the time comes.

Just write the best and hottest erotica you possibly can, send it off to the appropriate market, and start working on your next masterpiece. Eventually, you'll have so many manuscripts in circulation that you won't be worrying about each one because you'll be receiving something back in the mail almost daily.

Form Rejections

When you finally do get a response, it is likely to be a form rejection. A form rejection is exactly what the name implies — a pre-printed piece of paper that informs you that your submission will not be accepted by the magazine to which you've submitted.

I say "will not be accepted" rather than "rejected" because that's the sort of language these forms use. They are, with a few exceptions, rather gentle in their rhetoric.

Here's the wording of an old form rejection slip from Dugent Publishing. The slip itself measures about 4" x 5" (so the publisher can print about four little slips on each 8.5" x 11" sheet of paper) and bears the company logo as well as the names of the company's magazines at the bottom.

The text is simple and to the point:

> *Sorry we cannot use this*
> *material, but we appreciate*
> *your thinking of us.*
> *Please try again.*
> *The Editors.*

This was a fairly kind rejection, but such kindness is not always the case. For years, Larry Flynt Publications (publishers of *Hustler,* among other magazines) used to insert a 3" X 5.5" rejection card into the return envelope, and its wording was substantially harsher than the previous example:

> *Congratulations!*
> *You have been chosen to receive*
> *this beautiful hand-lettered*
> *rejection slip!*
>
> *We know you will be proud to add this*
> *attractive notice to your personal collection.*
>
> *For additional copies*
> *send your contributions to:*
>
> *(Company address and contact info)*
>
> *Note: In the event that your next*
> *contribution is accepted for publication*
> *we cannot send you another card,*
> *and you will just have to be*
> *satisfied with money. . . . Sorry.*
>
> *—The Editor*

This form is somewhat humorous in tone, but it could easily dash the hopes and spirit of a fledgling writer. In some cases, this may not be such a bad thing, since those who eventually succeed at writing are those who can take rejection and persevere, despite the great number of people who will say "No!" along the way.

If you receive a rejection like this one and still send another submission to the magazine, almost daring the editor to send you another form rejection letter, then you probably have the thick skin and determination needed to be published someday. (I happen to have two such cards in my extensive collection of rejection slips and letters, and although I have sold widely to many different publishers, I've never had anything accepted by Larry Flynt Publications.)

To be fair to Larry Flynt Publications, I did receive a form rejection from the company that was completely different, and perhaps a bit more writer friendly, than the card. The rejection letter, printed on the magazine's letterhead, read like most others, except for a single addition.

> *Dear Contributor,*
>
> *Thank you for submitting the enclosed for consideration in* Hustler Fantasies. *Unfortunately, the material does not conform to our current publishing needs. We do appreciate the effort involved, however, and look forward to reading your future letters and/or fiction.*

A fairly straightforward rejection letter. The difference? In addition to signing it, the editor underlined, "and look forward to reading your future letters and/or fiction." A simple gesture like that lets you know that while the work you submitted didn't work for them, they are impressed enough with your writing to want to see more. And they do want to see more, because they have a magazine to fill and they need words (and photos) to fill it.

If you persevere, keep submitting, and get a bit lucky, you won't have to endure form rejections for long.

Personalized Rejections

The most frustrating thing about form rejections is that they say nothing about *why* your story was rejected. In most cases, the editor doesn't have time to get into a discussion with a writer about rejected material and simply hopes that the writer will figure it out on his or her own.

But note that the first form rejection quoted above asked that I "please try again." A writer should do just that whenever an editor suggests it, even if it's just via a form rejection letter. If you've submitted to the same magazine over and over again, there's a good chance that the editor will begin to recognize your name. When that happens, he or she might be more inclined to seriously consider your work because you're obviously making an effort to sell to the magazine.

If you persist, you might get a personal message at the bottom of your form rejection. For example, the form rejection from Dugent Publishing carried a short note from the editor explaining what was happening with the story submissions they still hadn't rejected. (I had submitted several stories; only two were rejected, and the first page of each was included in the SASE along with the form rejection slip.)

Here's what the editor wrote (and by the way, *PBW* is short for the magazine *Plumpers and Big Women*):

> *Edo — Sorry, but we're going to*
> *have to pass on these two. We'll*
> *get you answers on the others (two*
> *of which went to* PBW) *as soon as possible.*

But although this was a personalized note, it still didn't tell me anything about why the stories were turned down.

I later learned in a telephone conversation with the editor that one of the stories, "Hard Work Made Harder" — about a couple of maintenance workers (a man and a woman) fixing up a kids' summer camp, whose close working conditions push them toward a sexual encounter — was turned down because it took place at a camp for kids. Even though the camp was deserted and the kids hadn't yet arrived, the mere mention of children was enough to gain an automatic rejection. The other story, "The House Hunt," was about a man who is always late for work because he lives too far from the office. He is shown an apartment by his boss (a woman), which is just down the block from the office. When she shows him the apartment, he realizes it's in her building and she wants him close by for something other than making it to work on time. I never did learn why this story was turned down. Luckily, rejection was only a temporary state for both stories.

"The House Hunt" was accepted a year later by another magazine produced by the same publishing company, and "Hard Work Made Harder" was sold to the same magazine that rejected it, but only after I revised it to make the kids' camp a dude ranch and gave it a new title: "Raunch on the Ranch." Rejection doesn't mean that a story is dead in the water. Think of it as merely treading water, waiting for the right time and the proper life boat to come to the rescue.

Keeping a Story on the Market

Whether you're writing fiction or nonfiction, science fiction or mystery, or a work of erotica, perseverance is always rewarded. Writing is hard work, and selling what you write is even harder, but success comes to those who persist.

This is especially true when it comes to marketing your work. If you give up after your first rejection, you will never sell your work to anyone. However, if you believe what you've written is good enough to be published, and you keep it on the market, continually on its way to or from an editor, there's an excellent chance that, in time, your story will find a market.

Take, for example, my story "Heat of Passion." I began selling stories to *Gent* magazine in the early 1990s. They were publishing most of what I sent them, and I was producing enough to test the waters of mass-market magazine publishing. After all, there were other magazines that paid better rates for fiction. So I sent the story somewhere other than *Gent*. Table 5 shows the story's chronology. Note that the response times were fairly reasonable back then: a couple of months for the first two magazines, and a few weeks for the third and fourth.

Table 5

Heat of Passion

Story	Publication	Submitted	Accepted/ Rejected	Published
"Heat of Passion"	*Gallery*	Sept 17, 1992	(R) Dec 7, 1992	--
	Fling	Dec 7, 1992	(R) Mar 24, 1993	--
	D-Cup	Mar 24, 1993	(R) Apr 27, 1993	--
	Busty Beauties	Apr 30, 1993	(R) May 17, 1993	--
	Gent	May 17, 1993	(A) Jun 1, 1993	Jan 1994

"Heat of Passion" was submitted to five different magazines over the course of 20 months before it sold. It took another eight months for the story to see print, some 28 months, or almost two-and-a-half years after the story was written. This may seem like a long time to wait, and it is. Getting a burger and fries at McDonald's takes just a few minutes, and an oil painting can be hung on the wall mere seconds after it's been completed, but with writing there is no instant gratification.

Publication requires an abundance of patience. Not surprisingly, it's those who hang in there the longest who enjoy the most success.

If you're still not convinced about keeping your story on the market, have a look at Table 6, which shows the marketing path of an erotic horror story of mine called "Skin Deep."

Table 6

Skin Deep

Story	Publication	Submitted	Accepted/ Rejected	Published
"Skin Deep"	*Tal Publications*	May 20, 1993	(R) Jun 14, 1993	--
	Nugget	Jun 18, 1993	(R) Sep 12, 1993	--
	Starry Nights	Sep 12, 1993	(R) Oct 26, 1993	--
	Hot Blood 7	Jan 17, 1995	(R) Jan 30, 1995	--
(Revised)	*Hot Blood 7*	Jan 31, 1995	(R) Feb 14, 1995	--
	Palace Corbie	6 Feb 14, 1995	(R) Mar 22, 1995	--
	Variations	Apr 10, 1995	(R) May 3, 1995	--
	Tesseracts 5	Jul 14, 1995	(R) Jan 23, 1996	--
	Whitley Strieber's Aliens	Jan 23, 1996	(R) Oct 16, 1996	--
	Editrice Nord (Italian)	Feb 14, 1995	(R) Mar 22, 1995	--
As "Pattern Baldness"	*Conspiracy Files*	Oct 15, 1997	(A) Nov 3, 1997	June 1998

The story is about a completely hairless female alien who comes to Earth to discover if humankind can accept a humanoid so different in appearance from themselves. The alien meets a man who happens to love hairless women, and the two have sex for days. When she returns to her ship, she reports to her superiors that while some humans truly appreciate the alien's differences, humankind in general is not ready for them. They decide to come back in a few years to check on us again and see if we might be ready then.

It was originally written for an anthology called *Bizarre Bazaar* but it was rejected. I then tried it out at *Nugget*, figuring the hairless aspect of the female might be popular with a fetish audience — no sale. *Starry Nights* was some small and forgettable publication. Next came the *Hot Blood* series of erotic horror anthologies. The editor there asked for revisions, which I did in short order and sent back to him. He nonetheless rejected it a couple of weeks later. After that, I tried *Palace Corbie* and *Tesseracts*, which were horror and speculative fiction anthologies, respectively. Then I tried the HWA anthology *Whitley Strieber's Aliens* and an Italian anthology having to do with aliens, but no sale on either count.

Unsure of what to do with the story, I let it sit. I was confident that it was a good story; I simply hadn't found the right market for it yet. A couple of years later, a colleague of mine, Scott H. Urban, told me he was putting together an anthology about conspiracies, in the tradition of *The X-Files*. He was turning the anthology in shortly and would need a story soon. I got to thinking about "Skin Deep," and took it out and had a look at it. I thought that the sex with the alien could cause the man in the story to lose his hair after the encounter. I revised it, giving the alien spaceship a very heavy radiation signature (suggesting that the aliens themselves live in a radiation-rich environment), toning down the sex a bit (this was an SF anthology, not an erotic anthology), and adding a scene at the end in which the man calls out for his alien lover and discovers she's gone. Then, as he's looking at himself in the mirror, he runs his fingers through his hair, only to have it come away in his hands. Finally, I added a new title, "Pattern Baldness," suggesting that many men lose their hair due to sex with alien females. I had a sale.

That the sale was made four-and-a-half years after the story was written, and that the story had to be revised twice (with a little tweaking here and there over the four-plus years) is immaterial. I believed in the story, kept it on the market, and even when I wasn't sending it out,

I was still considering it for every new market I heard about. Ultimately, the 72nd story I'd written became my 114th sale. The happy ending is that the story has been reprinted in my erotic horror collection, *Six-Inch Spikes*.

Don't ever give up on your work!

Robert Heinlein's Five Rules of Writing

1. You must write.

2. You must finish what you start.

3. You must refrain from rewriting, except to editorial order.*

4. You must put it on the market.

5. You must keep it on the market until it is sold.

(* Rule number three assumes that the story is absolutely as good as you can possibly make it and therefore requires no further revision.)

Don't Give Up

The submission history of "Skin Deep" might seem daunting to a new writer. After all, ten rejections and a wait of almost five years would be enough to make more sane individuals decide to try another field of work — any other field of work.

But ten rejections are hardly worth mentioning when compared to some of my other non-erotic short stories. The story "The Night Terror" had 20 rejections before finally being published in *Northern Fusion*, some five and a half years after it was written, and other stories such as "The Girl Next Door" and "Overdue Fines" were rejected 18 times each before finding a home. If you think the stories were rejected because they weren't very good, consider for a moment the story "Rat Food," which I wrote with David Nickle and which won the Bram Stoker Award from the Horror Writers Association in 1998. That story was written in 1990, rejected five times, accepted by J.N. Williamson for his anthology *Masques IV*, which, after a wait of several years, never materialized, and then was rejected seven more times before finally being published in *On Spec* in 1996. Over those six years, several editors had wanted it, but turned it down for one reason or another. Just because a story gets rejected doesn't mean you should hide it in your drawer. You simply have to work harder to find the right market for it.

Finally, to finish off this message of determination, I'll just mention that my story "But Somebody's Got to Do It" was rejected 24 times before it was finally published in my own short-story collection. During those 24 rejections, there had actually been three sales, but each and every time, the magazine that took the story folded before it could publish it. After the story was printed in my collection, however, it was reprinted within a year.

Again, don't give up.

Talent, Luck, Persistence

Here's a list and a rule to remember:

1. Talent.
2. Luck.
3. Persistence.

Any two of these three qualities is required to become a successful writer.

You can have talent and be lucky.

You can have talent and persist.

You can persist and get lucky.

Notice that one of the alternatives does not even require that you have talent. Of course, if you want to see your work published, you have to have some ability to string words together, but you don't necessarily have to have a blazing talent. However, if you don't have talent, then you must have persistence; more than that, you must have a dogged determination to succeed.

Why? Because as you write and submit your stories, many people along the way will tell you your work is not good enough. They won't

One thing that beginning writers never get, and I certainly didn't get in the beginning, is that publishing does reward perseverance. It really does. To stick with it, to write books, to get them published wherever you can. To do whatever you have to do to make a living is something that, after 15 years, publishing respects.

— *John Preston*

necessarily be polite about it either, especially when you're submitting to erotic markets.

Say that you do succeed in selling a novel. Say you spent two years working on the book and took another couple of years to sell it. But when you sell, you receive only a few thousand dollars (the basic first-novel advance runs somewhere between $1,500 to $5,000 for a main-stream erotic novel, and less for a novel published as part of a line of erotic books). This is not the tens or hundreds of thousands of dollars that you envisioned. Then the novel is published with a cover that embarrasses you, with a small print run that barely puts one book in each major book store. The publisher does nothing to promote the book, sales are dismal, and some of the reviews seem to take glee in trashing your creation. You've invested four years of your life for little money and little satisfaction, and in the end you wonder why on Earth you wanted to do this in the first place.

Persistence and determination are an integral part of a writer's career. If you don't believe me, heed the advice of novelist and short-story writer Dennis Etchison:

> I would also say: never give up. I once had a story rejected 72 times; it took me six and a half years to sell it. But I did. It's like going to a party where there are 60 people. You can't expect to please all of them. But if you can just meet the right one, then you can forget the others you never connected with.

12
THE WORKING PROFESSIONAL

Giving Editors What They Want

Editors at magazines and publishing houses like to conduct business like everyone else in the world. Their work and lives are easier when they work with other professionals. Therefore, you must provide quality work that conforms to the market's guidelines; you must provide the work on time and in a totally professional manner. You should be easy to work with and dependable, and you should take pride in your work.

These things might seem so simple that they don't even need to be stated, but there are many writers out there who aren't dependable, who produce the wrong material and submit it late, and who require more time from an editor than their contributions are worth.

In the end, the writer who conducts business like a pro ends up getting more regular work (sometimes as much as he or she can handle), while the others never advance to the next level in their careers.

Conducting Business Like a Pro

Working in any field as a freelancer requires that you present yourself as a professional in every way. After all, if there are six people providing the same service, the thing that might make working with you more desirable than working with the other five is that you conduct business in a thoroughly professional manner.

In short, operating like a pro can put money in your pocket.

Look at it for a moment from the editor's perspective. An editor at a mass-market magazine might be working on four or five regularly scheduled titles in any given week. Furthermore, the editor is not dealing only with you — and other fiction writers — but also with photographers, layout staff, graphic designers, advertisers, circulation staff, finance staff, and maybe even a model or two. Does he or she have a lot of time to spend on the phone with you, or to answer your letters about things like why your story was rejected? No, of course not. In fact, the less time the editor must spend on your work, the better he or she likes it.

That's right. The editor of the large-circulation magazine to which you've just sold a story is happy to buy your work, pay for it on time, and send you a copy of the issue in which your story appears, but he or she doesn't want to spend time chatting with you on the phone. Really, the editor doesn't want to talk to you unless something's broken or there's a fire to be put out.

A Few Words with . . .

James Marriott

On Erotic Book Publishing

EDO VAN BELKOM: What has happened in the past ten years to make the publishing of erotic books and novels more mainstream than it's been in the past?

JAMES MARRIOTT: I think that there has been a general loosening up of attitudes toward sexually explicit material in the past ten years. The 1990s saw a huge growth in the profile of anti-censorship feminism, and women's erotica imprints such as

Black Lace helped to make acceptable the idea that women as well as men enjoy erotica. As unreconstructed feminism had been the foremost opponent to sexually explicit material in the 1980s, the importance of pro-porn feminism can't be stressed highly enough.

There's also been the much-vaunted return of porno chic: films like *Boogie Nights,* an impressive number of books about the adult-film industry, and the growing popularity of slick, sophisticated adult films put out by Vivid, Michael Ninn, etcetera. As far as specifically books are concerned, though, it's not only the loosening of restrictions that's been important, but also a number of other factors. These include market forces (erotic fiction sells well); other, newer bugbears for the censors (the focus on violent films and the Internet has effectively taken the heat off books in most areas); and the fact that books enjoy an elevated cultural status which puts them outside other media. Book-burning is an attack on personal freedom; the burning of video-tapes doesn't seem to provoke the same classic liberal reaction.

EDO VAN BELKOM: Is there a specific readership that your books aim to please, or are you publishing a wide enough variety that there is usually something to suit every taste?

JAMES MARRIOTT: I think "every taste" is a bit too broad! Nexus is known for publishing erotica which is essentially non-vanilla. Within that, we have fem dom, watersports, CP, S/M, lactation fetishes, splosh-style messiness, foot fetishism, clothes fetishism, etcetera. Some of our books do focus on one particular theme, probably the most popular single themes being fem dom and CP, but we encourage authors to feature a variety. We won't, however, ask authors to write about something they themselves don't like; as with adult films, I think that authenticity shines through and will always be the key factor in a reader's enjoyment. This is why people who write erotica for purely commercial reasons usually fail.

EDO VAN BELKOM: What is the most common misconception about erotic novels? Is editing a line of erotic books much different than editing book lines in other genres?

JAMES MARRIOTT: I work on a number of different lines here: I do true-crime books, film guides, and career guides. All are different. Probably the most common misconception about erotic novels is that they are all the same, or that they must necessarily follow the same formulae. Not so. While there are classic scenarios, which some of our novels follow, in others we try to push the envelope a little in terms of plot and style: check out any books by Lindsay Gordon or Aishling Morgan to see what I mean.

Editing erotic fiction is different from working in other areas principally because the authors tend to be more interesting people. Another difference is that we (there are two other editors of erotic fiction in my "pod") can get on with doing the books without having to have everything rubber-stamped in interminable meetings, which is sadly the case for the nonfiction on which I work. Either we're trusted to do a good job or nobody else wants to dirty their hands by dealing with it. It's probably a mixture of both.

EDO VAN BELKOM: What is your slush pile like? Do you receive a higher proportion of inappropriate submissions than other editors?

JAMES MARRIOTT: Huge, and yes. We do send out material to be read by trusted readers. They don't reject anything, but we'll follow their pointers to a degree; they help to separate the wheat from the chaff. We do take on new authors, but at present Nexus has a strong existing author base, so there's not much need for new talent. Existing authors do burn out or simply stop writing, however, and there's always room for superlatively good new material.

EDO VAN BELKOM: What quality is most often lacking in the submissions you receive? What would you suggest writers pay the most attention to when writing an erotic novel?

JAMES MARRIOTT: The answer to the first [question] is originality. A lot of authors tend to assume that if we've used one plot in an existing novel, then we'll happily use it again. Most erotic fiction is hackneyed and unimaginative in the extreme. I do feel that readers of erotic fiction appreciate originality — most tend to read more than one book, and I'd feel we were short-changing the punters if we were to accept lower standards in the originality of the books we publish.

So I'd advise authors to think differently — and also to write about what turns them on, rather than what they assume the market wants. I can think of a good number of scenarios which I haven't seen explored, and I do occasionally make suggestions to existing authors. New authors, however, have to think for themselves.

James Marriott is editor of Virgin Publishing's Nexus imprint. His favorite number is 78 and his favorite cartoonist is Jim Woodring. He prefers New York to San Francisco. His ideal pet would be a squid or chimpanzee, but they're expensive and hard to come by in the UK. All donations gratefully received.

When I first began selling erotic short stories to *Gent,* the editors there were just names on a contract. In fact, I don't think I spoke to any of them for several years, at which point they began calling me.

Why? Well, I had gained a reputation around the Dugent offices for writing good short fiction. (This became clear when the editor of *Gent* called me one day asking for a story that he had previously rejected. Seems that even the stories of mine they'd rejected were better than what they were receiving in the slush pile. After that, I sold stories to them much more steadily.) I had also started selling enough stories on a yearly basis to become a regular contributor to Dugent's stable of magazines, and they knew I would likely be selling them more in the future. I was no longer some guy who, on a lark, sent them a single story that turned out to be usable. I now published five to ten stories a year in their magazines. I was a supplier, if you will.

With this excellent working relationship established, I also received calls from other editors at Dugent who needed stories for their publications. I remember being asked to supply a story for a new, all-black magazine called *Sugah.* Nye Willden (yes, the very same Nye Willden who had regularly bought stories from Stephen King for *Cavalier* magazine in the 1970s) called and explained what he wanted the story to be about and when he wanted it by. I gave him everything he asked for, and the story was published in Issue 1 of the magazine. I kept writing stories for *Sugah* (when you have a receptive market, write as much as you can for it, because you never know how long it's going to last), and they were used regularly until the magazine folded a few years later. (You see? What did I tell you?).

But once you've connected with an editor, it's a relationship that can often last beyond the life of the magazine.

When an editor to whom I had been selling stories for more than eight years left the company for which he worked, I called him to wish him luck finding a job elsewhere. (Editors tend to work in publishing their entire lives, and you never know where one might end up.) I also told him that when he found another job, he should look me up. He replied that he intended to keep in touch, and when looking for a new job he'd be using his relationship with me and the other writers he knew as a benefit to potential employers. After all, if he ended up editing another men's magazine, he'd have enough contacts to begin work almost immediately without having to meet everyone who'd worked for the magazine in the past.

And that's exactly what happened.

A couple of months later, I got a call from the editor. He had just been hired on by another magazine group across town, and was now editing a magazine that featured young girls, 18 years and over. He needed some fiction. Not only that, he had also passed my name along to several other editors at the company who were always looking for writers who could provide professional copy on deadline. I received calls from three different editors, and sold material to all of them.

Always conduct your business like a pro, and your freelance erotic-writing business will be sure to grow.

Pitching Stories and Articles

Once you've established a working relationship with an editor, it becomes easier to sell work to him or her. By then, the editor will have some idea of the quality of your work, even before you've submitted it. And once you've sold enough material to a particular editor, and there has been a consistency of quality in your work over a long period of time, it is entirely possible for you to sell your work even before it's written.

After I had been selling fiction to the Dugent family of magazines for several years, I found myself looking for more well-paying work to fill up my days. Although *Gent* editor Steve Dorfman had asked me to consider writing nonfiction for his magazines several times before, I had always turned him down. My feeling was that I was a fiction writer, and if I was going to write for men's magazines, I would contribute fiction. However, at that point, I decided to give him a call and let him know I was interested in writing nonfiction. As expected, he was enthusiastic about the prospect of a long-time fiction contributor writing nonfiction as well, and asked that I send him a few proposals for articles. If he liked them, he could give me the go-ahead on them, and I would be writing material that I knew would be bought and published, rather than doing the work on spec.

I e-mailed him the following:

E-mail
Item   233828598/06/15   16:44
Sub: Nonfiction

Steve,

Okay, you've asked me enough times about nonfiction, I suppose I really ought to give it a try. Now, I don't know how you work it with your other freelancers, but I wouldn't want to do an article without getting the go ahead from you on the basis of a query.

For *Leg Scene*, I'd like to suggest two articles:

One: "Making Legs Even Sexier" would be about all the ways women can accentuate their legs, including high heels, stockings, ankle bracelets and toe rings, tattoos, nail polish. The appeal of the article would be the erotic description of each of the items through prose or quotes from people who enjoy the different adornments.

Two: "Which is the Sexiest Part of a Woman's Leg?" This would be about which parts of the leg men find most attractive: toes, feet, ankles, calves, knees, thighs, and of course, the grand place where all legs lead to.

For *Gent*, I'd like to suggest five articles:

One: A companion article to the first legs article, "Making Breasts Even Sexier," which could profile different kinds of bras, pierced nipples, perhaps even pregnancy and breast-feeding as ways of making breasts more attractive. Again, the appeal would be in the descriptions of the breasts.

Two: A companion article to the second legs article, "Which is the Sexiest Part of a Woman's Breast?" Is it the nipple, the areola, the cleavage between them? Or is every inch is as sexy as the next?

Three: "A Man's Guide to Sucking Tit" would be full of quotes from women talking about how they like to have their tits sucked and what it does to them. Sometimes they like it hard, sometimes gentle, and sometimes they enjoy doing it themselves.

Four: "Learning to Flaunt It" would be an article all about showing off a woman's best assets. From being a tease to getting a man interested, to stripping and letting it all hang out, this article would cover the joys of having mammaries and knowing how to use them.

Five: "Titfucking from A to D." The best tit-fucks are to be had with a set of D-cups, but not all women are so fortunate. The article would begin with suggestions for less-endowed women, and then move on to the joys of big breasts and what to do with them.

And finally, for *Plumpers*, two articles:

One: "A Plumper Appreciation Guide" would be a guide on how to treat plumpers like goddesses and encourage them to feel comfortable and uninhibited about their bodies, and the rewards such treatment would reap.

Two: "What makes Plumpers so hot?" This would be an examination of why heavier women are sexier than their skinnier counterparts.

So there it is, my proposal for nonfiction articles for three of your magazines. I'm not sure what format your queries usually take, or which of these you might have done before, but if you want me to send them to you via snail mail, I'll gladly do it.

If you're wondering, in addition to writing plenty of short stories, I used to be a newspaper reporter and have done plenty of the type of nonfiction you use in your magazine. I'd appreciate the go-ahead on several of the articles at once so I could make the most efficient use of my research time.

Let me know what you think. I have time now to work on these articles and would like to get started on them before other work fills my plate.

All the best,

Edo

Keep in mind that these queries were for specialty magazines. The article ideas may sound silly to you, but they are anything but to the magazine's regular readers.

Notice that even though I had been dealing with the editor for years and he had asked me if I wanted to contribute nonfiction, I still took the opportunity to sell myself by saying, "If you're wondering, in addition to writing plenty of short stories, I used to be a newspaper reporter and have done plenty of the type of nonfiction you use in your magazine." If the editor is uncertain about any of your proposed articles, a few words of reassurance could be enough to tip the scales in your favor. Also note that I made sure he knew that I'd be doing these articles for the money and would work better if I knew he'd be buying them once they were written: "I'd appreciate the go-ahead on several of the articles at once so I could make the most efficient use of my research time."

As it turned out, the editor was more enthusiastic about some articles than others, but he ended up giving me the green light on all of them, saying he wanted to encourage me to write more for the magazine. I think I wrote five of the articles before the editor was let go from the magazine, and all five ended up in print, even though a couple ended up in other company's magazines. There is never any shortage of markets for erotic nonfiction. Even if you've written for a very specialized magazine, that magazine will always have a competitor.

Proposals

The preceding query was, admittedly, rather informal. Its conversational tone is acceptable only because I had been working with the editor for some eight years and had spoken with him on the phone on numerous occasions. He had also written the introduction to my chapbook collection of erotic science fiction stories, *Virtual Girls: The Erotic Gems of Evan Hollander*. If I hadn't had this connection to the editor, my queries would have been much more formal in tone and each article idea would have been fleshed out to give the editor a better idea of where the article would be going. The editor at Dugent knew I could do this work very easily, but a new editor might have thought I was just another reader who believes that because he thinks about sex a lot and can string a few sentences together, writing an article would be easy.

When you are dealing with a new editor, you must submit a proposal. A proposal is far more detailed than a simple query, but not as much work as writing a complete article or story. To illustrate what should and should not go into a proposal letter, I've provided here the proposal letter I wrote for my erotic short story collection, *Working Hard*. Early in 2000, looking for new markets and opportunities for my work (as all freelance writers do), I counted up the erotic stories I'd written about people at work and on the job and found that I had more than enough for a collection. Since these stories had already been written and published, it seemed worthwhile to compile them and see if I could find a publisher for the collection. I needed to write a bang-up proposal letter to catch an editor's eye. It's reproduced as Sample 6.

Notice that the first paragraph does not begin with boring lines like, "I'm writing you to enquire," or "I was wondering if," but instead gets immediately to the heart of the matter. The letter must catch the editor's attention, and mentioning sex in the first line is a good way to do that.

Once I'd put the collection in context, I explain, in the second paragraph, why I'm writing. I'm hoping that I've still got the editor's interest and he or she will be reading all the way to the end. I also explain what's in the collection and mention that the stories have been published before to give the editor an idea of their quality. Of course, the magazines listed might not impress the editor, but at least he or she knows that someone thought enough of the stories to publish them. Finally, I mention that the stories are about a wide range of working people — not just office workers, and not just ditch-diggers — and that both men and women figure prominently in the stories. Much erotica these days is geared toward women, and mentioning that women take the initiative in some of the stories hints that the collection might have a broad appeal.

Next, since the editor doesn't know me, I try to make myself look as good as possible in terms of erotic writing. I mention almost all of my erotica credentials. If this proposal were for a book of horror or mystery, I would be using an entirely different set of credentials. (This is one reason why it's a good idea not to limit yourself to a single field. You never know where the work might be.)

Sample 6

Proposal Letter

Edo van Belkom   **freelance writer**

69 Erotica Lane   **(905) 555-3208**
City, Province/State   **edress@emailaddress.com**

January 5, 2000

Editor, X Libris
Brettenham House
Lancaster Place
London, UK WC2E 7EN

Dear Editor:

People spend more than one-third of their day at work, whether it be in an office environment or elsewhere, and as a result, a large part of their waking lives are spent on the job. And since men and women think about sex all the time, it's not hard to imagine that people fantasize about sex in the workplace…while they're working and every day of their lives.

With that in mind, I'm asking if X Libris would be interested in taking a look at a collection of erotic short stories dealing with sex in the workplace called *Working Hard.* I have more than 20 short stories that could be included, each of them previously published in such men's magazines as *Gent, Nugget, Leg Show*, and *Petite.* The stories feature both white- and blue-collar workers, and men and woman equally taking the sexual initiative.

If you're not familiar with my name or my work, allow me to introduce myself. Under my own name, and that of Evan Hollander, I have published 150 short stories to date, dozens of them in popular mass-market men's magazines. I've published a chapbook collection of stories with Circlet Press called *Virtual Girls,* with three of the stories later recorded by model Amber Smith for the SexxxyAudio Book, *Amber.* I have won both the Bram Stoker Award and the Aurora Award for my short fiction, and have had stories reprinted in *Year's Best Horror Stories* and *Best American Erotica.*

In addition to my fiction, I also write nonfiction and am currently working on a "how-to" book called *Writing Erotica,* a follow-up to *Writing Horror,* which will be out from Self-Counsel Press in February 2000. So even if you're not interested in considering the short story collection, I ask that you please send me a set of writer's guidelines in the SASE provided so that I could refer to them in the new book.

Hope to hear from you.

All the best,

Edo van Belkom

In the last paragraph, I make one final attempt to make myself look like an experienced pro whose work has some merit, and then I ask if the editor would like to see the entire collection. (I also asked for a set of writer's guidelines for this book, since it made sense to kill two birds with one stone. A freelancer always has to maximize the return on his or her efforts.)

Did It Work?

Of the five proposal letters I sent out, (which, of course, included SASES), two editors said they were not currently looking for new titles, one did not respond (and I've since learned that this line specializes in erotica for women, so it was the wrong place to send the proposal from the start), one asked to see a sample from the collection (five of the 20 stories) to decide whether or not to look at the entire collection, and one asked to see the entire collection. That's a hit rate of 40 percent, which is excellent, considering these things usually pay off only one out of ten times.

Getting Paid

It's wonderful to have something you wrote published in a real magazine. But the novelty soon wears off for most writers, and getting paid for your work becomes a much higher priority.

Some might even say that getting paid is what it's all about.

With the exception of some small press magazines, most erotica is published by money-making operations. Erotica is a business, and, as in any business, people expect to be paid for the work that they do. After all, the printer isn't printing the magazine for free, and the ads inside the magazine were all paid for by the advertisers, so it's imperative that the writer be paid as well.

Word rates for erotica are quite respectable, with magazines paying three or four times per word what you might expect to be paid by a top mystery or science fiction magazine. For a short story in a men's magazine you could receive between $250 and $600 US — not bad for a day's work.

Most magazines pay on publication. Even though you've sold your story in January, you might not be paid for it until November when the

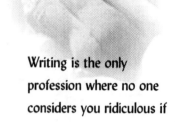

Writing is the only profession where no one considers you ridiculous if you earn no money.

— *Jules Renard*

issue in which it appears is finally published and on the stands. You'll likely receive a free contributor's copy of the magazine under a separate cover, but this is always an iffy thing and depends on the publishing company's procedures and the editor's attention to detail. If you don't receive a contributor's copy, receiving the check in the mail can serve as a reminder that the story is out and you can pick up a copy at your local newsstand.

Do erotica publishers really pay on time?

Yes, they do. Despite the type of material they publish, these are businesses that like to keep both their customers and suppliers happy. If you get burned on a payment for a story, you won't be sending that magazine any more work. When a few more writers get burned, the publishers quickly find themselves with nothing of quality to put in the magazine, and readership declines. Eventually the magazine folds.

As a writer of erotica, you are an important part of the publishing operation and your work has value.

Never think otherwise.

Receiving a Contract

Some publishers send an author a contract to notify him or her that they have accepted a story or article for publication. The contract usually outlines how much will be paid, when payment will be made, and what rights will be purchased.

Because newsstand magazines stay on the shelves for a month or so — three months in the case of a special — publishers are interested only in filling the magazine and not in what you do with the story afterward. As a result, they won't ask for any rights other than those that allow them to publish your story once.

However, if the company has a stable of half-a-dozen magazines, it might reserve the right to reprint your story in one of its other magazines at a reduced rate. Here's a clause from one of my short-story contracts with a magazine with which I've been dealing for almost ten years.

> *Also, please be advised that we reserve the option of reprinting the feature in one of our other magazines for our standard reprint rate — approximately 35% of the original purchase price.*

So if they paid you $300 to publish your story the first time, they have the option to reprint your story in a different magazine for $105. That doesn't mean they will be reprinting it again any time soon (I don't think I've ever had a story reprinted at this rate); it just gives them the ability to do so if they ever have the need. A reprint is a godsend for the writer, because the writer is being paid again for work already done. It's like found money.

Some publishers are more interested in reprinting stories in other publications and can be more aggressive in securing rights. Here's a clause from a short-story contract for a company to which I've only just begun to sell work.

> *Our rate for the story will be $400.00 with payment upon publication. This purchase includes first rights in North America, non-exclusive worldwide publishing, and electronic rights.*

According to this clause, the company retains the right to reprint the story anywhere in the world, and even on the Internet, for the $400. The word "non-exclusive" makes it a bit unclear whether or not they simply want the right to reprint the story and will be paying for any subsequent use either on paper or electronically, or they want all rights to the story without any further payment. In this situation, it is appropriate for you to make a call to the editor, and depending on the answer, you will have to decide whether payment is sufficient for the rights they're asking of you.

The questions you have to ask yourself are these: Is $400 adequate compensation if they reprint again and again without payment? Could you sell the story elsewhere for the same money, but without giving up world and electronic rights?

The good thing about each of these clauses is that they do not take the rights to the story away from the author. The author can still try to reprint his or her story elsewhere, as many times as possible.

For instance, take my short story "Sex in Time." Its first appearance was in the April 1995 issue of *Gent,* for which I was paid $250 US. In April of that same year, the story was reprinted in a chapbook of five of my stories published by Boston's Circlet Press called *Virtual Girls: The Erotic Gems of Evan Hollander.* Since Circlet is a very small operation, payment for the chapbook (which ran about 60 pages) was an advance of $100 (or $20 per story). Though the payment for the story was low at $20, I didn't have to do any additional work to earn that money. Furthermore, over the next five years, the book earned about $400 in royalties, so add another $80 for the story. Then in 1999, the audio-book company Sexxxy Audio picked up a copy of *Virtual Girls* and decided to make an audio book of three of the stories, read by swimsuit model Amber Smith and entitled "Amber." Payment for each of the three stories was $200, along with provisions for further payments if more copies of the audio book were to be produced in the future.

Table 7 shows the total earned by the one story to date (covering a period of four years).

Table 7

"Sex in Time" by Evan Hollander

SALES	PAYMENT
Gent, April 1995	$250
Virtual Girls, July 1995, Circlet Press.	20 (Advance)
	80 (Royalty)
"Amber," October 1999, Sexxxy Audio	200
	————————
	$550 Total

Now, this sort of thing hasn't happened with every erotic story I've written. Indeed, at the time I wrote most of them, I figured a single appearance in a magazine for one month was all I could hope for. However, I've found that once a story is in print, it can take on a life of its own. As a result, I like to think of my stories as assets that I produce and accumulate over the course of my career, which could earn a modest amount in reprint fees throughout my lifetime. A writer's body of work is the closest thing the profession has to a retirement plan.

Submitting an Invoice

If an editor doesn't send you a contract for your story, he or she might simply send you a letter (or, in this day and age, an e-mail) informing you of your story's acceptance and asking that you send an invoice for it.

If you've worked at all as a freelance writer, or in any business environment, you're probably familiar with invoices. They are bills you send to the company for the work they are buying from you.

The benefit of sending an invoice is that it places responsibility for the creation of the contract with the writer, and therefore you need not wait for the publisher to send you a contract. You can also ensure that you're paid the proper amount. (Some publishers have been known to have memory lapses when it comes to the amount to which they've agreed.) Invoices can make payments materialize that much more quickly, because your invoice will be paid much in the same manner as the bill for printing, photography, and other things. After the editor receives your invoice, it is passed along to the accounting department and — if all goes well — the check should soon be in the mail. An invoice also helps you avoid the question of rights. You are asked to send an invoice for a certain amount, the amount is paid, and you are left free and clear to submit the story elsewhere.

Sample 7 shows the invoice I use to bill publishers. Note that I print it on my letterhead which shows all my contact information. (It looks more professional, too.) I also keep it as simple as possible, including all the information the publisher needs to make the payment, and nothing more.

Selling All Rights

A lot of publishers of book-length erotica buy all rights to the work they publish. That means that for, say, $1,000, a book publisher will buy your novel outright, taking away any claim you might have to the work and paying you nothing further, no matter how many copies of the books are sold or what other media the work is adapted to.

If the book is sold to a foreign publisher, you receive nothing. If the book becomes a *New York Times* bestseller, you receive nothing. If an adult video is made from your story, you receive credit, but the publisher of the book takes all the money. Obviously, this is the sort of thing you want to avoid, whether it's for a book or short story. It might have been acceptable back when sex novels were produced on a regular basis and were the only outlet for that type of story, but the proliferation of the Internet, adult videos, and magazines has opened up a whole new marketplace. Who can tell where you might be able to resell your story in the future? It's best to keep as much control over your own work as possible.

Sample 7
Invoice

Edo van Belkom   **freelance writer**

69 Erotica Lane   **(905) 555-3208**
City, Province/State   **edress@emailaddress.com**

ITEM: "Learning The Tricks of The Trade"
        by Evan Hollander

FOR: May 2000, *Petite* Magazine
       Dugent Corporation
       14411 Commerce Way, Suite 420
       Miami Lakes, FL
       USA   33016-1598

RATE: $200 US

DATE: December 2, 1999

CONTRACTED BY: Jack Lisa

SIGNATURE: _____

Author: *Lord Soth, Mister Magick, Northern Dreamers, Death Drives a Semi,* and *Teeth*

Copyright information

If you want to read up on copyright law, the following books may be of some help regarding copyright law in Canada, the United States, and the United Kingdom, respectively.

Canadian Copyright Law, 2nd edition, by Lesley Ellen Harris. Toronto: McGraw-Hill Ryerson, 1995.

The Copyright Permission and Libel Handbook: A Step-By Step Guide for Writers, Editors and Publishers, by Lloyd J. Jassin and Steven C. Schecter. New York: John Wiley and Sons, 1998.

Richards Butler on Copyright, Designs and Patents: The New Law, by Robert M. Merkin. London: Longman, 1989.

The Check's in the Mail

As already mentioned, most erotic magazines are very good about paying their contributors, and receiving a check in the mail is the best (and sometimes only) notice a writer gets that his or her story has been published. The check is accompanied by a receipt that usually states what the check is for, so there will be a line reading something like —

```
2/15/00  PETITE May '00:
        erotic fiction "Learning the Tricks of the Trade"   $200.00
```

If the publisher is good about sending contributor's copies, one will likely arrive in a week or two. Remember that the check comes from the publisher's office, while the magazine comes from the printer or distributor, and one can come several weeks before the other. Don't worry if the magazine arrives before the check. But if a few months have passed, it's time to get anxious.

If the publisher isn't very diligent about contributor's copies (and there are a few that are not), receiving the check is your cue to head out to your local newsstand or convenience store to find your issue on the shelves. But keep in mind that there's sometimes a bit of a lag, and it may take a few weeks for the magazine to be shipped from the printer to the distributor to the seller.

The Check's Not in the Mail

With contracts and invoices changing hands, how often does it happen that you don't get paid for your work?

Well, with ten years and 60 or so erotic short stories and articles under my belt, nonpayment for the use of my work happened only twice. In one of these instances, I received a partial payment; in the other, I fell victim to bankruptcy proceedings.

Here's what happened in each case:

(1) Early in the 1990s I had been selling a few short stories to *Gent* and, although they were taking most of what I sent them, they still rejected the odd story. There were plenty of other magazines to which I could submit, so a rejected story wasn't a disaster. In fact, it worked to my benefit. After one particular story was rejected by *Gent*, I sent it to *Velvet*, knowing little about the magazine other than that it published fiction. The story was rejected by the editor of *Velvet*, but when I received the rejection letter, I was informed that he'd sent the story along to another editor. A short while later, I got a call from a woman editing a magazine called *40-Plus*. She not only wanted to use my story (at a rate higher than I would have received at *Gent*), but she also wanted to know if I'd like to provide a story to the magazine each month for the same amount.

Would I? This was the kind of opportunity a freelance writer always hopes for: a steady, well-paying gig. (And this happened when I was still working as a reporter, so it was all extra income.) Of course, you can write a story per month for any magazine you like, but it's difficult to do so on spec. Knowing that someone is waiting for a story, that it will be published, and that you will be paid for it is very strong motivation. In fact, it makes writing a real pleasure.

And so I began writing stories featuring older women at the rate of one per month, with the first, "The Arrangement," appearing in March 1992. By the time that story had appeared, I had written and submitted three others, "Reversal of Fortune," "House Calls," and "The Merry Widow." When I contacted the editor about payment for the first story, she complained about the publisher (who made all the payments) and said she would remind him to start cutting checks. The first story came and went, with no payment. Then the second story appeared, with no payment. I had the next story ready to go, but I didn't send it because there was no point if I wasn't getting paid for my work. So I waited.

And waited.

The fourth story came and went, and it was obvious that I wasn't going to be paid. The editor seemed as disgusted as I was, but whether she really was, or was in fact in on the deception, I'll never know. (Perhaps I was just a little too naïve at this point in my career, but this nonpayment came as a real surprise to me, especially after the editor sent me a very expensive box of chocolates for Christmas. I really thought I was on my way.)

So, what to do?

As I was in Canada, and the publisher was in the US (New York, to be precise), small claims court seemed more trouble than it would be worth, considering travel and other expenses. But there were other ways to get paid, and I thought I came up with a good one.

I sent a letter to the Internal Revenue Service complaining about the publisher, saying that if he claimed he'd incurred $1,200 in expenses with me and had not paid me, who knows what else he was claiming improperly on his tax returns.

The letter I sent to the publisher informing him of this certainly got his attention. According to the editor (with whom I kept in touch, but who never did anything to help me get my money), the publisher stormed through the office with my letter in hand, cursing me and vowing never to pay me a red cent.

Okay, so maybe coming on strong right away hadn't been the best tactic. But what could I do now that I'd shot my load with the IRS? I let a few weeks pass and then wrote the publisher again, this time basically groveling. I said I was sorry, but I was a freelance writer with a wife and child to support and I badly needed the money. If he could forgive me for my mistake, I'd sure appreciate it if he could help a guy out.

I just knew that he'd be walking around the office reading the letter out loud and making sure he let everyone know who was boss.

Did I get my money?

A few weeks later, I received a check for $772, which wasn't the full amount, but it was better than nothing. And things didn't turn out all that badly since, with the exception of the first story, I was able to sell the other three to *Gent* as reprints, earning more from the combined sales than if I'd sold them to *Gent* originally. I came out ahead, but most important is that I learned something about dealing with publishers that I've made use of throughout my subsequent career as a writer. Never come across as angry, upset, or anything other than absolutely polite and professional. In this case, I used the IRS as my first tactic, when it should have been my last resort. Since then, I've had great working relationships with dozens of editors and I've gotten plenty of work solely because of a professional attitude. What I learned from this incident was invaluable to me.

(2) A couple of years ago, Dugent Publishing, the company for which I'd been writing stories since 1990, was bought out by another company, Firestone Publishing. All the editors I'd been working with remained; and, in fact, since Firestone had been busy acquiring other magazines besides the ones in the Dugent stable, the editors I knew were working on more magazines than they had been before and needed more fiction and nonfiction to fill them.

I was asked to contribute stories for these new magazines. Not only was I being paid more than the regular rate, I was also able to submit my stories via e-mail and have them accepted before I'd even finished writing them. Once again, I'd thought I'd finally made some progress. After eight years, I was able to sell my work almost automatically. Whatever I wrote was being accepted, and there seemed to be no limit to the amount of prose they needed to fill these new magazines.

Sound too good to be true?

It was.

About four months into the new arrangement, Firestone failed to pay me for a story they published. This was a certain sign of a problem because in the previous eight years, I had always been paid on time. In fact, the check would often arrive before the issue in which my story was published.

I contacted the editor, and he said he would look into it. That was the beginning of a long string of "they'll be paying next week" type responses. Eventually, the editor became frustrated and gave me the name and number of a person in the business office whom I could contact directly. Once again, I received assurances that payment was coming soon, the final one explaining that the company had just got a loan to keep them going until some of their finances were freed up.

I stopped submitting stories and waited patiently for my payment to arrive. It never did. The next news I heard was that the company had gone into receivership. Apparently, Firestone had purchased a bunch of magazines without the financial resources to pay for the deal. In the end, they stretched themselves too thin and went bankrupt, which left me holding the bag for about $1,000 in unpaid stories.

Dugent Publishing was soon reorganized under the name Dugent Corporation, but the editor with whom I'd worked suddenly found himself out of a job when the company needed to cut costs. (A younger, cheaper editor took his place, and I continued selling to Dugent magazines, but the solid professional relationship I'd built along the way was gone.)

Bankruptcy proceedings were then taken on by the courts, and I became one of a few dozen claimants. I received regular mailings from the lawyers involved and did my best to fill out the forms (not understanding most of them, which arrived with absolutely no explanation), and I believe my claim was thrown out, even though the stories had been published and I'd provided the contracts I'd signed for each. I was left with no other choice but to eat the lost income, and hope that I would never fall victim to a similar set of circumstances again.

While both of these situations happened to me, they are rare occurrences in the publishing industry. I continue to do business with Dugent, but have diversified somewhat and now also write stories and articles for Dugent's competitor, the Score Group. Diversification is one of the best safeguards against having your entire livelihood taken away from you by the failure of a single company.

Finally, to be realistic, you can't stop writing and publishing because you're afraid of this sort of thing happening again. Nonpayment for merchandise and the bankruptcy of your customers are risks that all small businesses have to face. You're just as likely to encounter this sort of thing when operating a business that sells nails to the local hardware store as you are when selling erotica to mass-market magazines.

If and when it happens, take your lumps, keep working, and hope that it doesn't happen again, for your sake and for the sake of the company with which you're doing business.

Diversifying Yourself

If you want to earn an income from writing erotica, you have to write a lot of it. But no matter how much an editor likes your work, there's no way he or she would be willing or able to buy everything you send. Magazines need regular contributors, but they also need diversity, so if a magazine runs 12 issues a year you can't expect to sell it 12 stories each year. There will be other writers selling to the magazine, and readers might get bored with reading the same style of story each month. That's why it's a good idea to sell regularly to a diversity of publications.

If you're selling to an editor at a magazine who is buying everything you send, that's great; but don't let yourself start to believe that the sales will go on forever. Magazine editors have a tendency to change careers, move to other publications, or get fired, and if you've dealt with only one editor and that editor leaves, there's no guarantee that the next editor will have the same affection for your work. In fact, a new editor might not use you at all if he or she wants to begin with a clean slate.

Even when I was selling almost everything I was sending to *Gent*, I still looked for other magazines to which I could sell my work. That strategy paid off when, after eight years of working with the editor of *Gent*, he was unceremoniously let go by the company. Fortunately, the editor who took over was someone who had been editing another magazine in the Dugent stable, and who had been buying my stories for that magazine. I was able to continue selling to *Gent* as if there had been no editorial upheaval at all.

This approach is something I also practice in my other writing endeavors. At present, I have contracts with five different book publishers (Self-Counsel Press, Tundra Books, Quarry Press, Meisha Merlin, and DarkTales Publications), and I am constantly looking for more opportunities. Furthermore, I've also diversified in terms of the kind of work I do, so I write not only erotic stories, but other short fiction, novels, nonfiction, and book reviews. I teach writing classes and I edit books. If one company with which I do business folds, there is enough work with the others to keep me going until I can find a new market.

Being a historian is a lot of fun. I enjoy that kind of writing, and I love that kind of research. . . . Pornography is a much more personal thing to write, and I love writing it.

— *Leigh W. Rutledge*

13
THE EROTIC MARKETPLACE

Short Fiction

As I've said elsewhere in this book, the short erotic fiction marketplace is where a new or aspiring writer is likely to make a first sale. In addition to the numerous men's magazines publishing short erotic fiction, there are always anthologies being put together by erotic book publishers, and many small and literary magazines are open to stories with erotic content. There are even a few small magazines that are all about erotica and erotic writing.

Small-press magazines

Small-press magazines are somewhat more literary in nature and far more daring in content than their commercial brethren. Small magazines are more receptive to alternative sexuality, and may even sometimes experiment with the form itself. If you're curious about what's possible (or allowed), you might want to read through a sample copy before submitting. Who knows; your erotica might even be too plain for them. Better check it out first.

Paramour
PO Box 949
Cambridge, MA
USA 02140-0008

WHAP! Magazine: Women Who Administer Punishment
Retro Systems
PO Box 69491
Los Angeles, CA
USA 90069
E-mail: webmaster@whapmag.com
Web site: www.whapmag.com

Libido
PO Box 146721
Chicago, IL
USA 60614
Web site: www.libidomag.com

Yellow Silk: Journal of the Erotic Arts
Verygraphics
PO Box 6374
Albany, CA
USA 94706

Beau
Brush Creek Media
2215-R Market Street, #148
San Francisco, CA
USA 94114

Manscape
PO Box 1314
Teaneck, NJ
USA 07666

The Rubberist
Newmar Publications
PO Box 38
Carshalton, Surrey
England SM5 4QS

Professional magazines

Professional magazines are the slick type that you can find on any newsstand or in any convenience store. They definitely feature photographs of naked women and men within their pages, so if having your work published alongside such things doesn't appeal to you, try a small-press or literary magazine. However, if naked bodies don't bother you, you will find that these mass-market magazines represent a very large and high-paying market for erotic fiction. Also, once you've made your first sale to one of these magazines, your chances of making a second sale are considerably enhanced, since editors of these publications like to work with writers whom they know can produce quality material on a consistent basis.

A full list of publications would be impossible to compile, but there are several sources listed throughout this chapter that provide a fairly complete guide to these markets. In the meantime, here are a few of the more prominent professional publications.

Dugent Corporation
(Gent, Nugget, Petite)
14411 Commerce Way, #420
Miami Lakes, FL
USA 33016-1598

The Score Group
(Score, Voluptuous, Naughty Neighbors, Leg Sex, BabyFace)
4931 S.W. 75 Avenue
Miami, FL
USA 33155

Chic Magazine
H.G. Publications
9171 Wilshire Blvd., Suite 300
Beverly Hills, CA
USA 90210

Fox Magazine
Montcalm Publishing Corp
401 Park Avenue S.
New York, NY
USA 10016-8802

Hustler
Larry Flynt Publications
9171 Wilshire Boulevard Suite 300
Beverly Hills, CA
USA 90211

On Our Backs
3415 Cesar Chavez
San Francisco, CA
USA 94110

Erotica on the Web

With adult and erotic sites leading the way in the rapid expansion of
the Internet, the number of Web sites using erotic material grows every
day. But, unlike print magazines, Web sites aren't usually open to new
writers or unsolicited manuscripts. However, don't assume that it's impossible to sell to these markets.

Once you've found a site that publishes fiction and you think you
might be able to write material similar to what they've published, send
a query letter explaining who you are and what you'd like to submit.
More than likely, you'll receive no response, or a polite "No." But maybe
you'll get lucky, and someone will ask to see some of your writing. Submit your best work (because the goal here is to impress, not disappoint)
as a sample of what you can do. Once again, you'll probably receive a
"No, thanks," but maybe you won't. The thing about getting your foot
in the door, whether it be on the Web or in print, is that the second opportunity is never as hard to come by as the first, and the third is easier than the second.

If you're thinking that selling to the Web will be easier than breaking into print, forget it. Selling your fiction is difficult no matter who
you're selling to. The Web simply offers more places that you can submit to and be rejected from — and more markets into which you just
may be accepted.

Book-Length Erotica

The heyday of the sex novel is long gone, but book-length erotica is
making a comeback, led by the erotic imprints now being published in
England, especially those intended specifically for women.

A Few Words with . . .

Michael Crawley

On Writing Erotica for the Net

EDO VAN BELKOM: How did you get involved with writing erotic fiction for the Net?

MICHAEL CRAWLEY: It started with a writer's workshop I chair. A friend brought in an erotic men's magazine and suggested I write something for it. I did, but heard nothing back for a full year. In that time, the mag had gone bankrupt, found new funding, and had reappeared as a web-mag. They'd kept my submission all that time. I was asked if I could do something for them every month. The pay was right, so I agreed. At that time I wasn't "wired," but I had to be, to work for them, so I got on line. Once I'd surfed some, it seemed obvious that the adult sites were in sore need of material. I made up a file, bragging about how wonderful I was, and simply surfed. Every time I came to a site that used text, I sent my file to them. In all, I must have zapped that file to a thousand sites. Seven replied. Six became regular clients. It grew from there.

EDO VAN BELKOM: What sort of writing (fiction, letters, etc.) do you produce for the Net? How does writing erotica for the Net differ from writing other forms of erotic fiction?

MICHAEL CRAWLEY: I don't do letters for the Net, though I would if someone offered me enough. I produce an "advice" column — a "how to" — and I do erotic book reviews, but for the most part it's fiction. The fiction breaks down about 50/50 between plain text and illustrated. The illustrated works by the site sending me series of pictures and my writing stories around the pictures.

EDO VAN BELKOM: What is the market like for erotica on the Net? What kinds of erotica are most in demand? How does one go about doing market research?

MICHAEL CRAWLEY: The market is voracious. I can't keep up with the demand, although I write 60,000 odd (very odd) words a month. One way I am coping is by farming out work to pupils of mine and just editing their work. The demand, in terms of "content"? It's a broad spectrum, from sexy romantic to very hard core, with emphasis on B&D, S/M, and lesbian. In that, it's no different from the print market.

To research it, simply surf. There are a number of niche markets for various fetishes such as vampire erotica and smoking erotica that really need good writers.

EDO VAN BELKOM: How much of a connection is there between Web-based erotica and print versions? And how does publishing on the Web compare to being published in "dead tree" editions?

MICHAEL CRAWLEY: There are Web sites that are only that; print magazines that have branched onto the Web, and vice-versa. Web deadlines are often shorter than print. It isn't unusual for me to get a 9 p.m. request for "two thousand words by tomorrow morning." I always deliver. That's one reason my clients come back to me.

In print, we at least *think* about copyrights. If you sell on the Web, you assume your work will be stolen. That's fine by me. I write a piece, send it, and get paid for it. Once I've cashed the checks, as far as I am concerned, the text is "public domain." I have never had a Web site fail to pay me.

Michael Crawley has published 15 books in many genres, including The Watcher and the Watched, *under his own name, and a number of erotic novels as "Morgana Baron." Some of his titles can be found on Amazon.com. He has written two books on the craft of writing, both available from his own site, <69solution.com>. His short fiction and articles have appeared in magazines around the world, notably in* The Mammoth Anthology of Erotica *series. He has also written a number of courses on the craft of writing, and he teaches for Quality of Course Correspondence School in Ottawa. He can be contacted through his site or at <mcrawley@sprint.ca>.*

Erotica is also creeping into the mainstream, as depictions of sex and sexual situations become more common and more explicit in everything from romance and historical novels to suspense thrillers and science fiction. In fact, in the past there have been many erotic novels — Jacqueline Susann's *Valley of the Dolls* comes to mind — that pretended to be mainstream.

Any list that I could include here of mainstream publishers would be at once incomplete and misleading. While it's possible to include erotic scenes in a mainstream novel, the novels still have to be primarily about something else. However, there are some publishers with erotica imprints (a line of books that specializes in erotic subject matter), and a few of those are listed here.

Book publishers

Blue Moon Books
841 Broadway Fourth Floor
New York, NY
USA 10003

Liaison
Headline Book Publishing
Division of Hodder Headline
338 Euston Road
London, NW1 3BH
England

Nexus
Virgin Publishing Ltd.
Thames Wharf Studios
Rainville Road
London W6 9HT

Black Lace
Virgin Publishing Ltd.
Thames Wharf Studios
Rainville Road
London W6 9HT
England

Love Ain't Nothing But

Sex Misspelled

— Title, short story
collection
by Harlan Ellison

X Libris
A Division of Little, Brown and Co. UK
Brettenham House
Lancaster Place
London WC2E 7EN
England

Short-story collections

One thing that erotic publishers don't seem to shy away from is short-story collections. In other genres, single-author collections don't seem to sell as well as novels do, so publishing a collection is often an achievement in an author's career. Indeed, many authors with successful novel-writing careers will publish their collections with other (often smaller) publishers, so that the dip in their sales numbers will not affect sales of their next novel. But the erotica marketplace is more accepting of collections, and in this genre, it might be just as easy to publish a collection of previously published short stories as it is to publish a first novel.

Also, many mainstream publishers have been known to do a collection of erotic short stories while not doing much in the way of erotic novels. Such was the case with Cecilia Tan's collection, *Black Feathers: Erotic Dreams.* The book was beautifully packaged to look more like a literary book than a work of erotica, and was published by HarperCollins, a publisher without an erotica imprint.

Nonfiction

There never seems to be any shortage of erotic and sexual nonfiction on the shelves. Whether presented as serious scholarly research of human sexuality or an informal sexual "how-to," there are always new titles on the way and they seem to sell like proverbial hotcakes.

A case in point is the self-published book by Naura Hayden called *How to Satisfy a Woman Every Time . . . and Have Her Beg for More*, which is really a ten-page description of a single technique (extended foreplay) and 110 pages of quotes from other people's books, along with advice about health and fitness. Despite this (and because of a great title), the book has sold through 18 printings and is currently distributed by E.P. Dutton Inc.

A Few Words with...

Susie Bright

On Editing *Best American Erotica*

EDO VAN BELKOM: I guess the first question would be simply this: What do you look for when you are selecting stories for *Best American Erotica*?

SUSIE BRIGHT: Great literature with a wonderful erotic core. I've written about this from a lot of different angles in my prefaces to each *Best American Erotica* over the years, but that is the main message. I look for a wonderful yarn that uses sexuality to reveal the human character.

EDO VAN BELKOM: How diligent are you in reading the erotica that's published each year? Do publishers and writers send you their work? Is there any erotica that you just don't bother reading?

SUSIE BRIGHT: Your question makes me smile. I always worry that there's some great story out there that I'm missing somehow, and I suppose that tension helps keep me from being complacent. Yes, I receive some review copies, and some writers are self-promoters who send in their work. But I also have to just read every book review I can, peruse the literary journals, encourage fans to send me their suggestions, and just plain hang out in bookstores, looking, looking, looking. The only erotica I wouldn't "bother" with is something that is signed by "anonymous," since I need to credit the story; that's part of my philosophy. The only erotic books listed by "anon." these days are rather deliberate crap or some Victorian specialty.

EDO VAN BELKOM: I imagine you receive a lot of material that's inappropriate for *Best American Erotica* or just downright unsexy. Does it sometimes surprise you what some people consider to be erotic?

SUSIE BRIGHT: I wouldn't characterize it that way. I think anything can be erotic to the right individual, and there is sexual and literary potential in every part of life. The reason I reject stories is because of poor writing, poor craft, poor articulation, or an insincere, phony presentation, not the subject itself.

More than that, there are plenty of great stories that I do turn down because, frankly, the competition is much tougher these days. If I have three great stories that all take place onboard a ship, for example, I will probably choose only one of them, just for diversity in the volume.

EDO VAN BELKOM: Have there ever been any stories that went too far and were turned down by the publisher, either in the *Best American Erotica* series or your *Herotica* books?

SUSIE BRIGHT: The publisher of *Herotica,* in the early editions at least, was very nervous about S/M — this was in the feminist sex-war climate of the 1980s. We argued about that all the time, more in theory than in practice, because it was difficult to get anyone to send us any stories at all at that time, let alone one with an erotic power-play theme. However, I was also editing *On Our Backs* at the time, which was my magazine, so I had the freedom to publish anything, and I did — lots of provocative stories that made me burst out in a sweat or a scream when I read the original manuscript.

When I started *Best American Erotica* in 1993, I told the publisher I wanted total freedom with the story subjects, and they just looked at me like, "Well, of course!" which made me realize that the feminist publishing circles were in a different world about this sort of thing. Interestingly, Simon & Schuster told me that DC Comics threatened legal action against them for a story I ran last year on the theme of Batman. Simon & Schuster decided not to fight them, and is withdrawing the story from future printings. I was very disappointed by that, because I believe the author of this satire has the law on his side.

In general, if I read a story that makes me scared for some reason, I know then, for sure, it's a great story, and I really need to publish it! Not every wonderful story is a frightening one, of course, but when a writer has the power to outrage you, to push you past your limits, that's typically a sign of great talent!

Of course, some people write what they think are outrageous stories, designed to shock, but if that purpose is simply gratuitous, or they are unskilled, it neither shocks me nor tempts me to publish them.

EDO VAN BELKOM: How does editing erotic anthologies fit in with the other work, namely your sex-related nonfiction work like *The Sexual State of the Union*?

SUSIE BRIGHT: Well, it's my editor's hat, rather than my writer's hat. I love editing and working with other writers, composing anthologies and magazines, discovering new talent, etc. But I also love to express myself, so it's simply two things I'm in love with!

Susie Bright is the editor of the annual Best American Erotica *anthologies and* Herotica, Herotica 2, *and* Herotica 3. *As a nonfiction writer, she has penned the landmark volumes,* The Sexual State of the Union *and* Susie Sexpert's Lesbian Sexworld. *For more info, check out* <www.susiebright.com>.

If you're interested in how genuine erotic nonfiction books look and read, I suggest you pick up a copy of any one of a number of books by Graham Masterton, a former editor of *Penthouse* and a successful novelist in his own right.

Small and literary presses

Small and literary presses are usually more open to new writers as well as new ideas. If your erotic writing appeals to a small but eager readership, then a small press might be the right market for your work. Or if your erotic writing is out on the edge and no mainstream publisher would dare touch it, then the small press might embrace you with open arms.

Small presses are typically one- or two-person operations with little money to pay authors or generate publicity. However, the input of the author is more significant in the small press as compared to larger operations, and the writer and the publisher usually work together to make a book succeed. Some of the bigger names in the small-press business include —

Circlet Press Inc.
1770 Massachusetts Avenue, #278
Cambridge, MA
USA 02140
Web site: www.circlet.com

Cleis Press
PO Box 14684
San Francisco, CA
USA 94114
E-mail: cleis@cleispress.com

Alyson Publications
6922 Hollywood Boulevard, Suite 1000
Los Angeles, CA
USA 90028
Web site: www.alyson.com

Masquerade Books
801 Second Avenue
New York, NY
USA 10017

The Permanent Press
4170 Noyac Road
Sag Harbor, NY
USA 11963

The Olympia Press
36 Union Street
Ryde, Isle of Wight
England, PO33 2LE

Silver Moon Books
PO Box CR25
Leeds, England, LS7 3TN

Print-on-demand

The future of publishing might very well be in the realm of print-on-demand, or POD. POD simply means that rather than printing up thousands of copies of a single title, a publisher will produce, say, 100 copies and print more books only when those 100 have sold. Furthermore, POD can also mean that when an order for a copy of a book is received by the publisher, the publisher will then produce one copy of the book for the customer. This allows the publisher to keep dozens or hundreds of books in inventory, but does not require that he or she keep anything in stock. The contents of each book are stored on a computer disk or hard drive until someone requests the information in book form. The publisher makes no high initial investment on the printing of 1,000 or more books, and a small operation can begin to earn money with the first book they sell. POD books rival regular books in quality, but are still a bit more expensive, usually by $5 to $10. This price gap is coming down each year, and soon there will be no difference in price.

Because of POD, works that deal with fetishes or that do not have mass appeal (but nonetheless appeal to a small but loyal number of readers) will have a chance at a life not currently available to them. Older titles will be able to remain "in print" indefinitely, and some new authors might be able to break into print sooner than they would have otherwise.

My second short-story collection, *Six-Inch Spikes*, will be produced by a POD publisher. I chose this route because although almost all of the stories have been previously published in magazines and anthologies, the content of the book as a whole wasn't suited to any of my usual publishers. Yet DarkTales Publications, already producing horror titles in their POD publishing program, wanted to expand their operation to include works of erotic horror, and so *Six-Inch Spikes* was a perfect fit. You can contact them at —

DarkTales Publications
PO Box 675
Grandview, MO
USA 64030

E-book publishers

E-book publishers produce books as downloadable computer formats, not only for personal computers — Windows and MacIntosh — but also for e-book readers such as Rocket eBook, SoftBook, Palm Pilot, WinCe, and other text-reading systems. The advantages to e-book publishing are low overhead for the publisher, higher royalties for the author, and the ability for the publisher to make more titles available for extended periods of time. This might prove to be a boon to erotic fiction, although the Internet seems to be at the forefront of electronic publication of erotica at the moment and probably will remain so in the near future.

To find electronic publishers on the Internet, try entering key words like "e-book" or "electronic publishing" into your search engine.

Where to Find Market Information

Nothing is better than firsthand research: the aspiring writer picks up a few books and magazines and reads through them to figure out what the publisher is looking for and what needs to be written to make a sale. Spend and hour or so in your local bookstore leafing through some of the sort of books you've written and copy down any information that might be helpful to you from the books' copyright pages. If you're checking out magazine markets, copy down the magazine editor's name and the publication's address (or better still, buy a copy) and send off your story.

Put aside any shyness and just do it. I've gotten all kinds of stares from store owners who aren't too happy about me leafing through men's magazines and copying down addresses right there in the store. Look at it like this: in some way, we all have to suffer for our art.

However, if you simply can't or won't do it that way, try one or more of the following sources of market information.

The *Writer's Digest* Magazine "Fiction 50" and "Top 100"

Each June, *Writer's Digest* puts together a list of the top 50 fiction markets in the United States and publishes it in a special issue of the magazine. The list is a great reference for market information, but it doesn't list all that many magazines that publish erotica. Also, the list isn't entirely complete, as some of the absolute best fiction markets like *Playboy* and *The New Yorker* decline to be included on the list. However, a few of the 50 markets listed each year publish erotica, such as No. 36, LSF: *Lesbian Short Fiction*.

Writer's Digest also puts together an annual special issue featuring the "Top 100" nonfiction markets in the United States. In 1999, this list began with *Reader's Digest* and finished with *Response TV* at number 100. Several magazines listed publish erotic or sex-related nonfiction, including No. 4, *Cosmopolitan*; No. 20, *Men's Health*; No. 50, *Marie Claire*; and No. 69, *Playgirl*. Keep in mind that these are mainstream markets, and any erotic content therein will be quite mild in comparison to the slick newsstand sex magazines.

Writer's Digest Magazine
1507 Dana Avenue
Cincinnati, OH
USA 45207
Phone toll free (for a subscription): 1-800-333-0133

Annual Novel and Short-Story Writer's Market

Each year, Writer's Digest Books puts out a series of annually updated books providing market information about different writing fields. The best one for a fiction writer is the annual *Novel and Short Story Writer's Market*. This book lists hundreds of small and commercial magazines, literary journals, contests, agents, and book publishers, including most of the slick magazines that don't make it onto the "Fiction 50" list, such as *Hustler* and *Gent*. However, don't confuse this book with the annual *Writer's Market,* which tries to provide you with a little bit of market information on all types of writing and doesn't give enough information on fiction markets.

Novel and Short Story Writer's Market
Writer's Digest Books
1507 Dana Avenue
Cincinnati, OH
USA 45207

The Gila Queen's Guide to Markets

Published by writer Kathryn Ptacek, *The Gila Queen's Guide to Markets* is an irregular (almost monthly) magazine devoted to news and updates on all types of writing markets. As well as providing new listings and magazine updates, each issue puts a spotlight on the markets of a particular genre, so one issue will concentrate on romance, another will be on erotica, and so on.

The Gila Queen's Guide to Markets
Katherine Ptacek, Editor
PO Box 97
Newton, NJ
USA 07860-0097
E-mail: GilaQueen@worldnet.att.net

Market books on erotica

There are a couple of publishing companies that have produced books listing erotic markets for both fiction and nonfiction. These are handy reference guides, but the information in these books can very quickly become out of date, so the more recent the publication date, the better. One such book is *Putting Out: The Essential Publishing Resource Guide for Gay and Lesbian Writers,* edited by Edisol W. Dotson and published by Cleis Press, currently in its fourth edition.

Putting Out: The Essential Publishing Resource Guide for Gay and Lesbian Writers
Cleis Press
PO Box 14684
San Francisco, CA
USA 94114
E-mail: cleis@aol.com

Online market information

Just as checking out the racks at your local bookstore for markets to which you can send your fiction is a good idea, so too is surfing the Web. There are countless sites on the Web publishing erotica to accompany the nude photos that decorate sites' pages. Even if you're interested in publishing your fiction in dead-tree editions, the Web is still a handy place to find markets for your work. The following sites provide some market information on a regular basis, and some, like The Market List and *Write Market Webzine,* are fairly comprehensive sources. Best of all, they are listed for free on the Web.

The Market List
www.marketlist.com

Speculations
www.speculations.com

Write Market Webzine
http://www.writemarket.com

Writers Write Paying Market List
www.writerswrite.com/paying

Spicy Green Iguana
http://members.aol.com/mhatv/index.html

Join a writers' organization

While there isn't an official writers' organization for erotica writers, there are organizations out there for other genres such as romance, science fiction, mystery, and horror. If you have an interest in any of these, it's a good idea to join and seek out writers within the organization who share your interest in erotica. In the Science Fiction and Fantasy Writers of America organization, for example, many members write erotica in addition to science fiction, and for many years there was a Pornography Special-Interest Group that informally shared information about erotica.

Another idea is to join a writer's organization that has no interest in a specific genre, but instead is for professional writers, period. Doing so would also allow you to seek out and network with others who share your interest while being exposed to a wide variety of mainstream and genre news, information, and markets. For information on writer's organizations, see Appendix 1 at the back of the book.

14
AGENTS AND MARKETING

Do You Need an Agent to Sell Erotica?

New writers often approach me at writing conferences and ask, "How do I get an agent?"

My response is, "Why do you need an agent?"

Usually, they have just finished a book — or worse still, are halfway through writing a book — and will be needing an agent to sell it for them when they're done. More often than not, these writers want to be represented by an agent so their careers as "writers" (unpublished writers at that) will have some sort of validation.

Here are some things to remember about agents:

- If you're selling short stories to men's magazines and literary anthologies, you don't need an agent.

- If you're selling erotic novels to bottom-feeding erotic book publishers (low-paying, all-rights-acquiring types of publishers), they won't pay enough to interest an agent, and if you have an agent they probably won't want to deal with you anyway.

- If you haven't sold anything yet, you probably won't be able to get an agent who's worth having.

- Stay away from agents who advertise for clients at writers' conventions. Any agent worth having usually has a full list of clients and takes on new ones rather selectively.

- Do *not* pay any agent a reading fee. Legitimate agents make their money by selling the work of an author and charging that author a modest 10 percent to 15 percent commission. Reading fees are scams run by fly-by-night agents, who take on clients but never sell anything to publishers. They make their money by charging reading fees to prospective clients, and frequently recommending editing services that will take your money (often thousands of dollars) for "editing" your book, which, in the end, won't make the manuscript any more salable. Keep the following in mind: *Money always flows from the publisher to the writer, never the other way around.*

Many mainstream book publishers will look at neither unsolicited nor unagented manuscripts. This narrows the potential markets for your new novel somewhat, but it doesn't eliminate them completely. There's nothing to stop you from writing a polite query letter or proposal to an editor, explaining who you are and that you've finished a novel, and asking if you could please send along an outline and a few sample chapters. (See Sample 6, the proposal letter for my story collection, *Working Hard,* in chapter 12.) That gives the editor the chance to refuse you or to agree to look at the outline and sample chapters. If the editor likes the material, he or she might ask to see the entire manuscript. Now your manuscript is no longer unsolicited: it has been solicited by the editor. Certainly this is a long, hard way to go about it, but there is nothing easy about any aspect of the business. I've seen numbers suggesting that only one in every 10,000 novels is ever published, and the true ratio is probably much higher. Writing a novel is difficult and selling it is even harder, but if you give up after the first two or three (or 100) rejections, then you might not be cut out to be a writer in the first place.

Getting an Agent

Obviously, at some point in your writing career, you might require the services of an agent. But when?

When I completed my first novel, after having published 30 or more stories, I decided it might be time to acquire an agent. I was a member of the Science Fiction and Fantasy Writers of America, so I looked in the SFWA *Membership Directory* and found out which agents represented which writers. (This can be done with any decent writers' organization that has a good number of professional members.) I selected a top agent and wrote a letter asking if he'd like to look at my novel. He answered positively, read the novel, and declined to represent it.

It was just as well, because the book wasn't good enough for publication. Also, in retrospect, I may not have been represented as well as I would have liked by an agent with a long client list representing a lot of big names.

Agents make money by selling the work of the authors they represent. Obviously, agents will spend the most time on authors that make the most money, and will spend less time on authors that have less of a chance of doing so. After that first effort, I tried the same agent again, but this time with another novel (my erotic horror novel, *Teeth*). He refused to represent that one as well, saying it would be a difficult book to sell. In other words, the book might sell someday, but it wouldn't be worth the effort to him to sell it. It's a bit of a catch-22 situation: an agent wants a new author to have a book that's easy to sell before taking him or her on as a client; however, a book that's easy to sell doesn't really need an agent to represent it.

I forgot about getting an agent for a while and got a commission to write my first horror novel, *Wyrm Wolf*, without an agent. Since it was a work-for-hire book, there wasn't any point in hiring an agent to take 10 percent of the advance for negotiating a contract that had little room for negotiation. I wrote the novel, it did well, and about a year later I had two similar novel contracts in hand.

At that time I was approached by my current agent after he'd read a story of mine in an erotic horror anthology that two of his clients had edited for Pocket Books. So, after I'd tried unsuccessfully to get an agent to represent me, here was one interested in my work. I answered by saying that if the agent wanted to represent me, he had to represent my erotic horror novel *Teeth*, the one the first agent said would be a tough sell. The agent read it, liked it, and agreed to represent it. At that point, I told him about the other two contracts I had, and allowed him to negotiate them on my behalf. Since then, I've sold many books through my agent, including *Teeth*, which was indeed a tough sell but which eventually sold after being rejected more than a dozen times.

All of this is a long-winded way of saying that the time to go looking for an agent is after an editor has made an offer on one of your books. You answer by saying, "I'll have my agent call you," at which point you call the agent of your choice and say, "I've just sold a novel. Would you like to represent me?" Any agent would be a fool to turn down such a proposition.

Marketing Yourself

Many successful professional writers don't use agents at all. A new trend in contract negotiations is to use a lawyer who specializes in publishing and copyright law, who will negotiate a book contract for you and charge a fee for his or her services. This might cost more up front, but the lawyer won't be taking 10 percent of your royalties over the book's entire lifetime in print.

Some other writers don't use agents or lawyers at all, preferring to negotiate their own book contracts. (One famous author even provides his own contracts whenever he sells a short story.) This works up to a point, but once the dollar amounts get large enough, the editor-author relationship can become strained over money — as do many relationships. Here is where the true benefit of having an agent negotiate contracts and hound publishers for money on your behalf comes into play. They can pester and pursue publishers for your money, haggle over a few dollars, and call people names, but once the contract is signed, you are able to work with the editor without any of the animosity of the negotiating process clouding the working relationship.

Where to Get Advice

If you're not sure about something in a contract, there are people you can ask for advice.

If you are a member of a writers' organization, you can call, e-mail or write a letter to another member and ask his or her opinion on the matter, which will allow you the benefit of consulting with someone who has far more experience than you do and will provide you with practical advice as it relates to the genre. If you are a member of the Horror Writers Association, for example, you would be able to get advice from someone who has already dealt with the same magazine or publisher of which you're unsure. The Science Fiction and Fantasy Writers of America allows new writers to join as active members (full voting membership) after the writer has been offered a contract but before it has been signed. Therefore, a writer can join and receive the benefits of membership (and the advice of more experienced writers) before he or she has unknowingly signed a bad contract.

If you're not a member of any writers' organization — and unfortunately there is no Erotica Writers Association — you can still approach a professional writer whom you've met at a convention or some other function. Just be sure you're in need of advice on a writing matter, and not looking for information that you can easily obtain yourself by spending a couple of hours in the library reading through a few books. I've been called dozens of times by total strangers who have seen my name or photo in the newspaper. They want to know where a friend can send his or her novel, or they have a great idea for a story but need someone else to write it for them. There's a world of difference between that sort of question and, "I've just sold a novel to NewAuthor Publishing. Is $250 a decent advance for a first book?"

15
A FINAL WORD

So that's about it, everything I know about writing erotica. I hope it's enough to help you get started writing (and selling) prose in the genre.

If there's anything I've failed to emphasize enough over the course of this book, it's this: If you want to write prose fiction or nonfiction, it is imperative that you read. You don't necessarily have to start spending your days with your nose buried in erotic books and slick magazines, but you should be reading something each and every day, whether it's a newspaper, your favorite magazine, a novel, a collection of short stories, or a how-to book on repairing washing machines. When you read, you learn how words look when they're strung together on the page. You begin to hear the author's voice inside your head, and over time you can learn to discern whether something is well-written or merely adequate.

Once you've read a great deal and you've decided you want to try writing erotica, it's time to make a trip to the library (yes, there is plenty of erotic material in your local library, even if it isn't labeled as such) or bookstore, pick up a few volumes, and start reading again. Read the classics of the erotic genre, read trashy sex novels, read romances in which sex is alluded to, and read erotic horror in which sex is not only explicit, but is often described in gruesome (and sometimes gory) detail.

When you've got a good grounding in the genre and you know what kind of erotica you want to write, you'll be that much further ahead. If you know what kind of erotica you want to write, you'll have a rough idea about where you might want to send it once you're done. And once you've done that, half the battle is already won.

In short, read, write, send out your work, and read and write some more. If you succeed in publishing something, great. If you don't, the beauty of the erotic genre is that you'll have a lot of fun trying!

Best of luck.

Appendix I
Writers' Groups and Organizations

Writers' organizations usually have membership numbers in the hundreds or thousands (such as the Horror Writers Association and The Science Fiction and Fantasy Writers of America) and provide their members with regular market information through their newsletters or online publications.

The larger organizations can put you in touch with other writers who are struggling to sell their work just as you are, or can connect you with established pros who can provide you with advice based on the benefit of their experience. Most writers' organizations have quarterly or monthly newsletters and host annual general meetings, or meetings of local chapters. While every attempt has been made to ensure that the following information is accurate, contact information for writers' organizations can often change because the people who run them are primarily volunteers and, as such, things tend to move around a bit.

There aren't any organizations for writers of erotica, but every organization includes members who write erotica in addition to other genres. For example, I got in touch with Michael Bracken, a fellow contributor to men's magazines, through the Horror Writers Association.

There are also smaller writers' groups that are more local in nature, and almost every small town or county has one. Writers' groups are made up of a small number of avid writers with vastly different interests, while the writers in organizations all have an interest in the same genre. Both can be very helpful to new writers. To find the local writers' group in your community, try the library or your city hall.

Romance Writers of America (RWA)
3707 FM 1960 West
Suite 555
Houston, TX
USA 77068
Phone: (281) 440-6885
Web site: www.rwanational.com

RWA is the largest organization of romance writers in the world, with members in many countries around the globe. Members receive a bimonthly newsletter containing information about markets, contests, and conferences. The organization holds an annual conference featuring seminars and awards presentations. It also has more than 100 local chapters.

Horror Writers Association (HWA)
PO Box 50577
Palo Alto, CA
USA 94303
Web site: www.horror.org

Begun in 1984 under the name HOWL (The Horror and Occult Writers League), HWA is the only international organization for people who work within the field of horror. While the word "writers" appears in the name of the organization, membership is open to artists and illustrators, poets, reviewers, book publishers, and agents who work in the horror field. There are several classes of membership, from affiliate to active, but all members receive a newsletter, market updates, and announcements via an Internet mailer. HWA has a presence at most horror conventions and presents the Bram Stoker Awards (voted on by active members of the association) each year.

Science Fiction and Fantasy Writers of America (SFWA)

532 La Guardia Place, #632
New York, NY
USA 10012-1428
Web site: www.sfwa.org

An association of professional science fiction and fantasy writers founded in 1965 to inform its membership on matters of professional interest, to promote their general welfare, and to help them deal effectively with publishers, editors, and anthologists. Publishes a quarterly magazine, *The Bulletin,* the members-only *Forum,* as well as online updates via the Internet. SFWA has a presence at most major SF conventions and hosts annual events such as the Nebula Awards banquet and the author/editors' reception in New York City. Presents the Nebula Awards (voted on by the active members of the organization) each year.

SF Canada

Web site: www.sfcanada.ca

An association of Canadian professional science fiction and fantasy writers similar to SFWA, but with less stringent membership requirements.

Mystery Writers of America (MWA)

17 East 47th Street, 6th Floor
New York, NY
USA 10017
Phone: (212) 888-8171
Fax: (212) 888-8107
E-mail: mwa_org@earthlink.net
Web site: www.mysterynet.com/mwa/

One of the oldest and largest mystery writers' organizations. It has an international membership, with categories for published mystery writers, editors, booksellers, and writers in other fields; and unpublished writers who can demonstrate (via copies of query letters, rejection slips, verification of enrollment in courses) that they are serious about their work. Presents the Edgar Allan Poe Awards annually in New York City. MWA maintains a resource library for members, including a listing, available by mail order, of documents on crime-related topics.

Crime Writers of Canada
3007 Kingston Road
Box 113
Scarborough, ON
Canada M1M 1P1
E-mail: ap113@freenet.toronto.on.ca

Crime Writers of Canada is the association for writers of mystery and crime fiction and crime nonfiction in Canada. You don't have to be Canadian to join, and you don't necessarily have to have sold a work of mystery to be a member. Reviewers and others who work in areas that are related to the mystery and crime fields are welcome. The Crime Writers of Canada puts on events throughout the year such as "Devil of a Good Read" and other readings, and presents the Arthur Ellis Awards at a yearly banquet, usually held in Toronto.

Canadian Authors Association (CAA)
PO Box 419
Campbellford, ON
Canada K0L 1L0
Phone: (705) 653-0323
Fax: (705) 653-0593
E-mail: webmaster@CanAuthors.org
Web site: www.canauthors.org

An organization dedicated to the support and development of Canadian writing in all genres. Its slogan is "Writers helping writers." While the CAA is a national organization and hosts an annual meeting, there are many regional chapters across Canada. The CAA has a category of membership for aspiring writers.

Appendix 2
Reference Books

Writers not only need to read within the field in which they want to work, they must also be fairly well-read about the craft of writing itself. In the case of erotica writers, they also have to be well versed in the physical mechanics of sex so they can get the all-important details right. Fortunately, there have been a great many books written about the craft of writing, all kinds of volumes on human sex and sexuality, and even several good books specifically about writing erotica. Here is a brief list that can help you learn more about writing, about sex, and about writing about sex.

Books about Writing

Applebaum, Judith. *How to Get Happily Published.* 5th Edition. New York: HarperCollins, 1998.

Barnhart, Helene Schellenberg. *Writing Romance Fiction for Love and Money.* Cincinnati: Writer's Digest Books, 1983.

Block, Lawrence. *Spider, Spin Me a Web: A Handbook for Fiction Writers.* New York: William Morrow & Co., 1988.

Block, Lawrence. *Telling Lies for Fun & Profit: A Manual for Fiction Writers.* New York: Arbor House, 1981; Quill, William Morrow, 1994.

Block, Lawrence. *Writing the Novel: From Plot to Print*. Cincinnati: Writer's Digest Books, 1979.

Bradbury, Ray. *Zen in the Art of Writing*. Capra Press 1990; Bantam Books, 1992.

Crawley, Michael. *How to Fail as a Novelist*. Pug Enterprises Inc., 2000.

Crawley, Michael. *A Novelist's Commonplace Book*. Ottawa: Quality of Course, 1994.

Grant, Vannessa. *Writing Romance*. Vancouver: Self-Counsel Press, 1997.

Meredith, Scott. *Writing to Sell*. Cincinnati: Writer's Digest Books, 1995.

Movsesian, Ara John. *Pearls of Love*. Fresno: The Electric Press, 1983.

Pianka, Phyllis Taylor. *How to Write Romances*. Cincinnati: Writer's Digest Books, 1988.

Van Belkom, Edo. *Writing Horror*. Vancouver: Self-Counsel Press, 2000.

Van Belkom, Edo. *Northern Dreamers: Interviews with Famous Science Fiction, Fantasy and Horror Writers*. Kingston: Quarry Press, 1998.

Books about Writing Erotica

Allison, Jane. *A Writer's Confession*. San Diego: Chelsea Library Press, Manchester Publications, 1974.

Bailey, Mike. *Writing Erotic Fiction and Getting Published: A Teach Yourself Book*. London: Hodder Headline, 1997.

Barbach, Dr. Lonnie. *Pleasures: Women Write Erotica*. New York: Doubleday, 1984.

Benedict, Elizabeth. *The Joy of Writing Sex: A Guide for Fiction Writers*. Cincinnati: Story Press, 1996.

Eighner, Lars Lavender Blue. *Elements of Arousal: How to Write and Sell Gay Men's Erotica*. New York: Richard Kasak Books, 1994.

Feldhake, Susan C. *How to Write and Sell Confessions*. Boston: The Writer, Inc., 1980.

Kelly, Valerie. *How To Write Erotica*. New York: Crown Publishers Inc., 1986.

Palmer, Florence K., and Marguerite McClain. *Confession Writer's Handbook*. Cincinnati: Writer's Digest Books, 1980.

Parker, Derek. *Writing Erotic Fiction*. London: Marlowe and Company, 1996.

Rowe, Michael. *Writing below the Belt: Conversations with Erotic Authors*. New York: Masquerade Books, 1997.

Stern, Jerome. *Making Shapely Fiction*. New York: W.W. Norton & Company, 2000.

Books about Sex and Sexuality

Comfort, Alex. *The Joy of Sex*. 1971.

Estes, Clarissa Pinkola. *Women Who Run with Wolves: Myths and Stories of the Wild Woman Archetype*. New York: Ballantine Books, 1992.

Friday, Nancy. *Forbidden Flowers: More Women's Sexual Fantasies*. New York: Pocket Books, 1975.

Friday, Nancy. *My Secret Garden: Women's Sexual Fantasies*. New York: Pocket Books, 1974.

Grice, Julia. *What Makes a Woman Sexy?* London: Piatkus Publishers, 1988.

Masterton, Graham. *How to Drive Your Woman Wild in Bed*. New York: Signet (Penguin), 1991.

Masterton, Graham. *More Ways to Drive Your Man Wild in Bed*. New American Library, 1985.

Masterton, Graham. *Single, Wild, Sexy . . . and Safe*. New York: Signet (Penguin), 1994.

Masterton, Graham. *Wild in Bed Together*. New York: Signet (Penguin), 1992.

Pellegrino, Robert. *A Glossary of Sexual Terms: A Specialty Book*. Chicago: Novel Books Inc., 1965.

Stoppard, Miriam. *The Magic of Sex*. London: Dorlin Kindersely Ltd., 1991; Toronto: Random House Canada, 1992.

Taormino, Tristan. *The Ultimate Guide to Anal Sex for Women*. San Francisco: Cleis Press, 1997.

Tyler, Alison and Dante Davidson. *Bondage on a Budget*. New York: Masquerade Books, 1998.

Winks, Cathy, and Anne Semans. *The New Good Vibrations Guide to Sex: Tips and Techniques from America's Favorite Sex Toy Store*. 2nd edition. San Fransisco: Cleis Press, 1997.

Notable Books of Erotica

Baron, Morgana. *Rue Marquis de Sade*.

Bataille, Georges. *The Story of Eve* (1928).

Cleland, John. *Fanny Hill* (1748).

Delany, Samuel R. *Tides of Lust* (1973).

de Sade, Marquis. *Justine* (1791).

Eighner, Lars. *Whispered in the Dark* (1995).

Exander, Max. *Leathersex: Cruel Affections* (1994).

Farmer, Philip Jose. *Flesh* (1960).

Lawrence, D.H. *Lady Chatterly's Lover* (1928).

Miller, Henry. *Tropic of Cancer* (1934).

Nin, Anaïs. *Delta of Venus* (1969).

Preston, John. *Mr. Benson* (1992).

Réage, Pauline. *The Story of O* (1954).

Roquelaure, A.N. (Anne Rice). *The Claiming of Sleeping Beauty* (1987).

Travis, Aaron. *Beast of Burden* (1993).

Underwood, Miles. *The English Governess* (1960).